ON

RESOLVING INTERNATIONAL CONFLICTS

Studies in International Politics

The Leonard Davis Institute
for International Relations,
The Hebrew University of Jerusalem

RESOLVING INTERNATIONAL CONFLICTS

The Theory and Practice of Mediation

edited by
Jacob Bercovitch

BOULDER
LONDON

Published in the United States of America in 1996 by
Lynne Rienner Publishers, Inc.
1800 30th Street, Boulder, Colorado 80301

and in the United Kingdom by
Lynne Rienner Publishers, Inc.
3 Henrietta Street, Covent Garden, London WC2E 8LU

Library of Congress Cataloging-in-Publication Data
Resolving international conflicts : the theory and practice of
mediation / edited by Jacob Bercovitch.
p. cm.
Includes bibliographical references and index.
ISBN 1-55587-474-6 (hc: alk. paper)
ISBN 1-55587-601-3 (pb: alk. paper)
1. Mediation, International. I. Bercovitch, Jacob.
JX4475.R47 1995
341.5'2—dc20 95–16447
CIP

British Cataloguing in Publication Data
A Cataloguing in Publication record for this book
is available from the British Library.

This book was typeset by Letra Libre, Boulder, Colorado.

Printed and bound in the United States of America

The paper used in this publication meets the requirements
of the American National Standard for Permanence of
Paper for Printed Library Materials Z39.48-1984.

5

To the memory of my father,
the compleat mediator

Contents

Foreword

Jimmy Carter

To increase our knowledge and understanding of how international and intranational armed conflicts can be resolved is of vital importance today. At no time in history have the nations and peoples of the world been so interdependent. Technological advances in transportation and communication have had far-reaching effects, bringing enormous benefits, but also causing new problems. National and international institutions still have great difficulty in coping with the demands placed on them. The opportunities for ethnic conflicts, resource-based strife, and governance disputes are far more numerous, and the consequences of conflict far more severe than ever before. Ethnic conflicts are raging in the former USSR and the former Yugoslavia. We have also witnessed armed conflicts and violence spreading in Liberia, Somalia, Sri Lanka, Sudan, and Zaire.

The world has recently witnessed the end of the Cold War. With it came a dramatic change in superpower, East-West, and North-South interrelationships, and some new opportunities for the peaceful resolution of conflicts. We have seen as direct by-products of the end of the Cold War the termination of the Iran-Iraq War, an end to the wars in Cambodia and Nicaragua, the end of two wars in Ethiopia, the withdrawal of Soviet troops from Afghanistan, and a peace agreement between the Palestine Liberation Organization and Israel. For 1990 and 1991, the *SIPRI Yearbook* (1992) listed major armed conflicts, defined as prolonged combats incurring battle-related deaths of at least 1,000 persons, in thirty-one and thirty locations respectively. It would seem that the number of major armed conflicts dropped slightly in 1991 as interstate conflicts showed a slow but noticeable downward trend.

Conflicts within state borders have continued to predominate on the world scene and the resolution of the majority of these disputes remains elusive. Countries are increasingly turning to international organizations and other institutions for assistance in resolving disputes when attempts at direct negotiations fail. Although national and international institutions have always concentrated on wars between countries, the United Nations is now being seen as a legitimate dispute resolution mechanism, and the era of perceiving noninterference in a country's domestic affairs as a "sacred cow" appears to be waning. The United Nations has undertaken election-monitoring missions in several countries. The Carter Center's Council of Freely-Elected Heads of Government, which I chair, was invited to Panama, Nicaragua, the Dominican Republic, Guyana, Mexico, Paraguay, and Haiti to monitor those elections. The Carter Center also monitored the elections in Zambia and Ghana. By giving voice to opposition groups and by enfranchising minorities, free and fair elections have proved to be a valuable step in resolving disputes.

Third-party mediation is another important conflict resolution option. For example, talks between the government of Mozambique and the rebel movement RENAMO were convened by the government of Kenya in 1989; talks between the government of Ethiopia and the Eritrean People's Liberation Front (EPLF) were mediated by the Carter Center. The Carter Center also conducted peace talks between the government and the Sudanese People's Liberation Movement. Efforts continue to renew this peace negotiation. Reluctance to have other nations and institutions involved in an internal armed conflict resolution process is sometimes being replaced by eagerness as acceptance of the interdependence of the world becomes more prevalent. External actors can provide or withhold incentives (the proverbial "carrots and sticks") to use as peace dividends that can make or break the peace process. The Carter Center's International Negotiation Network (INN) convened two major consultations in 1992 and 1993 that examined conflicts in Africa, Asia, Europe, and Latin America, and discussed ways of sustaining the peace, the psychological dimensions of conflict, early warnings of conflict, and small arms transfers. These consultations provided a forum for open discussion between intergovernmental and nongovernmental organization leaders on their roles in conflict resolution.

If we believe that conflicts can be resolved without recourse to weapons and violence, then the involvement of nongovernmental actors, be they individuals or organizations, can lessen tensions between parties and facilitate the peaceful negotiating process. Central to the effectiveness of any NGO in mediating a conflict, however, is its credibility and neutrality with warring parties. We must also realize that there are alternatives to violence at the grassroots level across cultures and societies. We need to encourage regional solutions and incorporate indigenous methods of dispute resolution. Among those societies where warfare is practiced, levels of violence may differ remarkably. Conflicts and disputes in these societies are often handled through kinship organizations and other social structures. In some Asian cultures, harmony between peoples is highly valued and appreciated; elderly people often possess special prestige and are in a position to foster accord and maintain peace in their communities. We must keep in mind that there are many paths to peace and that only one involves violence.

We must support the study of conflict situations and look for creative opportunities for their peaceful resolution. I have learned from experience that it is especially important to understand the unique perspectives of contending parties. In negotiations that I conducted as president and in my post–White House years, I tried to put myself in the place of foreign leaders and to imagine how they view their nation's interest. I knew that any agreement we reached had to be in the interest of all parties if it were to be maintained, and had to have the unanimous agreement of all parties in order to be enforceable.

I believe that this volume is an important contribution to the field of conflict resolution and that it provides scholarly insights and creative alternatives of interest to scholars and practitioners alike.

Acknowledgments

Editing a book can be a demanding and even frustrating experience. It is also very much a joint endeavor, and as I look back at this book now I realize just how much the contributors have helped to shape it. I have discussed most aspects of the book with all of them on numerous occasions and benefited greatly from their advice. They provided an opportunity for me to learn more about the discipline. They have also been inordinately patient. My first debt of gratitude must go to all the contributors, who, as close friends of mine, had more of an influence on the book than some of them might care to admit.

Two individuals in particular played a very special role. Nils Petter Gleditsch, editor of the *Journal of Peace Research,* first suggested the idea for a volume of essays on international mediation and has supported the project through its many phases. Gabi Sheffer, director of the Leonard Davis Institute for International Relations at the Hebrew University of Jerusalem, nursed the project from an abstract idea to a publishing contract and finally a book in a way no other person could have. They both deserve special thanks.

The following individuals provided insights, help, and support when most needed: Bill Breslin, Peter Carnevale, Raymond Cohen, Ray Goldstein, Loraleigh Keashly, Lou Kriesberg, Pat Regan, Jeff Rubin, and David Singer—sincere thanks to all of you.

David Hornik at the Leonard Davis Institute read the entire manuscript several times over, improved its presentation and argument, and generally made excellent suggestions and editorial criticisms. The book benefited immensely from his knowledge and attention to detail. I very much appreciate David's work. I am also grateful to Lynne Rienner, who waited patiently for the manuscript and whose faith in it did not waver.

Canterbury University allowed me the time to complete the book during my leave, and the Lady Davis Fellowship at the Hebrew University of Jerusalem, where I spent most of 1993, provided the perfect financial and research support to keep the momentum going in a stimulating and rewarding environment.

I am grateful to the editorial board of the *Journal of Peace Research* and to the publishers of Sage Publications for permission to use the article by Paul Wehr and John Lederach, "Mediating Conflict in Central America," which appeared in the *Journal of Peace Research* vol. 28 (1), 1991.

This book was conceived when I was a single person, written largely as a married person, and completed as a parent. Throughout these incarnations Gillian Wess provided support, advice, encouragement, and occasional criticism. She has been tremendous in her support, even when I felt least like receiving it. The book could not have been done without her. Our young daughter, Liora, tried her best to ensure that the book not get done. She did, however, help to refine my mediation skills. I hope she reads the book in a few years' time, and appreciates that those hours spent away from her were not in vain.

I dedicate this book to the memory of my father as a way of expressing my appreciation for all that he taught me about mediation.

Jacob Bercovitch

Introduction: Thinking About Mediation

Jacob Bercovitch

A PERSPECTIVE ON MEDIATION

The ending of the Cold War and the fundamental changes that have taken place in international relations over the past few years may have altered the character or occurrence of conflict. They have not removed the causes of conflict, however, nor affected its intensity or the need to deal with it effectively. The new international system is as conflict-prone, many would argue even more so, as any previous system. The world today is literally covered with ethnic, religious, territorial, and nationalist conflicts that are as serious, costly, and intense as any in the past. And somehow they need to be managed or resolved.

Although the Cold War ended, neither history, as we were led to believe, nor conflict ended in 1990. The global changes of that year spawned a myriad of new problems, few of which require more urgent attention than the need to maintain peace and security within and between states. Regardless of whatever changes were brought about and how the distribution of power took shape, we quickly realized that conflicts were going to remain with us whether the international system was unipolar, bipolar, or multipolar. The expectation that conflicts would diminish or even disappear proved to be as erroneous as it was ephemeral. As long as conflicts are with us—and it is truly impossible to conceive of a system that will be conflict-free—the possibility of serious damage exists, as does the need to prevent or resolve such conflicts.

How, then, can we manage or resolve our conflicts? Throughout history, individuals, groups, communities, and more recently states, have searched for methods of dealing with conflict in more constructive and peaceful ways than the seemingly inevitable resort to hurling stones at each other. Some of these ways have been fairly ingenious (such as the whistling or singing competitions that we see in some communities) and others have been fairly obvious (such as talking to each other). Lying somewhere mid-point on a spectrum ranging from violence to the use of ritual as a way of managing conflict is the practice of mediation. This book is devoted to an analysis of this important form of conflict management. It is hoped that the concepts and case studies presented here will enable us to formulate better theories of mediation and will contribute to a more effective response to conflicts in international relations.

It is worth noting at the outset that as a response to conflict there is little that is novel about mediation. It has been used everywhere and has a rich and varied history. References to it abound in the Bible, Homer's *Iliad,* and Sophocles' *Ajax*. It is also found in arenas as diverse as neighborhood and personal conflicts, group conflicts, and organizational, environmental, and policy conflicts. In the present international system, where the sophistication and destructive capability of weapons make the violent pursuit of conflict both costly and irrational and where there is no adherence to a generally accepted set of rules or a central authority with the power to regulate international behavior, mediation can be seen as an ideal way of dealing with differences and settling conflicts between antagonistic and fiercely independent states. This is one of the main reasons why studies of mediation have proliferated in the last two decades or so. All these studies, despite differences in focus, orientation, and methodology, purport to describe how mediation can prevent the spread of a conflict and contribute to its resolution.

While there may be no definitive answers, scholars from disciplines as diverse as anthropology, psychology, political science, sociology, law, and communications have all attempted to further our understanding of how mediation works and under what conditions is it effective. Their collective efforts have often been bedeviled by the immensity of the scope of mediation, the secrecy that normally surrounds it, and the difficulty of studying mediation, and especially international mediation, in its natural setting. The upshot of all this is minimal consensus on a definition of mediation or on the best method of conducting research on mediation, and little relevant information on its frequency and success in international relations. Scholars of mediation, whether engaged in case studies of an anecdotal nature or large-scale comparative studies, appear to inhabit their own little islands. To ensure that they are not out of touch with each other and that their own little islands actually converge to form a body of knowledge, students of the field, whichever research strategy they adopt, have to define mediation and indicate its unique features, find connections between structures and mediation behavior, and learn to compare and evaluate the contribution of mediation in a large number of cases. All these avenues of research are represented in this book.

Whether we pursue research that uses quantitative methods to study many instances of mediation and achieve a high degree of generalizability, laboratory experiments or computer simulations to achieve a high degree of control in the precision and measurement of variables, single cases of mediation to achieve a high degree of descriptive accuracy, or theoretical modeling to increase universal understanding, is a less important issue than the necessity of making our concepts and research strategies explicit and of communicating across disciplines, theories, and methods. Neither the relevance nor the findings of any research on mediation can be rejected a priori. Multiple approaches—both theoretical and methodological—are required to achieve a convergence of findings that can improve both our understanding and the practice and performance of mediation. We can make this kind of progress by adopting, as we do here, a research perspective that permits us to evaluate how mediation affects, and in turn is affected by, the context, the participants, the strategies, and the nature of a conflict.

Our approach to mediation recognizes that it is practiced in numerous arenas; that it is, in many ways, a continuation of the parties' own conflict-management efforts; and that it involves the noncoercive intervention of a third party (who may be an individual, an ad hoc group, an organization, or a state) who seeks to influence or resolve a particular conflict. This is its primary objective, which mediators fulfill through reliance on persuasion, appeals to logic, the use of information, and the application of social-influence strategies. The mediators' objective of changing, reducing, or resolving a conflict legitimates their intervention. The material, political, or other resources mediators invest in the process provide the rationale for their own motives and interests. The intertwining of the parties' interests, the mediators' interests, and the overall interest of changing the course or outcome of a conflict (without which interest mediation would be neither invited nor accepted) is one of the unique features of mediation.

The perspective suggested here recognizes that mediation involves (1) a relationship between two protagonists and a mediator, (2) behavior of some sort, within a context, and (3) the outcomes consequent to that behavior. The outcomes may have been caused by direct mediator behavior, or they may have been facilitated indirectly by mediators removing barriers to their occurrence, permitting them to occur, or not preventing them from occurring. This may appear to be a fairly broad conception of the possible impact of mediation, but it is one with decided advantages. It allows us to embrace a spectrum of outcomes (and not just the binary success versus failure), it permits us to analyze the relationship between different kinds of mediation behavior and outcomes, it reveals the complexity of the causal link between a mediator, the parties in conflict, and an emerging outcome, and it acts as a guide in evaluating mediation outcomes from the perspective of the parties, the mediators, or the observer or scholar.

The inclusion of a mediator, in any arena, turns a dyadic conflict into a triadic relationship. This transformation may be wholly planned or totally accidental. At its heart, however, are the mediator's attempts to affect the behavior, perception, and choice of outcome of the adversaries. A mediator enters a conflict and becomes part of a voluntary and unique conflict system. That system comprises two parties in conflict, each with its own concerns and interests, a set of issues that may or may not be clear to all, divergent attitudes, and behavior that is at best incompatible and at worst downright hostile. No mediator enters such a system for altruistic reasons only. Whether individuals, organizations, or states, mediators enter a conflict system to do something about it, passively or assertively, and to promote or protect any interests they may have. In this sense, a mediator is not unlike another party in the conflict-management process whose behavior and performance—what it wants to do, chooses to do, or is permitted to do—are as conditioned by the context and circumstances as the behavior of the adversaries themselves. To understand mediation and its impact, we have to know something about the context, the issues, and the parties involved.

The peculiarities and distinctive features of mediation relate to the fact that it is not a quasi-legal process, nor is it extraneous to the parties' own conflict-management efforts. To be successful, mediation must be congruent with, and complementary to, a given conflict in its context, and to treat mediation as either a legal process or a disinterested input is to miss important features that explain the relationship between a mediator and the parties. This volume makes that relationship very explicit.

Mediation begins with the interaction of two conflict parties within a unique context. These parties' reaction to their conflict and to the act of mediation is the result of their particular experience, society, culture, and structure. These features in turn affect how a mediator intervenes, what strategies and outcomes are pursued, and mediation's impact on the parties and the outcome. Studies on mediation should be organized and mediation itself should be analyzed in terms of a broad framework that places mediation at the very heart of a conflict. This sort of framework encourages us to explore how different contexts impinge on mediation, what conditions are most conducive to success, what behaviors mediators use in different contexts, and how mediators relate to different parties. Only when such analysis has taken place can an evaluation of the impact of mediation—always a tentative and perilous matter—be undertaken.

It is important to bear in mind that neither mediator roles nor mediation performance can be stipulated in advance. Generic principles promoting better outcomes should be viewed with caution, as mediation is a dynamic and flexible process and adaptability is its prized attribute and its key to success. This adaptability is a source of strength for the practitioner but a source of bewilderment for the scholar. Our ultimate aim here is to understand this complex, responsive, and heterogenous process and to provide a solid basis for assessing its performance. Only in this way can we move the study of mediation from infancy to maturity.

THEMATIC ORGANIZATION

The chapters in this book proceed developmentally from theoretical considerations through an examination of the relationship between a mediator and the parties, an exploration of the mediation context, an illustration of the possible range of application in international relations, and finally to the presentation of how novel approaches can expand the role and relevance of mediation.

In their chapter, Bercovitch and Houston show just how relevant and widespread mediation has become in international relations. The authors review the literature on mediation, establish the background for assessing its occurrence, and examine the conditions—both structural and behavioral—that determine its performance and effectiveness in international relations. They use a theoretical framework and a large number of mediation cases in the post–1945 era to show how aspects of a context such as who the parties are, who the mediator is, and what the conflict is all about have an impact on both the nature and outcome of mediation. Mediation is found to be a reciprocal process and a contingent form of political influence. The best guides to its effectiveness are the issues involved, the intensity of the conflict, the parties' previous relations, and the mediation strategy.

The second part of the book examines a question in the mediator-parties relationship that has often been asked in analyzing prerequisites for successful mediation: that of bias and impartiality. Is it necessary, possible, or even desirable for mediators to be totally unbiased and impartial? The relationship between a mediator and the parties in conflict is voluntary. That means that a mediator has to be acceptable to both parties. Mediators need not be perceived as impartial or unbiased (is there such an entity in international relations?) to be acceptable; they do need to be seen as having access to resources and the ability to get the conflict parties out of a no-win situation. It is resources and the ability to effect a change, not the appearance of impartiality, that are the sine qua non of effective mediation.

Carnevale and Arad examine the notion and consequences of mediator impartiality. In a paper that utilizes laboratory research experiments, they demonstrate that effective mediation may well be undertaken by biased or partial mediators, and that decisions concerning the acceptability of mediators do not simply reflect the mediators' alignment. Numerous actors, partial and impartial, may serve as mediators in international conflicts. A perception of "fair decisions fairly arrived at" appears to be more important in the approval of a mediator than the attachment to a dated notion of bias and impartiality.

A further exploration of the mediator-parties relationship and the notions of bias and impartiality, this time in actual conflict situations, is undertaken by the authors of the next two chapters. Wehr and Lederach analyze the Esquipulas peace process in Central America in 1987 and find that in a number of cases a mediator from within the conflict environment, an "insider and partial," is more likely to succeed than an "impartial outsider." This is certainly the case when a mediator is connected to and known by both conflict parties, shares their culture, and is expected to live with the consequences of mediation. Such mediators inspire trust, an effective resource in mediation. The Contadora experience in Central America suggests that there may be other international conflicts where mediators need be neither neutral nor even external to the conflict. In many contexts the events, persons, and attitudes may legitimate a mediator in the form of a sympathetic and respectful insider rather than a "neutral" outsider.

Of all the actors in international relations, none could have a stronger claim to impartiality and neutrality than the United Nations. As a supranational organization, the UN was set up to transcend state interests and embody global concerns, and in the new political climate it finds itself with greater decisional latitude and involvement in more and more conflicts (such as in Sudan, Somalia, Bosnia, Cambodia, Zaire, and others). Skjelsbæk and Fermann examine the factors that account for the involvement of the United Nations in so many international conflicts. They find that the personal skills and moral status (derived from the Charter) of the Secretary-General and the degree of cooperation between the permanent members of the Security Council are the most important assets in the scope and effectiveness of UN mediation. It would seem that impartiality does not define mediation; nor is it bound up with its successful performance by individuals, states, or even international organizations.

The importance of the context in international mediation is treated in Part 2 of the book. Many mediation attempts fail because the parties in conflict make different assumptions about the process and have different expectations regarding its outcome. When the parties have different assumptions about conflict and different ideals, goals, and values about social reality, mediation and conflict management in general are unlikely to be effective. An exchange of meanings, a shared common ground, and an awareness of cultural differences are prerequisites to successful mediation or conflict management. The chapters by Cohen and by Mandell discuss the relationship between culture and mediation in theory and in practice.

Cohen's chapter raises questions about the need for mediators to be sensitive to the context and the value differences within a conflict. A new form of mediation, cultural mediation, may be called for to help negotiators remove their cultural blinders and perceive reality in essentially the same fashion. The value of mediation that ignores cultural forces or consigns them to the periphery is very limited indeed.

Mandell focuses his attention on Kissinger's mediation efforts between Israel and Syria after the 1973 Yom Kippur War. His analysis shows that Kissinger's task-oriented "toing and froing" could not have produced a durable settlement. As a mediator Kissinger was tempted by Western negotiation procedures and by the prospect of playing a central role, but he completely ignored basic cultural disharmony between the parties and failed to get them to agree on common norms. Any settlement emerging from such mediation could only have been temporary and short-term. A successful mediation is predicated on the awareness of cultural differences and the creation of shared norms.

The new international environment is characterized by much conflict and many structural problems. In the absence of an explicit framework defining international response to these problems, mediation has emerged as a consistent and effective instrument. It is no longer narrowly focused on conflicts between states, but has now become relevant in internal, ethnic, and global environmental conflicts. The principles and practices of mediation have become central to the international community's response to conflict, and Part 3 presents a series of case studies that demonstrate the range and contribution of mediation in international relations.

Rupesinghe's chapter examines problems of mediation in a protracted conflict within a state. In such conflicts the human costs, often borne by the civilian population, are high and the chances of settlement pretty low. To achieve a successful outcome, mediation must proceed on a number of tracks. An official, formal track can deal with high politics and achieve agreement on principles, but only a series of citizen-based, informal tracks, using a number of channels of mediation, can create the conditions for a sustainable reconciliation. Mediation in internal conflicts requires a change of attitudes and behavior of the elites as well as the peoples that can only be accomplished by multiple mediation avenues. Their absence contributes to the risk of wider escalation.

Of the conflicts that have erupted since 1989, none has posed a more serious challenge to the international community than the turmoil in the former Yugoslavia. A variety of responses and policies have been developed to deal with the conflict. Individuals, former statesmen, single countries, groups of countries, and international organizations have all attempted some form of mediation—regrettably without much success. Webb, Koutrakou, and Walters examine the European Community's ability to mediate a conflict in its very midst. They find that most mediation attempts have been ill-fated, whether because they were dictated by domestic political considerations or because they proceeded along one dimension only. To be effective in complex internal conflicts, mediation must proceed along several avenues, develop clear objectives, and use all the tools available to it. Complex conflicts call for complex mediations, and any other response will simply fail.

Threats to international peace and security can now come from a variety of sources, among the most important of which are environmental. Issues such as pollution, soil erosion, desertification, and deforestation generate conflicts as intense as any political issue. Environmental conflicts also usually transcend national jurisdiction and involve multiple issues and parties, technical uncertainty, and considerable disagreement on their implications. Shmueli and Vranesky examine the structure of mediation that is most pertinent to environmental conflicts and highlight the roles mediators enact in such conflicts. Successful mediation in environmental conflicts requires a search for multilateral consensus and the management of an enormous complexity of information and organization. Given such difficulties, environmental mediation is best embedded in an international structure such as the Organization of Economic Cooperation and Development (OECD) or the United Nations Conference on the Environment and Development (UNCED).

The final chapters of this book seek to expand our conception and the theoretical range of mediation. These chapters challenge some of our basic assumptions about conflict, resources, goals, and mediators' identities and interests. They represent something of a departure from traditional conceptions of mediation and a significant step in the evolution of a wider scope for mediation roles.

Kriesberg argues for a conception of mediation that is context-derived. The structure of a conflict, its context, the presence or absence of other actors, political pressures rising from within, and the overall relations between the parties all have a considerable impact on who can mediate a conflict and how that mediator can behave. The chapter suggests that mediation services may be provided by different actors, both formal governments and informal individuals (or quasi-mediators), each implementing a unique role to "unblock contextual problems" at different phases of the conflict. Moving from a conflict to a settlement requires a series of steps and transitions; quasi-mediators may have a crucial role in the initial phases, and having mapped the road, may allow formal mediators to take the parties through the negotiation and implementation phases.

Keashly and Fisher expand our conception further by introducing the consultation, or problem-solving, model and arguing for the matching of mediation models to conflict situations. The consultation approach is based on generic principles of conflict; it emphasizes an analysis of conflict, interests, and needs, focuses on perceptions and cognitions, requires honest communication, and is facilitated by a skilled third party or mediator. At the heart of this chapter is the contingency approach, which suggests that effective mediators who can properly read the conflict cues begin with one mediation strategy, usually consultation, and when they achieve the results anticipated move on to a more formal strategy. Ideal mediation should be matched to the sequential stages of escalation until the parties themselves are in a position to coordinate their de-escalation.

The chapters in this volume make it evident that resolving conflict through mediation requires the conscious efforts of human beings working in a very fraught and complex arena. How well their efforts are understood by people in the mediating profession and scholars determines how successful mediation is going to be. Mediation does have its own forms, logic, rules, and mechanisms. Understanding its many facets requires an understanding of the parties' positions on different issues, their overall relationship, their resources, and their motivation to settle their conflict. Mediation cannot be viewed simply as an addendum to negotiation, or as a set of techniques imported by someone completely removed from the dispute to correct the perceptual errors of those in conflict. It is an integral part of the process of negotiation and conflict management in which each actor, the mediator included, interacts with the others, exerts an influence, and seeks to promote a specific outcome. This is both the objective and rationale of international mediation.

To understand how mediation works means understanding the context of a conflict as well as the background, interests, needs, and resources of the participants. The nature of the influence process and the modalities of influence used by a mediator are dependent on these factors. The form the mediation takes, the role of a mediator, even the criteria used to evaluate mediation outcomes are all functions of the broader context of a conflict situation. This is why we often describe mediation as a contingent or reciprocal aspect of conflict management. One misses a lot if one ignores the reciprocal interaction between the mediators and the mediated.

Mediators in international relations are agents of influence, promoters of cooperation, and catalysts for change. They achieve their objectives through the use of information, communication, facilitation, interpretation, and the waving of carrots and sticks. Mediation should not be confused with altruism; mediators are usually cognizant of their own interests and they have motives, consciously expressed or not, that they wish to see promoted or protected. This interplay of actors, motives and interests, resources, and context gives mediation its unique features.

International mediation is an effective form of conflict management. The chapters that follow try to create a shared arena of discourse on mediation and convey the richness and complexity of the process by illustrating how, and under what conditions, mediation works. It is hoped that this book can also help us to develop clear and practical political policies for conflict management, and to define the mediation instruments most effective in achieving these objectives.

CHAPTER ONE

The Study of International Mediation: Theoretical Issues and Empirical Evidence

Jacob Bercovitch and Allison Houston

Conflict is one of the most pervasive—and inevitable—features of all social systems, however simple or complex they may be and irrespective of their location in time and space. This is true of personal, group, and organizational, as well as international systems. Wherever it occurs, conflict is significant, newsworthy, and challenging. It can lead to mutual satisfaction and growth or it may produce acrimony, hostility, and violence. Our interest in the study of conflict is undoubtedly related to our desire to manage it in a way that maximizes its potential benefits and minimizes its destructive consequences.

There are a number of ways of dealing with or managing conflict. These may range from avoidance and withdrawal, through bilateral negotiation, to various forms of third-party intervention. Third-party intervention in conflict, particularly of the nonbinding, noncoercive kind, is in many ways as old as conflict itself. It has played an important role in industrial and preindustrial societies. Its popularity as a way of dealing with conflict grows each year, as does its applicability to different realms. Unresolved problems and conflicts create the conditions for third-party intervention of one form or another.

Yet notwithstanding its popularity, longevity, ubiquity, and importance, we know far less about this form of conflict management than we imagine. Systematic analyses, let alone empirical studies, of third-party intervention in general and mediation in particular have been very rare. The phenomenon has for too long remained little studied and poorly understood. The purpose of this chapter is to redress this balance somewhat and present an overview of the behavioral literature on mediation. We intend to do so by organizing our material around the question that we believe is central to an understanding of this problem: namely, what factors and conditions determine the success or failure of mediation? Although the focus of this chapter is the international environment, many of the findings presented below can contribute to enhancing the effectiveness of third-party intervention and mediation in other contexts.

THE NATURE OF INTERNATIONAL MEDIATION

The practice of settling disputes through intermediaries has had a rich history in all cultures, both Western and non-Western (Gulliver, 1979). Although there are considerable differences in the way mediators from different cultures deal with a conflict, all the approaches have value in terms of managing or settling disputes. In the international arena, with its perennial challenges of escalating conflicts, shrinking resources, and rising ethnic demands, and with the absence of generally accepted "rules of the game," the potential application of mediation is truly limitless.

Even a cursory survey of recent international disputes reveals the extent and heterogeneity of mediation. In the last decade or so, we have seen the involvement of such parties as the United Nations (in the Vietnam-Kampuchea dispute, the Iraq-Kuwait dispute, and the Yugoslav dispute), the pope (in the Beagle Channel dispute), the Organization of African Unity (in the Tanzania-Uganda dispute), the Organization of American States (in the Nicaragua dispute), the Arab League and Algeria (in the Iraq-Kuwait dispute), the United States (in numerous efforts in the Middle East). Less formal mediation efforts (by the Quakers, for example, or by prominent politicians such as President Carter, Lord Owen, or Prince Sihanouk) occur on a daily basis.

As a form of international conflict management, mediation is likely to occur when (1) a conflict has gone on for some time, (2) the efforts of the individuals or actors involved have reached an impasse, (3) neither actor is prepared to countenance further costs or escalation of the dispute, and (4) both parties welcome some form of mediation and are ready to engage in direct or indirect dialogue (Bercovitch, 1984).

Whatever its specific characteristics, mediation must in essence be seen as an extension of the negotiation process whereby an acceptable third party intervenes to change the course or outcome of a particular conflict. The third party, with no authoritative decisionmaking power, is there to assist the disputants in their search for a mutually acceptable agreement. As a form of conflict management, mediation is distinguishable from the more binding forms of third-party intervention, such as arbitration and adjudication, in that it is initiated upon request and it leaves the ultimate decisionmaking power with the disputants (Folberg and Taylor, 1984; Moore, 1986).

In an arena such as the international one, where a large and highly diverse number of actors coexist, where each guards its sovereignty and independence zealously, and where each views the resort to violence as a viable option, mediation with its ad hoc basis, voluntary nature, and non-binding character offers a relevant and useful response to the problems posed by ethnic, regional, and global conflicts.

The scope of mediation activities in the international arena is truly immense. This is reflected in the abundance of definitions offered by various students of the discipline. Doob, one of the "founding fathers" of the field, uses the term in a very broad sense indeed. He defines it as "the efforts of one or more persons to affect one or more other persons when . . . the former, the latter or both perceive a problem requiring a resolution" (1993:1). Mediation thus purports to offer a solution to any problem the disputants perceive as such. Other definitions of mediation stress its objectives. Mitchell defines it as "any intermediary activity . . . undertaken by a third party with the primary intention of achieving some compromise settlement of issues at stake between the parties, or at least ending disruptive conflict behavior" (1981:287). Some definitions highlight specific attributes in mediation or its dynamic phase structure. Folberg and Taylor see mediation as "the process by which the participants, together with the assistance of a neutral person or persons, systematically isolate disputed issues in order to develop options, consider alternatives, and reach a consensual settlement that will accommodate their needs" (1984:7).

The reality of international mediation is in some ways closest to Doob's definition, but it is also more restricted. Mediators may intervene to protect the parties or to promote their own interests. They may or may not possess the required attributes of neutrality and visibility. They may be external to the dispute or they may come from within the dispute environment. Their mediation may be passive or active, and it may purport to change some aspects of behavior or to affect the perceptions of the parties. Mediators may act as individuals or as members of a larger ad hoc group. Taking all these features into account, we see international mediation as a reactive process of conflict management whereby parties seek the assistance of, or accept an offer of help from, an individual, group, or organization to change their behavior, settle their conflict, or resolve their problem without resorting to physical force or invoking the authority of the law (see Bercovitch et al., 1991:8; but compare Dryzek and Hunter, 1987; Wall, 1981).

This may be a broad definition, but the terminology here is quite significant. Such a definition permits us to study cases in different contexts, to employ different methods, and to make comparisons between cases. Above all, we feel it forces us to recognize that mediation is a dynamic and complex social process comprising parties in dispute, a social environment or a context, a particular dispute or problem, and a mediating agent. Our basic contention here is that the success or failure of any mediation is ultimately dependent on each of these clusters or categories of factors.

STUDYING THE CONDITIONS FOR EFFECTIVE MEDIATION

The relationship between international mediation and successful outcomes (by which we mean a cease-fire, a partial settlement, or a full settlement) is frequently mentioned, rarely defined, and widely misunderstood. There are some, such as Meyer, who emphasize the unique aspects of mediation and the impossibility of generating any useful conclusions about mediation outcomes across a wide array of cases. To Meyer, the "task of the mediator is not an easy one. The sea that he sails is only roughly charted and its changing contours are not clearly discernible. He has no science of navigation, no fund inherited from the experience of others. He is a solitary artist recognising at most a few guiding stars and depending on his personal powers of divination" (1960:161).

The notion that success or failure in mediation is essentially the product of idiosyncratic factors beyond the reach of ambitious social science scholars is echoed by another experienced mediator, Simkin, who notes that "the variables [in mediation] are so many that it would be an exercise in futility to attempt to describe typical mediator behavior with respect to sequence, timing or the use or non-use of the various functions theoretically available" (1971:118).

Other avenues of research, despairing of the ideographic consequences of single-case description and clearly influenced by propositions in organizational development, find the key to mediation success in normative or prescriptive approaches. These approaches, in a laudable desire to improve the effectiveness of mediation, offer in a fairly generic fashion a set of recommendations that, if pursued, could lead to successful outcomes in all types of disputes from the interpersonal to the international (Burton, 1969, 1972, 1979, 1984; Doob, 1971; Fisher, 1983; Mitchell, 1981). Such approaches usually offer very little reliable evidence to support their notion of what constitutes success in mediation and how best to achieve it. They are also predicated on the somewhat dubious assumption that all disputes, in all contexts, can be successfully mediated.

The anecdotal single case and the normative approach represent different foci of research. Neither approach, however, offers a reliable explanation of when mediation succeeds and why. The descriptive approach emphasizes unique aspects of a dispute, and assumes that all cases are different and that nothing meaningful can be said about kinds of mediation and dispute outcomes. The normative approach concerns itself with a wide range of disputes and collectivities, emphasizes subjective elements of perception and communication, assumes that no dispute is too intractable for an experienced third party, and usually ends up as advice for mediation practitioners. Neither approach has really stimulated much-needed empirical research (Brookmire and Sistrunk, 1980; Carnevale and Pegnetter, 1985; Mitchell and Webb, 1988; Ott, 1972; Rubin, 1980; Young, 1967).

International disputes are not static or uniform events. They vary in terms of the situation, parties, intensity, escalation, response, meaning, and possible transformation. These features define the context of a dispute and cannot but affect its course and outcome. Mediation is shaped by the context and characteristics of a situation. The specific rules, beliefs, attitudes, behaviors, and symbols that make up international conflict impinge on, perhaps even govern, the process of mediation. As a social process, mediation may be as variable as the disputants themselves. To be successful, mediation must be above all adaptive and responsive. It must reflect different problems, different parties, and different situations. Thus, for mediation to be effective it must relate to and reflect the wider conflict.

With this in mind, we wish to suggest an approach to the study of mediation that does take the context and other factors into account; we refer to it as the contingency approach. This approach was used in a series of earlier studies (Bercovitch, 1986; Bercovitch et al., 1991; Bercovitch and Houston, 1993; Bercovitch and Langley, 1993; Bercovitch and Wells, 1993). The approach stipulates variables with specific operational criteria, each of which may have an impact on mediation effectiveness. At the heart of this approach are clusters of context, process, and outcome variables. Each cluster refers to specific characteristics of the party, the dispute, the mediator, and the outcome. Mediation outcomes, whether successful or not, are logically seen as the result of the interaction of context and process variables. Our conception of the contingency approach is depicted diagrammatically in Figure 1.1.

The contingency approach offers a useful framework by which to organize and integrate much of the literature on mediation. It also allows us

Figure 1.1 A Contingency Model of Mediation

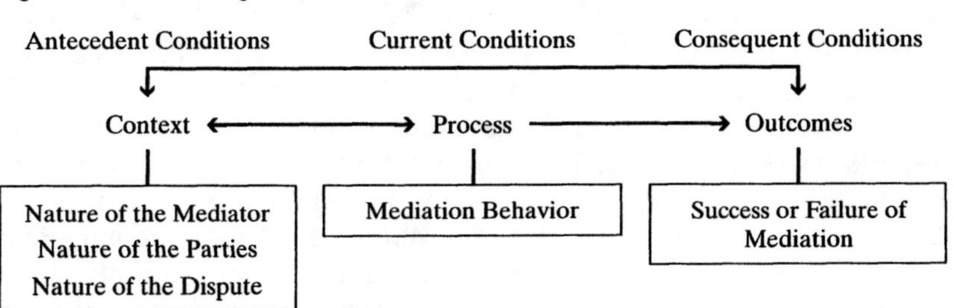

to evaluate the impact of different kinds of mediation and assess the relationship between dispute characteristics and mediation (Bercovitch, 1989), or evaluate the most successful mediation strategies (Bercovitch and Wells, 1993).

Mediation must not be analyzed or understood in terms of a simple cause and effect model in which a particular strategy invariably produces a desired outcome. Mediation in general, and international mediation in particular, is not merely an exogenous input that can be applied uniformly and indiscriminately to all disputes. Nor can it be presented only as a set of rules, the rigid pursuance of which can affect or influence the disputants, their behavior, or their perceptions. The relationship between mediators and the disputing parties is reciprocal. Those involved in a dispute wish to influence the mediator and the mediator certainly hopes to influence the parties. The contingency approach enables us to focus on this reciprocal relationship through either a detailed study of a single mediation or the utilization of a large number of mediation cases.

We will pursue the latter course in the hope that our efforts constitute a valuable step on the road to theory building.

METHODOLOGY

To start with, we should obtain information on the incidence of international disputes and international mediation. A great many quantitative studies describe the occurrence and analyze important patterns of international disputes. These are well summarized by Maoz (1982), Cioffi-Revilla (1990), and Bremer (1993). None of these studies, however, addresses itself specifically to the question of how disputes are managed or terminated. It is with this aspect that we are particularly concerned.

Our empirical examination was conducted through the utilization of an original data set of international disputes from 1945 to 1990, which was developed by us as part of a larger research project on the correlates of international mediation. For operational purposes, we define an international dispute, as Singer and Small do (1982), as an organized and continuous militarized conflict involving at least one state and resulting in at least 100 fatalities (Bercovitch et al., 1991). We identified 241 disputes that meet our criteria. The geographical distribution of these disputes is shown in Figure 1.2.

Compiling a list of all mediation events in international disputes is an ambitious task. Routine informal, institutional mediations are carried out behind closed doors between various international actors on a daily basis. Our task here is to examine the "nonroutine" mediation attempts that were mentioned in public sources. Of the 241 international disputes identified, 137 were actually mediated. Some disputes were mediated once,

Figure 1.2 Geographic Region of Disputes

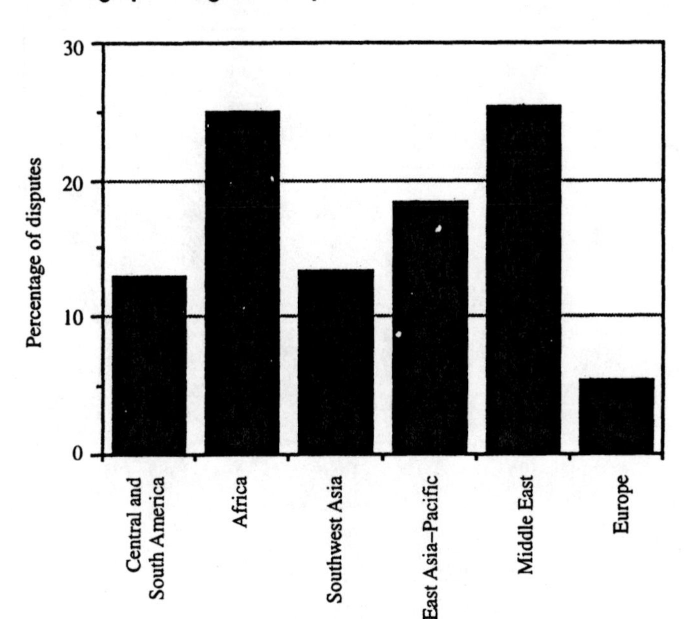

others experienced multiple mediations. A thorough search of the *(London) Times*, *New York Times*, and *Keesing's Archives* revealed 593 separate mediation cases. That is, 593 reports of formal or institutionalized, nonviolent, and nonjudicial interventions of an outsider or third party of some sort occurred in these disputes. Figure 1.3 shows the relationship between the number of disputes and the rate of mediation at successive historical periods.

If we examine the prevalence of mediation vis-à-vis other conflict-management activities, we get a fairly clear picture, in Figure 1.4, of just how widespread the resort to mediation as a form of international conflict management really is.

Overcoming the problem of data availability brings us to the second major issue: namely, exploring outcomes and relating them to a whole host of contextual factors. Devising an index of successful mediation outcomes is a complicated matter. There is little or no agreement on which episode constitutes the outcome or how to identify a terminal point in dealing with a dynamic and ever-changing process. Furthermore, mediation outcomes may be perceived and in turn defined very differently indeed by an observer, by the parties involved, by the international com-

Figure 1.3 Disputes and Mediation Cases by System Period

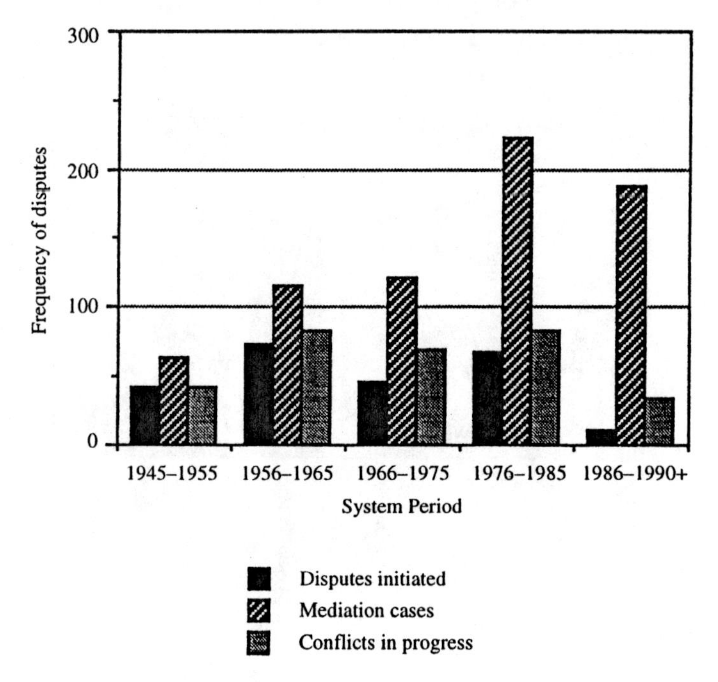

Figure 1.4 Conflict Management Type

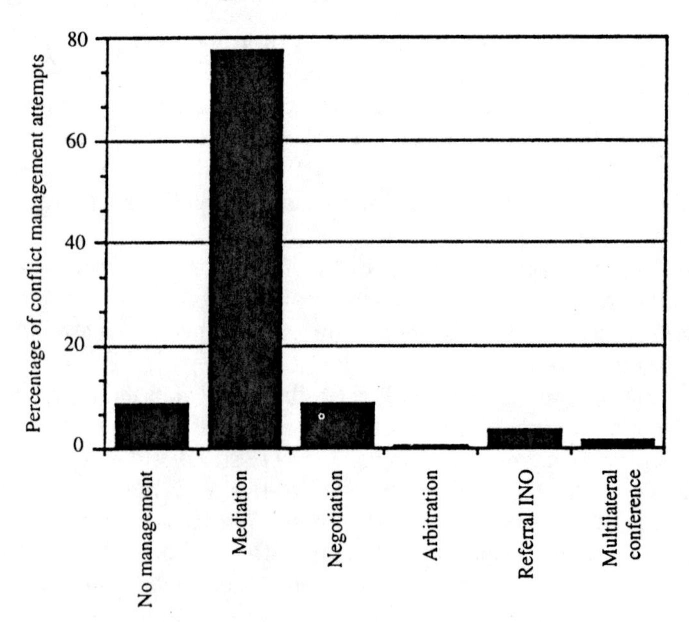

munity, or by the mediator himself/herself. Outcomes may be considered successful at one point only to be deemed unsuccessful a few years later. Mediation outcomes may also be defined as successful or unsuccessful depending on the extent to which they meet certain normative criteria (for example, has mediation produced greater fairness, efficiency, legitimacy, and so on?).

Each of these perspectives has its limitations. Here we have decided to modify Haas's success index (1986) and focus on the behavioral consequences of mediation rather than on such factors as efficiency, legitimacy, satisfaction, or short- or long-term success. We define a mediation as successful when it has made a considerable and positive difference to the management of a conflict and the subsequent interaction between the parties. Mediation is deemed to be partially successful when it has initiated negotiations and a dialogue between the parties. It is defined as being of limited success when it has achieved a cease-fire or a break in hostilities only. We contrast this with a second outcome category, failure, which is defined as occurring when mediation has had no discernible or reported impact on the dispute or the parties' behavior (Bercovitch et al., 1991). The distribution of mediation outcomes can be seen in Figure 1.5 (we have excluded from our analysis "no mediation" and "mediation offered only," 122 cases, as it is inappropriate to regard these as either failed or successful attempts).

It might be tempting to assume that mediation can produce a successful outcome in most types of international disputes. Yet as shown in Fig-

Figure 1.5 Mediation Outcomes

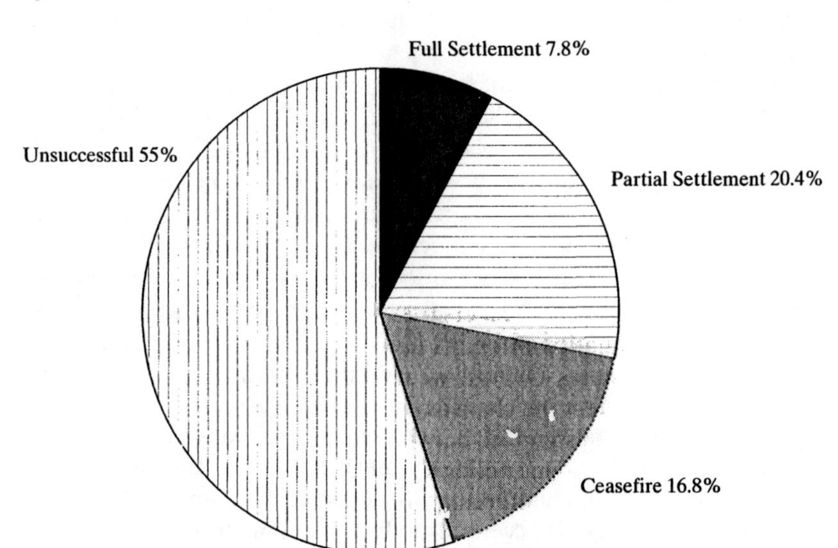

ure 1.5, an analysis of the data indicates that this is not the case. Fully 55 percent (325 cases) of mediation attempts were unsuccessful, compared with only 45 percent (267 cases) of successful cases (we collapse all three gradations of successful outcomes into one measure). The relatively low number of successful mediation outcomes may be explained in terms of our very strict behavioral definition of success in international disputes. Others (for example, Frei, 1976) consider mediation successful when it is offered only.

The basic question we wish to address concerns the kinds of mediation cases that are successful. Which contextual attributes or factors explain successful mediation? Can such attributes or factors be used as "information inputs" by decisionmakers in determining whether or not to initiate mediation? We would like to suggest that these questions and others are best answered within the conceptual framework presented above in Figure 1.1.

CONTEXT VARIABLES

Characteristics of the Parties

Parties' political context. A traditional hypothesis in the study of international relations suggests that democratic states are less likely to initiate conflict than nondemocratic states. Mack and Snyder (1957) conclude that the greater ability of democratic states to channel and accommodate internal discontent makes them less likely to exhibit external aggression. Maoz and Abdolali (1989) found little empirical support for this hypothesis. What they did determine was that democratic states are unlikely to find themselves in a dispute with one another. What we want to know is just how responsive democratic states, and indeed other states, are to international mediation when they are in conflict. Does the type of political system affect the chances of successful conflict management?

The political context can be divided into five regime types: monarchies, one-party states, military regimes, multiparty democratic states, and others. Although we find that democratic states account for 30 percent of all those states involved in mediation attempts, they usually resort to mediation only when their adversaries are nondemocratic states. Only 6.7 percent of all mediation attempts involved disputes where both parties were democratic states. Overall, we find that the kind of political system does not greatly affect the chances of mediation success.

However, if we distinguish between symmetric dyads (disputes where both parties share the same political system) and asymmetric dyads (where the disputants are from different political systems) we find that there is a 53 percent probability of successful mediation in symmetric disputes compared to only 41 percent in asymmetric disputes. Mediation is easier when the parties share a political system or have a basic adherence to the same set of cultural norms and values. Shared norms and sociopolitical similarity minimize misperception and facilitate a successful conclusion to a conflict.

We can also examine how such factors as internal composition, cultural and ethnic differences, and degree of homogeneity affect the success or failure of mediation. Conflict management by third parties can occur only between adversaries that have well-defined and legitimate identities. A mediator's job is hardly likely to prove easier if the incumbent government of one of the adversaries is experiencing an insurgency, rebellion, or any other serious internal threat. Mediation has a better chance of success when each disputant is accorded legitimacy. Disunity or lack of cohesion within a state makes it difficult for both the adversaries as well as a mediator to engage in any meaningful form of conflict management. The successive failures of mediation attempts in Lebanon, Cyprus, and the former Yugoslavia illustrate this point only too well.

The relationship between internal unity and successful conflict management has been alluded to by many (for example, Burton, 1968; Modelski, 1964). Raymond and Kegley state that "the greater the cultural differences between disputants, the less likelihood of successful mediation" (1985: 38). Kressel and Pruitt (1989) support this argument by suggesting that internal discord within a state has a negative impact on its interactions with other states. The greater the fractionation within a state, the greater the chances of mediation failure. This may seem intuitively plausible. When we analyze the relationship between homogeneity, ethnic composition, and mediation outcomes we find that mediations where one or both of the parties are culturally fragmented have a 54.4 percent chance of success. Where one or both of the parties have no significant cultural minority, the chances of successful mediation are as high as 64.4 percent. Where one or both parties have a significant cultural minority, the chances of mediation success are only 38.4 percent.

Parties' power. Another contextual factor relates to the relative power status of the parties in conflict. Is there a relationship between the power and capabilities of states, or their discrepancies, and mediation effectiveness? Ott (1972) and Young (1967) suggest that the smaller the power differences between the adversaries, the greater the effectiveness of international mediation. Logically this seems quite obvious. In cases of clear power disparity, the stronger adversary may not be prepared to make any concessions or compromises that are essential to mediation success. Yet others, such as Deutsch, argue that conflicts in which there is "a mutual recognition of differential power and legitimacy" (1973:46) will be more easily resolved. The presence of a fairly unambiguous advantage by one of the parties may well create a clearer incentive toward a settlement.

The idea that mediation is most effective in disputes involving adversaries with equal power receives strong empirical support from a reinterpretation of Butterworth's data (1976). In a study examining power resources and the impact of international mediation, a clear pattern emerged showing high mediation impact (that is, abatement or settlement of a dispute) when power capabilities were evenly matched and low impact or no impact when power disparity was high (Bercovitch, 1985). In this chapter, we wish to replicate this examination with a much larger data set. The parties' relative power was measured using the Cox-Jacobson scale, incorporating measures of states' gross national product (GNP), military spending, GNP per capita, territorial size, and population (Cox and Jacobson, 1973). We find that where the power disparity between parties is small (0–4 on our scale), that is, where there is little difference in the power resources possessed by each party, the chances of successful mediation are 51.4 percent, compared to only 33.3 percent where power disparity is great (11+ on our scale).

Previous relations between the parties. An international dispute is not an isolated event; it has a past and presumably some sort of a future. It may occur between parties who have had a history of friendship or one of enmity. Past events and interactions cannot be discounted. Indeed, the previous relationship between the parties is cited by Deutsch (1973) as one of the main variables affecting the course and outcome of a conflict.

To assess the impact of the dynamics of a relationship, we divided the parties' previous relationships into five distinct categories: friendly, antagonistic (unfriendly but without previous conflict), conflictual (previous low-level conflict), one previous dispute between the parties, and more than one previous dispute. We found that where the parties' previous relationship was friendly the probability of successful mediation was 80 percent. Where the parties had had one or more than one previous dispute (such as in the Korean, Arab-Israeli, and Pakistan-Indian conflicts) the probability of success was only 40 percent and 46 percent respectively. Clearly the historical context of a dispute exerts a strong influence on the manner of its management and likely outcome.

The Nature of the Dispute

There is general agreement in the literature that "the success or failure of mediation is largely determined by the nature of the dispute" (Ott, 1972: 597). Naturally the choices of conflict management modes and the chances of successful mediation are affected by the importance each adversary attaches to the issues in the dispute. When vital interests are affected (for example, issues of sovereignty or territorial integrity), intermediaries will be quite unlikely to have any impact. Can we, however, go beyond this rather obvious point and identify dispute aspects more specifically and assess their effects on international mediation? In this section we try to do that.

Duration and timing of intervention. To begin with, the duration of a dispute and the timing of initiating mediation may to a large extent determine the likelihood of its success. To be effective, mediation must take place at a propitious moment. However, little agreement occurs on how to recognize when a conflict is "ripe" for mediation. Edmead (1971) claims that mediation is more likely to succeed if it is attempted at an early stage, certainly well before the adversaries cross a threshold of violence and begin to inflict heavy losses on each other. Others, such as Northedge and Donelan (1971), Ott (1972), and Pruitt (1981), suggest that mediation is more effective when a dispute has gone through a few phases and must certainly not be initiated before each side has shown a willingness to moderate its intransigence and revise its expectations.

An analysis of the mediation data set and direct interviews with experienced intermediaries both lend support to Northedge and Donelan's proposition (Bercovitch, 1984). It seems that mediation is slightly more effective when it follows, rather than precedes, some "test of strength" between the disputants. At some stage in a dispute, here at around seven to thirty-six months (by which stage the adversaries presumably have exhausted other modes), mediation efforts show the greatest degree of success (50.2 percent), compared to a 47.4 percent chance of success for earlier interventions. Attempts made at over thirty-six months are considerably less successful in mediation (38.6 percent).

Fatalities and intensity at time of intervention. Closely related to the timing of mediation is dispute intensity. The costs incurred by the parties from continuing a conflict may at some point become so overwhelming that further losses are deemed intolerable and unacceptable. Here again the literature on mediation offers two contradictory points of view. Jackson (1952) and Young (1967, 1968) suggest that the greater the intensity of a dispute, the higher the likelihood that mediation will be accepted and be successful (as a way of cutting losses, if nothing else). An opposing view contends that the greater the intensity and the higher the losses, the more polarized the parties' positions will become and the more determined each party will be to reject any mediation effort and attempt to "win" at all costs (Brockner, 1982; Burton, 1969; Modelski, 1964).

To test these hypotheses, we evaluated the intensity of an international dispute by the number of fatalities and related this to mediation outcomes. We found a clear and significant relationship between low fatalities and successful mediation. Just over 39 percent of mediation attempts had any degree of success in disputes with more than 10,000 fatalities, compared to 64 percent of successful outcomes in low-fatality (100–500 fatalities) disputes. Although we examined fatalities in isolation from other variables, they are clearly an important factor in determining the success or failure of mediation.

Issues. The literature on mediation abounds with ideas linking mediation effectiveness to the nature of the issues in dispute. Ott sees the "absence of vital national security interests, particularly questions of territorial control" (1972:616) as a necessary precondition for successful mediation. Randle contends that "should a dispute affect vital security interests of the parties, no amount of mediation by a third party is likely to prevent the outbreak of hostilities" (1973:49). And Lall, himself a practitioner as well as a student of international mediation, contends that "it is one of the principles of international negotiation that when territory is at stake, the party in possession tends to resist third party involvement" (1966:100). What they all seem to say is that the adversaries' perception of the issues is a key factor in determining whether or not to accept a mediation initiative and in influencing whether it will have much success.

Issues in conflict are the underlying causes of a dispute. They may not always be clear, but they refer to what the dispute is all about. Often more than one issue may be involved, and the parties themselves may not agree on what constitutes a disputed issue or on its relative importance. Here we suggest five categories to describe and reflect the tangible and intangible types of issues that may characterize international disputes: sovereignty, ideology, security, independence, and all other issues (including ethnicity).

Sovereignty disputes refer here to disputes where the adversaries have incompatible claims to a specific piece of territory (for example, Argentina-England dispute over the Falklands/Malvinas, Iraq-Kuwait Gulf War). Ideology disputes are defined as disputes based on strong disagreements over the nature of a political system, basic values, or beliefs (for example, Iran-Iraq, Korean, U.S.-Panama conflicts). Security disputes are disputes over frontiers, borders, and territories (for example, 1967 Arab-Israeli war, India-Bangladesh dispute, U.S.-Libya dispute). Independence disputes are fought by countries seeking to liberate themselves from another state and to determine their own national selfhood (for example, Mozambique-Portugal, Lithuania-USSR, Bouganville-PNG disputes).

Looking at the data set, we see that sovereignty (36.3 percent) and security (23.6 percent) are the most prevalent issues in contention in international disputes. A more interesting feature is that ideology disputes (50.4 percent chance of success) are more amenable to mediation than security disputes (where only 40.7 percent of mediation attempts had some success) and sovereignty disputes (44.7 percent success). Where disputes were over issues of resources and ethnicity, the chances of successful mediation were even higher (70 percent and 66.7 percent respectively). The nature of the issue can, and does, affect mediation outcomes.

There can be no doubt that issues in dispute, and how they are perceived, make a difference to the probability of achieving a successful or unsuccessful outcome. This argument is implicit in much of the writing on mediation. Here we provide some preliminary evidence to suggest the kinds of issues that are best handled by international mediation. Other studies (for example, Kochan and Jick, 1978; Kressel, 1972) offer different views.

The Nature of the Mediator

The identity and characteristics of a mediator have been cited by some (Brett, Drieghe, and Shapiro, 1986; Carnevale, 1986; Young, 1968) as predictors of success. Others, such as Harbottle (1979), Kockan and Jick (1978), and Ott (1972), do not view the mediator as a critical determinant, relegating him/her to a secondary position. Thus it seems possible to argue, on one hand, that the personal characteristics of mediators as major agents differentiate effective from ineffective mediation, or on the other hand that personal traits are largely irrelevant. What really matters is the nature of the dispute. Either way, it would be useful to investigate the relationship between mediators' characteristics and the effectiveness of their mediation.

Mediation is a voluntary process. This means that mediators cannot mediate unless they are perceived as reasonable, acceptable, knowledgeable, and able to secure the trust and cooperation of the disputants. Jackson, himself an experienced international mediator, makes this quite clear: "It would be difficult, if not impossible, for a single mediator, who was distrusted by one of the parties, to carry out any useful function" (1952: 129).

Effective mediation also depends not only on the mediator's knowledge of conflict and conflict management but also on his/her prestige and authority, originality of ideas, access to resources, and ability to act unobtrusively. In a theoretical discussion, Wehr (1979) lists the attributes required for successful mediation as including knowledge about conflict situations, an ability to understand the positions of the antagonists, active listening, a sense of timing, communication skills, procedural skills (for example, chairing meetings), and crisis management.

The list of desired personal attributes for a successful international mediator is very long indeed. Among the attributes that experienced international mediators cite as particularly important are intelligence, stamina, energy, patience, and a sense of humor (Bercovitch, 1984). Such personal qualities are associated with success in other areas of human endeavor; they are, of course, no less important in international mediation. Trust, credibility, and a high degree of personal skill and competence in the mediator are also necessary preconditions for effective mediation (Karim and Pegnetter, 1983; Landsberger, 1960).

Another characteristic that has traditionally been cited as being strongly associated with effective mediation is even-handedness or impartiality. Young claims that "a high score in such areas as impartiality would seem to be at the heart of successful interventions in many situations" (1967:81). His views are echoed by Jackson (1952), as well as Northedge and Donelan (1971), who claim that parties will have confidence in a mediator only if he/she is perceived as impartial.

We are, however, doubtful of the importance of this attribute. The traditional emphasis on impartiality stems from the failure to recognize mediation as a reciprocal process of social interaction in which the mediator is a major participant. It is entirely sensible to see mediation as "assisted negotiation" (Susskind and Cruickshank, 1987); to regard mediation as an exogenous input is both erroneous and unrealistic. A mediator engages in behavior that is designed to elicit information and exercise influence. Mediators are accepted by the adversaries not because of their impartiality but because of their ability to influence, protect, or extend the interests of each party in conflict (Faure, 1989; Kressel and Pruitt, 1985; Smith, 1985; Touval, 1985; Touval and Zartman, 1985).

To exercise any degree of influence, mediators need "leverage," or resources to search for information and move the parties away from rigid positions. Leverage or resources buttress the mediator's ability to facilitate a successful outcome through the balancing of power discrepancies and enhancing of cooperative behavior. The mediator's task is also essentially one of reframing and persuasion (Edmead, 1971; Frei, 1976; Gross-Stein, 1985; Touval and Zartman, 1985). These strategies are most successful, as Touval and Zartman (1985) observe, not when a mediator is unbiased or impartial but when he/she possesses resources that either disputant values. Effective mediation in international relations is more a matter of mediators' utilization of resources, leverage, and influence commensurate with their position to enhance fairness than it is of impartiality (Brookmire and Sistrunk, 1980).

One of the most effective resources any international mediator can possess is legitimacy. Leaders of states and high-level officials such as foreign or prime ministers have legitimacy and can bring it to bear together with their status and respect (Ott, 1972; Touval and Zartman, 1985). Under the proper auspices and sponsorship of high-ranking mediators, an environment of credibility, trust, and joint interests may be established. The presence of a powerful and legitimate mediator allows the parties to back down from fixed positions, make concessions, and "save face" (Pruitt and Johnson, 1970). Leaders and representatives of large governments with more resources at their disposal will be more likely to be successful mediators than other actors.

Mediator rank. One way in which we can examine this notion empirically is to classify all mediators according to rank. Mediators have different ranks and possess different resources, both of which they use in different ways in different disputes (Bercovitch, 1992). Reflecting the diversity of possible mediators in the international environment, we have ranked mediators along a dimension ranging from government leaders and representatives of regional and international organizations to private individuals.

In relating rank to mediation outcomes, we find that mediators with the best success rate are leaders and representatives of regional organizations (62.4 percent and 50 percent respectively). They are followed by leaders or representatives of small governments (54.8 percent and 56.8 percent respectively). Interestingly, both leaders and representatives of large states fare rather worse than expected (40 percent and 31.3 percent respectively), as do representatives of international organizations (only 23.8 percent).

Regional organizations (such as the Organization of African Unity, the Organization of African States, Contadora group, and the Economic Community of West African States) with common ideals, perspectives, and interests appear to offer the best chances of successful outcomes in international mediation. In contrast, international organizations such as the United Nations have a very poor record in the area of mediation. One may argue that an organization such as the United Nations usually deals with the more intractable disputes that resist mediation and other forms of conflict management, whereas regional organizations deal with less serious disputes. A more compelling argument asserts that regional organizations always mediate within the same cultural and value system—and this, it seems, promotes agreement more than any other factor.

Previous relationship with the parties. We can also assess mediators' influence, leverage, and legitimacy by examining their previous relationship with the adversaries. The importance adversaries assign to a continuing relationship with a mediator may well influence their perception of a dispute and their behavior. Where a mediator is aligned with one of the parties or shares a common experience or goals with one party and future interactions are important to both, each disputant may show greater flexibility and confidence in the outcome. Mediator alignment, past relationship with the adversaries, and the mediator's own interests affect both mediator behavior and mediation outcomes.

Frei (1976) found that mediators who shared religious, ideological, or economic values had a higher chance of success than other mediators. We examined the consequences of mediator alignment by looking at the political structure of mediator-parties relationships. Thus mediators may come from the same political bloc as one or both of the parties, a different bloc, be unaligned, or have no previous relationship with the parties. We found that those mediators who came from the same bloc as both adversaries had a significantly higher chance of being successful (62.18 percent) than mediators from the same bloc as one of the parties only (31.4 percent) or a mediator from a different bloc (51 percent). Mediators from the same bloc have a strong self-interest in maintaining peace and stability, and a greater chance of doing so.

PROCESS VARIABLES

The Initiation of Mediation

Thus far we have evaluated the impact of different contextual factors on mediation. Here we consider the mediation process itself—the way it is initiated and conducted.

A question that invariably confronts all potential mediators and parties to conflict is whether or not they should take the step of initiating mediation. It is agreed that to be effective mediation must take place under the most propitious conditions, but just whose decision should it be to intiate mediation?

Since mediation is essentially a voluntary process, it is logical to assume that a conflict will be most constructively and effectively dealt with through mediation when both the parties are willing to commit themselves to the process. Hiltrop (1985) suggests that mediation is most successful when both of the adversaries request it. In cases where only one party is interested in seeking mediation assistance, or interested third parties propose it, the effectiveness of mediation may be reduced considerably.

An analysis of our data set clearly indicates that mediation is most likely to be successful (62.3 percent) when initiated by both parties to a dispute, as opposed to only one of the parties requesting mediation (41.3 percent). Surprisingly, mediation also appears to be highly successful (60 percent) when regional organizations initiate proceedings, perhaps because of common interests and relationships shared with the parties. In contrast, mediation initiated by a mediator or by international organizations achieved only 41.2 percent and 29.7 percent success rates respectively.

Mediation Environment

One of the central tasks of mediation is to accentuate cooperation and tendencies toward agreement. This is best achieved when the parties' conflict management takes place in a neutral environment, free from the external pressures and influences of constituents and media. Such an environment allows the mediator to have procedural control over the process and the parties to concentrate on the more substantive issues. In a neutral environment, a mediator is able to create a level playing field by guaranteeing each party free and equal access to information and resources, maintaining the flow of communication between the parties, and, where necessary, balancing power differences between the parties.

Our data confirm the importance of environment in the success of mediation. Mediation on neutral ground (including mediator territory) provides the conditions most conducive to successful mediation, achieving a 49.5 percent and 54.4 percent chance of success respectively. This is in contrast to mediations held on the parties' territories (45 percent) or mediations that have moved among a number of different sites (36.4 percent). An appropriate site, then, can considerably influence the success or failure of mediation.

Strategies of Mediation

Evaluating the relationship between what mediators do and the outcomes of their efforts is, on the whole, based on ex post facto reflections by mediators (and they may be quite reluctant either to claim success or to take responsibility for failure) or on direct observations of their performance (rarely, if ever, available in international relations). Although conceptualizing or measuring mediator behavior, roles, and strategies is difficult, many agree with Kochan and Jick (1978) and Touval (1982) that it is the most crucial variable affecting mediation outcomes.

There are many typologies for describing mediation strategy and behavior (Bercovitch, 1984; Kochan and Jick, 1978; Kolb, 1983; Kressel, 1972). Here we follow Touval and Zartman (1985), who classify mediator behavior along a continuum ranging from low to high intervention. We identify three main strategies that encompass the spectrum of mediator behavior (Bercovitch et al., 1991). At the low end of the spectrum are communication-facilitation strategies where a mediator takes a fairly passive role, largely as a channel of communication or go-between for the parties, and exhibits little control over the process or substance of mediation. In the second set of mediation strategies, procedural strategies, a mediator exercises more formal control over situational aspects or the process of mediation. Here a mediator may determine such factors as the mediation environment, the number and type of meetings with the adversaries, the agendas covered in those meetings, the control of constituency influences, and the distribution of information and resources to the parties. In the most active range of mediator behavior, directive strategies, the mediator sets out to affect the content and substance as well as the process of mediation. A mediator may achieve these goals by providing incentives, offering rewards and punishments, issuing ultimatums, and introducing new proposals.

Which of these strategies is most effective in international disputes? Kochan and Jick (1978), for instance, found that industrial mediators who used directive strategies were more successful than mediators who used communication strategies. Carnevale and Pegnetter (1985), on the other hand, in their survey of mediators found communication-facilitation strategies to be more effective than other kinds. In an earlier study, Bercovitch (1986) found that communication strategies were the most commonly used but directive strategies were the most successful.

Here we examine the relationship between different mediation strategies and mediation outcomes. A clear pattern emerges that shows that the likelihood of achieving a successful mediation outcome is 52.3 percent when directive strategies are employed and only 32.2 percent when communication-facilitation strategies are used. This relationship is particularly strong when disputes are intense (Donohue, 1989; Hiltrop, 1989). Mediators who possess the ability, opportunity, and resources to initiate and engage in active mediation are more likely to produce a successful outcome than powerless mediators who put their faith in communication strategies only. Procedural strategies, while used in only 16 percent of all mediation attempts, have a 48.4 percent chance of success.

Mediation operates within a system of reciprocal social influence in which the parties and the mediator seek to influence each other. Mediation behavior is not based on a specific predetermined plan of action but reflects the changing context of a dispute and the interests and needs of all concerned. A mediator has to be seen as a full, if external, participant in a conflictual decisionmaking system. As such, it is not at all surprising that possession of resources and an active strategy provide the basis for successful mediation.

CONCLUSION

Third-party assistance or mediation is one of the most promising approaches to constructive conflict management. To understand it better, we need to study what mediators do, how they do it, and the consequences of their actions. In this chapter, we have sought to organize what is known about mediation, extract propositions about how it works, and identify a number of factors that are hypothesized to affect its outcomes. Although we restricted ourselves here to the field of international mediation, our findings are intended to be applicable to other mediation arenas.

Our understanding of mediation is predicated on the notion that mediation is related to the overall context in which it occurs. The overall context affects mediation and is, in turn, affected by it. Hence mediation can best be seen as an extension of bilateral conflict management, not a replacement of it. The nature and effectiveness of mediation depend as much on who the parties are and the character of their dispute and interaction, as on who the mediator is and his/her behavior. Mediation is a contingent form of political influence; its performance and results are contingent on context. To overlook this point is to mistake the nature of mediation in international relations.

Here we have gathered information on a large number of mediation cases and tested various propositions to identify the factors that are closely correlated with the success or failure of mediation. The results of our analysis offer some exciting insights into the most significant factors and are summarized in Figure 1.6. It emerges that components of all four of the clusters of our framework have a direct impact on mediation outcome. Our results reveal that all the factors, from the disputants themselves—who they are, their past relationship, their sociopolitical norms and power, the actual dispute, the issues at stake, its intensity and duration—to the mediator and the way he/she influences the process of conflict management, determine the success of mediation.

Figure 1.6 Factors Associated with Successful Mediation

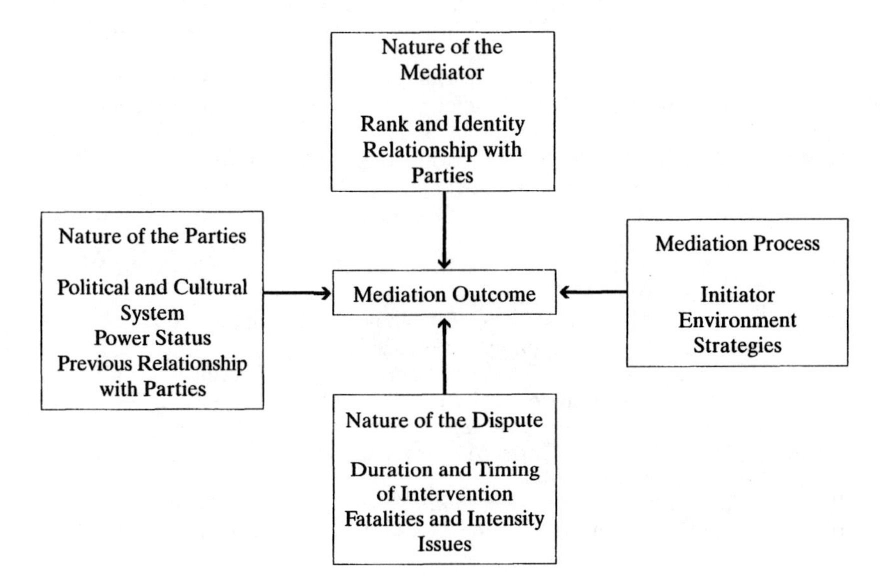

The approach and method adopted here are deliberately limited in their scope. Future research will be directed toward specifying more clearly how each factor, in itself and combined with others, transforms a conflict system. We hope that the approach we have taken and the results presented here take us some way toward viewing mediation in the proper perspective. By viewing it accurately, studying it in actual situations, and acknowledging its richness and diversity we can provide the necessary guidelines for more effective mediation in international relations.

REFERENCES

Bercovitch, J. (1984). *Social Conflicts and Third Parties: Strategies of Conflict Resolution.* Boulder, Colo.: Westview.

Bercovitch, J. (1985). "International Mediation: Incidence and Outcomes." Unpublished paper. University of Canterbury, Christchurch, N. Z.

Bercovitch, J. (1986). "International Mediation: A Study of Incidence, Strategies and Conditions of Successful Outcomes." *Cooperation and Conflict* 21: 155–168.

Bercovitch J. (1989). "International Dispute Mediation." In K. Kressel and D. Pruitt, eds., *Mediation Research.* San Francisco: Jossey-Bass, 284–299.

Bercovitch, J. (1992). "The Structure and Diversity of Mediation in International Relations." In J. Bercovitch and J. Rubin, eds., *Mediation in International Relations: Multiple Approaches to Conflict Management.* New York: St. Martin's.

Bercovitch, J., Agnoson, J. T., and Wille, D. (1991). "Some Contextual Issues and Empirical Trends in the Study of Successful Mediation in International Relations." *Journal of Peace Research* 28: 7–17.

Bercovitch, J., and Houston, A. (1993). "Influence of Mediator Characteristics and Behavior on the Success of Mediation in International Relations." *International Journal of Conflict Management* 4: 297–321.

Bercovitch, J., and Langley, J. (1993). "The Nature of the Dispute and the Effectiveness of International Mediation." *Journal of Conflict Resolution* 37: 670–691.

Bercovitch, J., and Wells, R. (1993). "Evaluating Mediation Strategies: A Theoretical and Empirical Analysis." *Peace and Change* 18: 3–25.

Bremer, S. N. (1993). "Advancing the Scientific Study of War." *International Interactions* 19: 1–26.

Brett, J. M., Drieghe, R., and Shapiro, D. L. (1986). "Mediator Style and Mediation Effectiveness." *Negotiation Journal* 2: 277–285.

Brockner, J. (1982). "Factors Affecting Entrapment in Escalating Conflicts." *Journal of Research in Personality* 6: 247–266.

Brookmire, D., and Sistrunk, F. (1980). "The Effects of Perceived Ability and Impartiality of Mediator and Time Pressure on Negotiation." *Journal of Conflict Resolution* 24: 311–327.

Burton, J. W. (1968). *Systems, States, Diplomacy and Rules.* Cambridge: Cambridge University Press.

Burton, J. W. (1969). *Conflict and Communication.* London: Macmillan.

Burton, J. W. (1972). "The Resolution of Conflict." *International Studies Quarterly* 16: 5–29.

Burton, J. W. (1979). *Deviance, Terrorism and War.* Oxford: Martin Robertson.
Burton, J. W. (1984). *Global Conflict.* Brighton, Sussex: Wheatsheaf Books.
Butterworth, R. (1976). *Managing Interstate Disputes, 1945–1974.* Pittsburgh, Penn.: University of Pittsburgh Press.
Carnevale, P. (1986). "Strategic Choice in Mediation." *Negotiation Journal* 2: 41–56.
Carnevale, P., and Pegnetter, R. (1985). "The Selection of Mediation Tactics in Public Sector Disputes: A Contingency Analysis." *Journal of Social Issues* 41: 65–81.
Cioffi-Revilla, C. (1990). *The Scientific Measurement of International Conflict.* Boulder, Colo.: Lynne Rienner.
Cox, R., and Jacobson, H. (1973). *The Anatomy of Influence.* New Haven: Yale University Press.
Deutsch, M. (1973). *The Resolution of Conflict.* New Haven: Yale University Press.
Donohue, W. A. (1989). "Communicative Competence in Mediators." In Kressel and Pruitt, *Mediation Research,* 322–343.
Doob, L. W. (1971). *Resolving Conflict in Africa.* New Haven: Yale University Press.
Doob, L. W. (1993). *Intervention: Guides and Perils.* New Haven: Yale University Press.
Dryzek, J. S., and Hunter, S. (1987). "Environmental Mediation for International Problems." *International Studies Quarterly* 31: 87–102.
Edmead, F. (1971). *Analysis and Prediction in International Mediation.* New York: UNITAR Study.
Faure, G. O. (1989). "The Mediators as Third Negotiators." In E. Mautner-Markhof, ed., *Process of International Negotiations.* Boulder, Colo.: Westview, 415–426.
Fisher, R. (1983). "Third Party Consultation as a Method of Intergroup Conflict Resolution." *Journal of Conflict Resolution* 27: 301–344.
Folberg, J. and Taylor, A. (1984). *Mediation: A Comprehensive Guide to Resolving Conflicts Without Litigation.* San Francisco: Jossey-Bass.
Frei, D. (1976). "Conditions Affecting the Effectiveness of International Mediation." *Peace Science Society (International) Papers* 26: 67–84.
Gross-Stein, J. (1985). "Structures, Strategies, and Tactics of Mediation: Kissinger and Carter in the Middle East." *Negotiation Journal* 1: 331–347.
Gulliver, P. H. (1979). *Disputes and Negotiations: Cross-Cultural Perspectives.* New York: Academic Press.
Haas, Ernst B. (1986). *Why We Still Need the United Nations.* Policy Paper no. 26. Berkeley, Calif.: University of California, Department of Political Science.
Harbottle, M. (1979). "The Strategy of Third Party Intervention in Conflict Situations." *International Journal* 35: 118–131.
Hiltrop, J. M. (1985). "Mediator Behavior and the Settlement of Collective Bargaining Disputes in Britain." *Journal of Social Issues* 41: 83–99.
Hiltrop, J. M. (1989). "Factors Associated With Successful Labour Mediation." In Kressel and Pruitt, *Mediation Research,* 241–262.
Jackson, E. (1952). *Meeting of Minds.* New York: McGraw-Hill.
Karim, A., and Pegnetter, R. (1983). "Mediator Strategies, Qualities and Mediation Effectiveness." *Industrial Relations* 22: 105–114.
Kochan, T. A., and Jick, T. (1978). "A Theory of Public Sector Mediation Process." *Journal of Conflict Resolution* 22: 209–240.
Kolb, D. M. (1983). "Strategy and Tactics of Mediation." *Human Relations* 36: 247–268.

Kressel, K. (1972). *Labor Mediation: An Exploratory Survey.* New York: Association of Labor Mediation Agencies.
Kressel, K., and Pruitt, D. G. (1985). "Themes in the Mediation of Social Conflict." *Journal of Social Issues* 1: 179–198.
Kressel, K. and Pruitt, D. G., eds. (1989). *Mediation Research: The Process and Effectiveness of Third-Party Intervention.* San Francisco: Jossey-Bass.
Lall, A. (1966). *Modern International Negotiation.* New York: Columbia University Press.
Landsberger, H. (1960). "The Behavior and Personality of the Labor Mediator." *Personnel Psychology* 13: 329–348.
Mack, R. and Snyder, R. (1957). "An Analysis of Social Conflict: Toward an Overview and Synthesis." *Journal of Conflict Resolution* 1: 212–248.
Maoz, Z. (1982). *Paths to Conflict: International Dispute Initiation.* Boulder, Colo.: Westview.
Maoz, Z., and Abdolali, N. (1989). "Regime Types and International Conflict, 1816–1976." *Journal of Conflict Resolution* 33: 3–35.
Meyer, A. (1960). "Functions of the Mediator in Collective Bargaining." *Industrial and Labour Relations Review* 13: 161.
Mitchell, C. R. (1981). *Peacemaking and the Consultant's Role.* Westmead, U.K.: Gower.
Mitchell, C. R. and Webb, K. (1988). *New Approaches to International Mediation.* Westport, Conn.: Greenwood.
Modelski, G. (1964). "International Settlement of Internal Wars." In J. Rosenau, ed., *International Aspects of Civil Strife.* Princeton, N.J.: Princeton University Press.
Moore, C. W. (1986). *The Mediation Process: Practical Strategies for Resolving Conflict.* San Francisco: Jossey-Bass.
Northedge, F. S., and Donelan, M. (1971). *International Disputes: The Political Aspects.* London: Europa.
Ott, M. C. (1972). "Mediation as a Method of Conflict Resolution." *International Organization* 26: 595–618.
Pruitt, D. G. (1981). *Negotiation Behavior.* New York: Academic Press.
Pruitt, D. G. and Johnson, D. F. (1970). "Mediation as an Aid to Facesaving in Negotiation." *Journal of Personality and Social Psychology* 14: 239–246.
Randle, R. F. (1973). *The Origins of Peace.* New York: Free Press.
Raymond, G. A. and Kegley, C. W., Jr. (1985). "Third Party Mediation and International Norms: A Test of Two Models." *Conflict Management and Peace Science* 9: 33–51.
Rubin, J. Z. (1980). "Experimental Research on Third Party Intervention in Conflict." *Psychological Bulletin* 87: 379–391.
Simkin, W. (1971). *Mediation and the Dynamics of Collective Bargaining.* Washington, D.C.: Bureau of National Affairs.
Singer, J. D., and Small, M. (1982). *Resort to Arms.* Beverly Hills, Calif.: Sage.
Smith, W. P. (1985). "Effectiveness of the Biased Mediator." *Negotiation Journal* 1: 363–372.
Susskind, L., and Cruickshank, J. (1987). *Breaking the Impasse.* New York: Basic Books.
Touval, S. (1982). *The Peace Brokers: Mediators in the Arab-Israeli Conflict 1948–1979.* Princeton, N.J.: Princeton University Press.
Touval, S. (1985). "The Context of Mediation." *Negotiation Journal* 1: 373–378.
Touval, S., and Zartman, I. (1985). "Mediation in Theory." In S. Touval and I. Zartman, eds., *International Mediation in Theory and Practice.* Boulder, Colo.: Westview.

Wall, J. (1981). "Mediation: An Analysis, Review and Proposed Research." *Journal of Conflict Resolution* 25: 157–180.
Wehr, P. (1979). *Conflict Regulation.* Boulder, Colo.: Westview.
Young, O. R. (1967). *The Intermediaries: Third Parties in International Crises.* Princeton, N.J.: Princeton University Press.
Young, O. R. (1968). *The Politics of Force.* Princeton, N.J.: Princeton University Press.

PART ONE

BIAS, NEUTRALITY, AND POWER IN INTERNATIONAL MEDIATION

CHAPTER TWO

Bias and Impartiality in International Mediation

Peter J. Carnevale and Sharon Arad

Mediation is very much a matter of influence. The mediator wants to affect the disputing parties and their attitudes, perceptions, and behaviors about the conflict and about the mediation. And the disputing parties want to affect the mediator—not only who mediates and when, but the manner in which the mediation will produce acceptable if not favorable outcomes. The central questions about mediation, then, are about influence: What attributes of the mediator will foster success (for example, acceptance of the mediator, cease-fire, settlement)? What characteristics of the dispute, or of the disputants, will enhance the likelihood that mediation will occur, and work? What strategies and tactics of mediation are likely to be used, when, and with what effect?

These questions about influence point to the preferred approach to the study of mediation: the analysis of contingencies. In the contingency approach, mediation is an adaptation to shifting circumstances in a fluid and dynamic world. And influence in mediation, such as the impact of mediator strategies and tactics, is contingent on a variety of factors—including contextual and process variables such as characteristics of the dispute and attributes of the mediator (see Bercovitch, 1991; Carnevale, Lim, and McLaughlin, 1991).

This chapter focuses on the set of mediator attributes that pertain to impartiality and bias. The discussion is largely speculative, limited to a large extent by a shortage of statistical studies of impartiality and bias in international and other arenas of mediation. Nevertheless, there is a smattering of relevant cases to draw on, and a few laboratory studies—several to be presented below—that suggest general principles about how bias and impartiality may operate.

THE INTERESTED MEDIATOR

Mediators have interests and incentives that motivate their involvement in conflict (see Carnevale, Lim, and McLaughlin, 1989; Rubin, 1992).

Young (1972), for example, states that mediator involvement in disputes is guided by cost-benefit calculations: "It is perfectly possible for situations to arise in which there is a distinct role for an intermediary but in which no third party finds it worth his while to assume this role" (p. 55). When mediators have interests, they have something at stake in the conflict. These stakes may stem from the issues at hand or from the broader political and economic context and relationships with either side.

Benefits to the mediator may be humanitarian or material; they may include a salary for professionals as well as intangible rewards such as prestige, gratitude of the disputants and others from the broader community, a sense of personal satisfaction, reputation benefits that may facilitate a political career, and political and economic influence gained or protected. Costs include expenditure of time and energy, loss of tangible resources, sense of frustration (especially in the event of failure), expenditure of political capital, and so on (see Gulliver, 1979:217; Mitchell, 1988; Touval and Zartman, 1985).

A biased mediator has something at stake and is closer to one side than the other—politically, economically, and culturally. An impartial mediator is ostensibly balanced, even "neutral" in the sense that he/she has no opinion regarding the conflict at hand, however unlikely that might be. But the terminology of bias loses meaning—or takes on new meaning—in a close analysis of how influence can operate in mediation.

Influence in mediation can stem from either the mediator's impartiality or the mediator's interests and biases. There are several basic forms of bias in mediation which will be discussed later, and the different forms interact to affect mediator acceptability and effectiveness. For example, as will be shown in the data to be presented below, mediator bias in combination with mediator evenhandedness can enhance the effectiveness of mediation.

INFLUENCE VIA IMPARTIALITY

The idea that mediators need to be impartial in the conflicts they face is pervasive. Consider Young's often-quoted statement: "the existence of a meaningful role for a third party will depend on the party's being perceived as an impartial participant (in the sense of having nothing to gain from aiding either protagonist and in the sense of being able to control any feelings of favoritism) in the eyes of the principal protagonists" (1967: 81). Stulberg (1987) goes so far as to require that a mediator be "(1) Neutral. A mediator must have no personal preference that the dispute be resolved in one way rather than another. . . . (2) Impartial. A mediator must treat all parties in comparable ways, both procedurally and substantively. . . . (3) Objective. A mediator must be able to transcend the rhetoric and emotion of the parties" (p. 37). Given this, one might think that the very best mediator is a "Eunuch from Mars," distant and disinterested, indifferent to the conflict and issues at hand. Why?

In this argument, impartiality is the main source of the mediator's influence. The mediator is more likely to be accepted and more effective in eliciting information, and the mediator's suggestions will be compelling, to the extent that he or she is untainted by any affinity with the opposing side. A suggestion from an impartial mediator is imbued with fairness. This, together with the idea that perceived fairness and trust in the mediator are key predictors of settlement in mediation (and there is evidence for this; Carnevale and Pruitt, 1992), indicates that the impartial mediator has an influence advantage. The basic idea is that mediators need to steer a precise course between the disputants lest they alienate one side and lose their credibility and acceptability.

What if one or both parties come to believe that the mediator is hostile or biased against them? Such beliefs have been shown to reduce disputant receptivity to mediators (Welton and Pruitt, 1987). With a biased mediator, the disfavored party will be less likely to heed the mediator's suggestions for settlement, less likely to divulge information about underlying interests, and less likely to accept the mediator as a mediator in the first place—all of which might otherwise contribute to the successful resolution of conflict.

INFLUENCE VIA INTERESTS AND BIASES

Another view, articulated by Touval and others, regards mediation as an extension of negotiation, as "three-cornered bargaining" where the mediator is a player in a "realist" framework of international or interpersonal politics (Touval, 1975, 1982, 1985, 1992; see also Touval and Zartman, 1985; Zartman and Touval, 1985). Mediation is seen as a policy instrument and a preferred alternative in a choice situation. In this framework, it is better to accept a particular mediator—despite any apparent biases—than to reject that mediator, particularly given a "hurting stalemate" and that continued conflict is costly (Zartman and Touval, 1985). And from the perspective of the mediator, it is better to mediate than not mediate given that vital interests need to be protected or extended.

In other words, real bias can play an important role in mediation when the bias adds to the mediator's capacity and desire to influence. A mediator may have access to the other side, and the potential to deliver concessions and agreements, despite an apparent bias.

Examples include the Algerian mediators in the Iran hostage crisis, who had "the required revolutionary credentials and the necessary international connections needed for the job" (Slim, 1992:228; see Sick, 1985). Consider also the Anglo-American mediation of the Italy-Yugoslavia dispute over Trieste in 1954 (Campbell, 1976), the American mediation in the Israeli-Arab conflict, and so on (Touval, 1975). And examples are plentiful in domestic contexts: a management negotiator accepts mediation by a prolabor mediator when that mediator is seen as having greater capacity to influence the intransigent union negotiator (Kressel, 1972).

In addition, the party that is favored may want to preserve its relationship with the mediator and the disfavored party may seek to earn the mediator's goodwill (Touval, 1975). This effect is heightened to the extent that the mediator has benefits to provide, such as the resources to reward concessions and cooperation. One may want to accept a large-power mediator in an effort to gain closer ties with that mediator and move the mediator closer to oneself than to the adversary, as Sadat did in wanting mediation by U.S. secretary of state Kissinger (Bobrow, 1981).

Not unrelated is the concept of the "Insider-Partial" developed by Wehr and Lederach (1991), a type of mediator who emerges from within the conflict and whose involvement stems from a positive, trust-based connection to the parties and to the future relationship between disputant and mediator. Lieb (1985) notes that Iran and Iraq agreed on mediation by the Algerians, specifically by Boumedienne, a Muslim leader and member of the Muslim community: that is, a "member of the same family" (p. 82).

These observations not only challenge the view that mediator bias and interests are totally incompatible with success but suggest that they can enhance influence and success. A biased mediator may not just be the only one available to mediate the conflict, but may also be the one with the greatest influence over the party that most needs to change.

EFFECTS OF MEDIATOR BIAS ON MEDIATOR BEHAVIOR

Touval (1975) observes that mediator acceptability is not a single-act decision at the start of negotiation, but is earned and recognized throughout. In the book by Kalb and Kalb (1974), Kissinger is described as constantly concerned about his credentials as an "even-handed" mediator. Touval and Zartman note that a mediator can disconnect his or her biases. What do mediators do to temper perceptions of bias?

In the 1966 mediation of the India-Pakistan conflict over Kashmir at Tashkent, Aleksei Kosygin, premier of the Soviet Union, stressed his evenhandedness despite stronger ties to India. Signs of this included his efforts to maintain balanced press coverage of both sides, balanced references to each side in Soviet speeches, and even ritualistic alternation of whose name was mentioned first (Thornton, 1985:156).

Another example is the mediation by the United States in the early stages of the dispute between Great Britain and Argentina over the Falkland Islands. Despite more substantial ties to Britain, the United States presented a neutral front and made apposite statements to the point that the British feared an unfavorable mediated agreement (Smith, 1985:369–370). It has been suggested that the United States wanted to preserve relations with both sides (Purcell, 1982).

In a laboratory study, we (Carnevale, Lawler, and Fobian, 1985) demonstrated that mediators can temper their biases for one side especially when they have long-term interests with the disputants. We hypothesized that biased mediators who had the potential of future interaction would be especially concerned about appearing biased, and would make a greater effort to equalize outcomes between the disputants in order to preserve their acceptability.

The experimental design involved two factors: the extent of mediator bias (biased vs. unbiased) and the potential of future mediation (potential vs. no potential). Each subject—a university student—was seated in front of a computer and told that he or she would be interacting via the computer in a simulated negotiation with two other participants. They were led to believe that each had been randomly assigned to represent one of three countries: two of the countries (Country West and Country East) were in conflict and would negotiate with one another, and the third (Country North) would act as a mediator of the negotiations. Actually, each participant was assigned to North, the mediator, and told that his or her task was to "facilitate an agreement between the two negotiators."

The task is shown in Table 2.1. The numbers represented monetary payoffs, and if there were going to be an agreement, the negotiators would have to agree on one letter. The subjects were shown the negotiators' lists and could see that the payoff values of West and East were negatively correlated; also, they were told that neither East nor West would see the other's payoffs.

Negotiators (the computer program) made a bid (a letter from the list), and the mediator (the subject) was then asked to make a nonbinding recommendation to the negotiators for a point at which he or she felt the negotiators should settle (also a letter from the list). At the end of six rounds the negotiation was stopped and subjects were asked to respond to a questionnaire.

In the biased conditions of the experiment, the subject's payoffs were positively correlated with West's payoffs and negatively correlated with East's (see Table 2.1). In the unbiased condition, the subjects' payoff list had the same value for all letters in the list (315, the middle value of the list in the biased-mediator conditions). There also was a manipulation of expected future interaction: in the potential-future-mediation conditions, subjects were told there would be five different negotiations and that they

Table 2.1 Payoff List Seen by a Subject in the Bias Conditions

Proposal	North[a]	West	East
A	420	840	220
B	409	819	241
C	399	798	262
D	388	777	283
E	378	756	304
F	367	735	325
G	357	714	346
H	346	693	367
I	336	672	388
J	325	651	409
K[b]	315	630	430
L	304	609	451
M	294	588	472
N	283	567	493
O	273	546	514
P[c]	262	525	535
Q	252	504	556
R	241	483	577
S	231	462	598
T	220	441	619
U	210	420	640

Notes: a. North's payoff was 315 for all levels in the unbiased condition.
b. Midpoint and equal-sacrifice point.
c. Approximate equal negotiator outcome.

would be the mediator in the first one and would also mediate the last four if the negotiators wanted them to. In the no-potential-future-mediation conditions, there would be only one negotiation.

The main dependent variable was the payoff value that the mediators gave to themselves, averaged across rounds (see the North column in Table 2.1). In the unbiased condition, where the mediators' payoffs were equal across all possible outcomes, we used the payoffs that corresponded to the payoff list to North in the biased condition. As can be seen in Row 2 of Table 2.2, biased mediators gave themselves less, and equalized negotiators' outcomes more, when there was a potential for future mediation than when there was not. It was as important to the biased mediators who

Table 2.2 Data on the Behavior of Biased Mediators

	No Future Mediation		Future Mediation	
Dependent Variable	Biased	Unbiased	Biased	Unbiased
Favor West more than East	4.07	2.94	3.50	3.13
Overall recommendations	352.00	303.00	329.00	306.00
Important to appear unbiased	4.00	4.56	4.56	4.53

had future mediation to appear unbiased as it was for the unbiased mediators (Row 3 of Table 2.2).

There was an interesting effect regarding the behavior of the unbiased mediators. The outcomes of the unbiased mediators were indifferent across all possible outcomes (315 for A through U) yet their recommendations were near level K, the midpoint on the scale. If they wanted to maximize equal outcomes for the negotiators, they would have recommended P.

There are at least two possible explanations for this: (1) they followed an equal-sacrifice rule, with each negotiator giving up the same amount from his or her maximum payoff, or (2) they wanted to make recommendations that appeared fair to the negotiators, who did not know one another's numerical payoffs but could see that K is the midpoint. The latter interpretation suggests that mediators are more concerned about the appearance of fairness than about the reality of fairness.

EFFECTS OF MEDIATOR BIAS ON DISPUTANT REACTIONS TO MEDIATION

The experiment just described suggests that mediators are able to alter their behavior—they can bend over backwards—to temper their biases and attempt to preserve their acceptability to disputants. This suggests that evenhanded mediator behavior in mediation may eclipse the initial apparent expected bias of the mediator.

In other words, there may be two basic forms of bias in mediation: (1) *bias of content,* which pertains to mediator behavior: for example, one side being favored over the other in a mediator's settlement proposal, and (2) *bias of source characteristic,* which pertains to expectations that stem from the mediator's closer personal, political, or economic ties with one party. Pruitt (1983) argues that the former type of bias makes it difficult to mediate effectively with the nonfavored party but that it is possible in some circumstances for disputants to ignore the latter kind of bias. Both forms of bias may have important effects on judgments of the mediator and the mediator's proposals. But the evidence is sketchy.

In one of our earlier laboratory studies, we reported that (1) the content of mediator proposals had a greater impact on the mediator's acceptability than the source characteristics of the mediator, and (2) mediators who made favorable proposals were mistrusted when the mediator had unfavorable source bias. The latter effect was labeled a "Trojan Horse" effect, that is, something favorable from someone you expect to be against you is distrusted (Wittmer, Carnevale, and Walker, 1991).

In a follow-up study, we (Carnevale and Conlon, 1988) had university students play the role of negotiators in a laboratory task similar to the one described earlier. The students dealt with a mediator (actually a computer program) that made outcome recommendations. There were two independent variables:

1. *Mediator source bias*: (1) unfavorable bias: mediator outcomes were negatively correlated with one's own (opposite); (2) favorable bias: mediator outcomes were positively correlated with one's own (identical); (3) interest in agreement: mediator outcomes were contingent only on agreement being reached; or (4) disinterested: mediator had nothing at stake.
2. *Mediator content bias*: mediator outcome recommendations in the negotiation were either: (1) favorable to the student; (2) evenhanded; (3) unfavorable to the student; or (4) the mediator did not make outcome recommendations.

The data shown in Table 2.3 pertain to the students' evaluations of how fair they thought the mediator was in the negotiation. In general, mediators who made evenhanded suggestions were seen as most fair, and behavior in mediation was more important than the initial alignment or source characteristics of the mediator. Moreover, the data indicate that (1) mediators who made proposals that were unfavorable were seen as more fair when the initial expectation was that the mediator would be on one's own side, which was labeled a "cushioning" effect; and (2) mediators gained in acceptability when the initial expectation was that the mediator would be aligned with the other, but then made proposals that were clearly evenhanded, which was labeled a "fairness pays" effect.

Table 2.3 Perceived Fairness of the Mediator as a Function of Two Forms of Mediator Bias

	Mediator Recommendation			
Mediator Alignment	Favorable	Evenhanded	Unfavorable	None
Favorable	2.44	3.57	2.29	3.88
Unfavorable	2.27	4.36	1.20	3.07
Impartial-interested	2.20	4.25	1.43	4.06
Impartial-disinterested	2.19	4.60	1.53	3.71

Taken together, these data suggest that bias in mediation has at least two facets—bias of behavior, and bias of general alignment—and these two forms of bias interact to influence the mediator's acceptability.

PARTISANS AND NONPARTISANS

In a recent study, we (Arad and Carnevale, 1994) demonstrated that perceived bias is in the eye of the beholder. We enlisted the aid of two groups of individuals: those who held partisan, pro-Israeli views of the Israeli-Palestinian conflict (mostly Jewish students at the University of Illinois), and those who were nonpartisan, that is, relatively neutral, less knowledgeable, and less personally involved in the conflict. The subjects were given a mediator's proposal for the resolution of the Israeli-Palestinian conflict in Jerusalem and were asked to evaluate its fairness as well as the trustworthiness of the individual who proposed it. We manipulated the favorableness of the mediator's proposals (content bias) as well as favorableness of the mediator (source bias), and expected partisans and nonpartisans to differ in their reactions. A 2 × 2 × 4 factorial design examined:

1. *Partisanship* of the subject, either partisan (pro-Israeli; students in Israeli fraternities and clubs) or nonpartisan (neutral);
2. *Content bias* of mediator proposals, where the substance of the proposal was either (a) pro-Israeli or (b) evenhanded;
3. *Source bias,* where the mediator was labeled as being (a) pro-Israeli, (b) pro-Palestinian, (c) neutral, or (d) of unknown persuasion.

Partisans. Research on self-serving bias in judgments suggests that judgments of fairness often derive from self-interest (Thompson and Loewenstein, 1992). This suggests that partisans, individuals who have a position and are ego-involved, that is, the pro-Israeli subjects, should use self-interest as a standard for judgments of fairness and trustworthiness of the mediator. Partisans should be particularly keen as to whether or not the content of the mediator's proposal is favorable, and should see favorable proposals as particularly fair and the mediator who makes favorable proposals as trustworthy.

Nonpartisans. A nonpartisan is a neutral individual who does not favor either side in a conflict. But that is not to say that nonpartisans are without sentiment. Indeed, nonpartisans often go to great lengths to preserve their neutrality, which often is reflected in their adopting middle positions on the issues. We suggest that nonpartisans in a conflict will also make self-serving judgments of fairness and trustworthiness, but of a sort that derives from their position of neutrality. Individuals who are neutral in a conflict should favor the middle position, that is, should adopt neutrality and evenhandedness as a standard for evaluations.

Thus, for nonpartisans we expected evenhandedness (equality) and neutrality to be important standards for judgments of fairness and trustworthiness of the mediator. In other words, nonpartisans should be particularly keen as to whether or not the mediator's proposal is evenhanded, and should see evenhanded proposals as particularly fair and the mediator who makes them as trustworthy. And trust in the mediator, for nonpartisans, should be tied to the neutral source characteristic of the mediator.

The data in Table 2.4 support the expected differences between partisan and nonpartisan subjects in self-serving bias in judgments about mediation. Partisans and nonpartisans differed in the standard used for evaluating mediator trustworthiness: partisans used favorableness of the mediator's proposals, whereas nonpartisans used evenhandedness of the mediator's proposals.

Table 2.4 Mean Perceived Proposal Fairness and Mediator Trustworthiness as a Function of Partisanship and Content Bias

	Content Bias of the Proposal	
	Pro-Israeli	Evenhanded
Proposal Fairness		
Pro-Israeli Ss	3.43_a [3.15_a]	2.78_b [2.91_a]
Nonpartisan Ss	2.20_c [2.48_b]	4.37_d [4.19_c]
Trust Mediator		
Pro-Israeli Ss	4.20_a [4.12_a]	3.37_b [3.52_b]
Nonpartisan Ss	3.07_b [3.52_b]	4.13_a [3.62_b]

Source: Arad and Carnevale (1994).

Note: Higher numbers correspond to a 6-point scale. For Proposal Fairness, 1 = extremely unfair/biased and 6 = extremely fair/unbiased. For Trust Mediator, 1 = extremely untrustworthy/unreliable and 6 = extremely trustworthy/reliable. Means in brackets are Least Squares Means, i.e., means adjusted for the covariate. For Proposal Fairness, the covariate is Trust Mediator. For Trust Mediator, the covariate is Proposal Fairness. Means of the same type (observed, adjusted) that share the same subscript are not statistically different.

Also, as can be seen in Table 2.5, when mediator proposals were relatively unfavorable (evenhanded) partisans were positively influenced by mediator source characteristics, a "cushioning effect" of source bias consistent with our earlier study.

Taken together, the data indicated that relative to partisans, nonpartisans value neutrality and evenhandedness. In other words, what is fair and evenhanded mediator behavior in the eyes of nonpartisans is likely to be seen as unfair and biased mediator behavior by partisans.

BIAS, IMPARTIALITY, AND INFLUENCE

If the central questions about mediation are about influence, as suggested at the beginning of this chapter, then the central questions about bias and impartiality are about how they affect mediator influence: When is mediator bias or impartiality likely to foster or hinder success? What characteristics of the dispute, or of the disputants, will enhance the likelihood

Table 2.5 Mean Perceived Proposal Fairness and Mediator Trustworthiness as a Function of Partisanship of the Subject and Source Bias of the Mediator (evenhanded mediator proposal conditions only)

	Proposal Fairness Partisanship		Trust Mediator Partisanship	
Source Bias	Pro-Israeli	Neutral	Pro-Israeli	Neutral
Pro-Israeli	2.45[a]	4.28	4.15[a]	3.94
Neutral	3.14	4.40	3.59	4.73
Pro-Palestinian	2.33[a]	4.12	2.89[a]	3.77
Unspecified	3.18	4.77	2.82	4.00

Source: Arad and Carnevale (1994).
Notes: Higher numbers correspond to a 6-point scale. For Proposal Fairness, 1 = extremely unfair/biased and 6 = extremely fair/unbiased. For Trust Mediator, 1 = extremely untrustworthy/unreliable and 6 = extremely trustworthy/reliable.
a. Numbers relevant to the "cushioning hypothesis" of mediator source bias (see text).

that either biased or impartial mediation will occur, and work? What strategies and tactics of mediation are likely to be used, and with what effect, by biased and impartial mediators?

We suggest that bias and impartiality both play a role in mediation, and both can add to a mediator's ability and desire to influence and to the disputants' willingness to be influenced. The evidence to date—cases identified by Touval and others, and a few laboratory studies—indicates that biased mediators can succeed regardless of their biases and perhaps even because of them, and can act in an evenhanded manner with some degree of success. And different forms of mediator bias interact to influence negotiators' perceptions about mediation.

The Arad and Carnevale data suggest that a mediator who intends to make an unpopular suggestion ought first to convince the recipient of the suggestion that the mediator has his or her best interests at heart. Such a mediator will benefit from a "cushioning effect." This may be something of a trick that requires dexterity and finesse (Zartman and Touval, 1985), or careful "juggling of partialities" as Tome (1992) calls it, so that the mediator's credibility is maintained with all sides.

There is little doubt that apparent impartiality can enhance the attractiveness and influence of a mediator, as when the Vatican was selected as mediator in the Chile-Argentina Beagle Channel dispute (Princen, 1987). Both sides rejected U.S. mediation, apparently thinking that U.S. interests in the natural resources of the Beagle Channel would be a hindrance, and both preferred a mediator who had no direct interests in the contested resource.

But the evidence indicates that mediator bias can be an important basis of influence in mediation and can contribute to positive outcomes (Wehr and Lederach, 1991). Bias and interests may motivate an otherwise disinterested mediator who may be capable of delivering acceptable outcomes. Even in divorce and child custody mediation, a context that one would think completely devoid of mediator bias, mediators departed from strict neutrality in cases where the conflict was driven by destructive behavior in one of the parents (Kressel, Frontera, Forlenza, Butler, and Fish, 1994). The mediators who were less concerned with neutrality were more cognitively active—they were more likely to generate, test, and refine hypotheses about the conflict, and more likely to search for dysfunctional attitudes, perceptions, and behaviors. And in these cases, more information came out that increased the likelihood of a durable settlement. Mediators who were concerned about "neutrality" were less likely to probe for important information, and less likely to put difficult but important issues on the table.

Moreover, professed mediator neutrality can sometimes exacerbate conflict. For example, there is reason to believe that the Argentines launched their invasion of the Falkland Islands in April 1982 in part because they expected the United States to maintain neutrality and prevent European ships from entering Western hemispheric waters (Purcell, 1982). This was clearly a false view. Pruitt (1983) argues that a clear-cut, public message on siding with Britain in the coming military confrontation would have prevented the invasion. "When an invasion is on the way, a clear-cut statement of support for the intended target can do more to quell the controversy than an effort to mediate" (p. 2).

It is worth noting in this context that a policy position can lock a third party into neutrality: the United States had interests to protect in remaining neutral, namely, to preserve the relationship with the anticommunist Argentine leadership. If Argentina had expected that the United States would join the British, would they have invaded the Falklands in April 1982? The notion of early detection and prevention, called "strategic mediation" by Kerr (1954), may offer a particularly effective long-term strategy of third-party intervention.

But mediator interests can also exacerbate conflict. Disputants will sometimes be intransigent as a stratagem to extract rewards and benefits from a mediator who has interests to protect or extend (see Zartman and Touval, 1985). There is laboratory evidence that negotiators sometimes use their cooperation with an adversary as a vehicle for extracting benefits from a mediator—particularly when they know the mediator has a stake in the outcome of the dispute and has compensation to offer (Harris and Carnevale, 1990).

CONCLUSION

When mediation participants are all partisan but on different sides, they view mediator behavior through a lens of self-interest. However, some conflicts, especially international ones, involve not only the partisans but others who are not directly involved but who have interests that derive from human welfare concerns or from strategic, political, and economic factors. These others may be relatively neutral, less involved, and less knowledgeable about the conflict, yet their opinions and actions may be important for the overall success of mediation. The results of the Arad and Carnevale study described above highlight a practical problem in mediation, in which the mediator may need the trust not only of the disputing parties but also of nonpartisan others: the same evenhanded mediator behavior that may impress nonpartisans is likely to be seen as biased mediator behavior by the disputants.

Bias and impartiality serve influence processes in mediation, albeit via different routes. The partial mediator sometimes engenders a political process characterized by leverage, weight and counterweight, or carrots and sticks (Zartman and Touval, 1985). Sometimes the partial mediator is trusted and accepted (Kressel, 1972; Wehr and Lederach, 1991). And sometimes the impartial mediator engenders a consensual process driven by perceived fairness and trust in the mediator. What is needed is a general model that specifies the boundary conditions of the effects of mediator bias and impartiality in light of their impact on influence processes in mediation.

NOTE

The authors are grateful to Jacob Bercovitch and Arie Kacowicz for their helpful comments on an earlier draft. This material is based in part on work supported by National Science Foundation Grant BNS-8809263.

REFERENCES

Arad, S., and Carnevale, P. J. (1994). "Partisanship Effects in Judgments of Fairness and Trust in Third Parties in the Palestinian-Israeli Conflict." *Journal of Conflict Resolution.*

Bercovitch, J. (1991). "International Mediation and Dispute Settlement: Evaluating the Conditions for Successful Mediation." *Negotiation Journal* 7: 17–30.

Bercovitch, J., and Rubin, J. Z., eds. (1992). *Mediation in International Relations.* New York: St. Martin's.

Bobrow, D. B. (1981). "The Perspective of Great Power Foreign Policy: Steps in Context." In J. Z. Rubin, ed., *Dynamics of Third Party Intervention: Kissinger in the Middle East.* New York: Praeger.

Campbell, J. C. (1976). *Successful Negotiation: Trieste 1954.* Princeton, N.J.: Princeton University Press.

Carnevale, P. J. (1986). "Strategic Choice in Mediation." *Negotiation Journal* 2: 357–361.

Carnevale, P. J., and Conlon, D. E. (1988). "The Perceived Fairness and Acceptability of Biased Mediators." Paper presented at the International Conference on Social Justice and Societal Problems, Leiden, The Netherlands, August.

Carnevale, P. J., Lawler, E., and Fobian, C. (1985). "Bending Over Backwards in Biased Mediation." Unpublished manuscript. Department of Psychology, University of Illinois.

Carnevale, P. J., Lim, R., and McLaughlin, M. (1989). "Contingent Mediator Behavior and Its Effectiveness." In K. Kressel and D. G. Pruitt, eds., *Mediation Research: The Process and Effectiveness of Third Party Intervention.* San Francisco: Jossey-Bass.

Carnevale, P. J., and Pruitt, D. G. (1992). "Negotiation and Mediation." *Annual Review of Psychology* 43: 531–582.

Gulliver, P. H. (1979). *Disputes and Negotiations*. New York: Academic Press.

Harris, K. L., and Carnevale, P. J. (1990). "Chilling and Hastening: The Influence of Third-Party Power and Interests on Negotiation." *Organizational Behavior and Human Decision Processes* 47: 138–160.

Kalb, M., and Kalb, B. (1974). *Kissinger*. Boston: Little, Brown.

Kerr, C. (1954). "Industrial Conflict and Its Mediation." *American Journal of Sociology* 60: 230–245.

Kressel, K. (1972). *Labor Mediation: An Exploratory Survey*. Albany, N.Y.: Association of Labor Mediation Agencies.

Kressel, K., Frontera, E. A., Forlenza, S., Butler, F., and Fish, L. (1994). "The Settlement-Orientation vs. the Problem-Solving Style in Custody Mediation." *Journal of Social Issues*.

Lieb, D. (1985). "Iran and Iraq at Algiers, 1975." In S. Touval and I. W. Zartman, eds., *International Mediation in Theory and Practice.* Boulder, Colo.: Westview.

Mitchell, C. R. (1988). "The Motives for Mediation." In C. R. Mitchell and K. Webb, eds., *New Approaches to International Mediation.* Westport, Conn.: Greenwood Press, 29–51.

Princen, T. (1987). "International Mediation—The View From the Vatican: Lessons From Mediating the Beagle Channel Dispute." *Negotiation Journal* 3: 347–366.

Pruitt, D. G. (1983). "Negotiation and Mediation in the Falklands Crisis." Paper presented at the symposium "When Third Parties Take Sides: The Case of the Falklands," Sixth Annual Scientific Meeting of the International Society of Political Psychology, St. Catherine's College, Oxford University, July.

Pruitt, D. G., and Carnevale, P. J. (1993). *Negotiation in Social Conflict.* Pacific Grove, Calif.: Brooks/Cole.

Purcell, S. K. (1982). "War and Debt in South America." *Foreign Affairs* 61: 660–674.

Rubin, J. Z. (1992). "Conclusion: International Mediation in Context." In J. Bercovitch and J. Z. Rubin, eds., *Mediation in International Relations*. New York: St. Martin's.

Sick, G. (1985). "The Partial Negotiator: Algeria and the U.S. Hostages in Iran." In S. Touval and I. W. Zartman, eds., *International Mediation in Theory and Practice*. Boulder, Colo.: Westview.

Slim, R. (1992). "Small State Mediation in International Relations." In Bercovitch and Rubin, *Mediation.*

Smith, W. P. (1985). "Effectiveness of the Biased Mediator." *Negotiation Journal* 1: 363–372.

Stulberg, J. B. (1987). *Taking Charge: Managing Conflict.* Lexington, Mass.: D. C. Heath.

Thompson, L. L., and Loewenstein, G. (1992). "Egocentric Interpretations of Fairness and Interpersonal Conflict." *Organizational Behavior and Human Decision Processes* 51: 176–197.

Thornton, T. P. (1985). "The Indo-Pakistani Conflict: Soviet Mediation, Tashkent, 1966." In Touval and Zartman, *International Mediation.*

Tome, V. (1992). "Maintaining Credibility as a Partial Mediator: United States Mediation in Southern Africa, 1981–1988." *Negotiation Journal* 8: 273–289.

Touval, S. (1975). "Biased Intermediaries: Theoretical and Historical Considerations." *Jerusalem Journal of International Relations* 1: 51–69.

Touval, S. (1982). *The Peace Brokers: Mediation in the Arab-Israeli Conflict, 1948–1979.* Princeton, N.J.: Princeton University Press.

Touval, S. (1985). "The Context of Mediation." *Negotiation Journal* 1: 373–378.

Touval, S. (1992). "The Superpowers as Mediators." In Bercovitch and Rubin, *Mediation.*

Touval, S., and Zartman, I. W., eds. (1985). *International Mediation in Theory and Practice.* Boulder, Colo.: Westview.

Wehr, P., and Lederach, J. P. (1991). "Mediating Conflict in Central America." *Journal of Peace Research* 28: 85–98.

Welton, G. L., and Pruitt, D. G. (1987). "The Effects of Mediator Bias and Disputant Power Over the Mediator on the Mediation Process." *Personality and Social Psychology Bulletin* 13: 123–133.

Wittmer, J., Carnevale, P. J., and Walker, M. (1991). "General Alignment and Overt Support in Biased Mediation." *Journal of Conflict Resolution* 35: 594–610.

Young, O. R. (1967). *The Intermediaries: Third Parties in International Crises.* Princeton, N.J.: Princeton University Press.

Young, O. R. (1972). "Intermediaries: Additional Thoughts on Third Parties." *Journal of Conflict Resolution* 16: 51–65.

Zartman, W. I., and Touval, S. (1985). "International Mediation: Conflict Resolution and Power Politics." *Journal of Social Issues* 41: 27–45.

CHAPTER THREE

Mediating Conflict in Central America

Paul Wehr and John Paul Lederach

INTRODUCTION

A regional process of conflict resolution has recently evolved in Central America the principal framework for which has been the Esquipulas II agreement of 1987. In this chapter we analyze mediation within Esquipulas, first from a regionwide perspective, then as it has been used to moderate and resolve conflicts within Nicaragua. How mediation has been applied in this historical case may have implications for how students and practitioners of third-party intervention conceive of the role of mediator.

We begin with a discussion of mediation as a theoretical concept and how our analysis of the Esquipulas case and our personal involvement in Nicaraguan mediation have influenced our conceptualization of the role of intermediary. We develop the concept of the Insider-Partial as a mediator type. We then proceed to discuss the development of mediation within Esquipulas as a historical *process* that moves through time, produces, responds to, and transforms events. Process implies action and in mediation third parties act to move conflict toward settlement. Since mediators create this process, who they are and what they do is necessarily of concern to this chapter. Oscar Arias Sanchez, for example, has been a key mediator-negotiator in Esquipulas.

We go on to examine the Esquipulas mediation in terms of the *structure* it has created for conflict resolution—the rules, agenda, principles, timelines, and organizations fashioned to move conflictants toward settlement. The principle of simultaneity of implementation (Hopmann, 1988) and the commissions for carrying it out illustrate the structure of Esquipulas mediation.

Reprinted with permission from a special issue of *Journal of Peace Research,* vol. 28, 1 (1991) by Sage Publications Ltd., London.

We next discuss the Esquipulas mediation as *context,* the larger environment influencing third-party efforts. Conflict research has addressed the importance of the immediate mediation setting for inducing settlement. Just as important is the wider context or environment influencing the conflict toward or away from resolution. In the case of Esquipulas, that context appears to have been of special import. The change of U.S. presidential administrations and the presence of international volunteers and nongovernmental organizations are noteworthy examples of contextual determinants of mediation success in Nicaragua.

Our chapter concludes with a discussion of some theoretical and practical implications of the outsider-neutral and insider-partial mediator roles illustrated by Esquipulas mediation. Our major recommendations are for a more inclusive set of mediator types and more systematic selection of mediators to reflect that range. Mediators, we conclude, must become more aware of the influence of context on mediation outcomes and how it can be made more supportive of mediation efforts.

CONCEPTS OF MEDIATION

Our concept of mediation has been very much influenced by our on-site involvement as observer and practitioner in Central American conflict resolution. One of us spent a year as mediator of one of the two major conflicts in the Nicaraguan civil war. The role of mediator has been characterized in numerous ways in the mediation literature, reflecting the various levels at which mediators work and the quite different personalities, skills, attributes, and positions they bring to their work. Our experience in Central America leads us to add to those characterizations a model of mediation we see as having particular relevance for third-party intervention in developing nations. We will first discuss some of those roles and definitions of mediation, and then how our concept relates to them and how it could expand the concept of mediation.

The Outsider-Neutral

One common conceptualization of mediation roots the mediator's effectiveness in *externality* (coming from outside the conflict situation) and *neutrality* (having no connection or commitment to either side in the conflict). In the North American field of intergroup and interpersonal conflict management, for example, mediation is commonly defined as a rather narrow, formal activity in which an impartial, neutral third party facilitates direct negotiation. Mediators' neutrality is reinforced by their coming from outside the conflict, facilitating settlement, then leaving. In North America this distance of mediator from disputants is heavily emphasized;

mediators are referred to as "third-party neutrals." Ethics codes bind mediators to that principle. Mediators' neutrality protects the legitimacy and authority that are created primarily through their professional role, position, and function—a rational-legal type of authority as Weber (1947) described it. This neutrality-based intervener is what we call the Outsider-Neutral.

Outsider-neutrals maintain distance from the disputants (see Figure 3.1). They are chosen because they have no connection with either side that will affect the outcome and are thereby judged to be unbiased. Outsider-neutrals are connected to disputants through the conflict alone, relating to them only during the mediation process in ways relevant to the function of mediation. Only small parts of the lives of conflictants and interveners intersect: those related to the conflict.

Figure 3.1 Neutrality-based Model

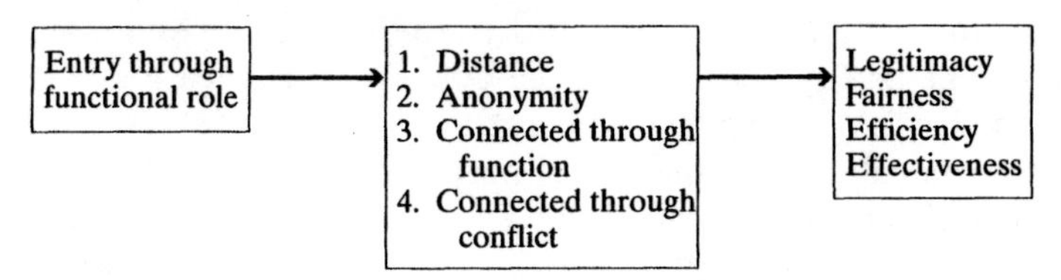

According to this view, the assurance of neutrality in mediation creates the necessary perception of mediator legitimacy, professionalism, and fairness. The mediator works to present a neutral self, to perform credibly in a way that defines the situation in which the mediation/negotiation performance takes place as neutral and impartial (Goffman, 1959). Neutrality and impartiality are defined negatively, in terms of what the mediator *is not.* The third party is *not connected* to either disputant, is *not biased* toward either side, has *no investment* in any outcome except settlement, and does *not expect any special reward from either side* (Moore, 1986: 15–16).

The International Mediator

International mediation is conceived with much greater breadth and diversity than is the North American view of intergroup and interpersonal mediation. The complexity of international and intercultural disputes calls forth perhaps a greater variety of mediator roles; hence we find the mediator-broker (Touval, 1982) and the mediator-conciliator (Yarrow, 1978) among many others. Each conceptualization emphasizes a different role played or function performed by international third parties. Touval's able discussion of the different mediator roles and conceptualizations suggests that the concept of international mediator remains somewhat open. There are other terms that from our review of the third-party literature appear similarly imprecise. Neutrality, for example, is on occasion to be translated as evenhandedness, or even balance, as in Yarrow's characterization of Quaker conciliation as "balanced partiality."

Theorists generally do not see mediator neutrality and impartiality as requisites for successful international mediation. In fact, in some cases mediator connectedness and bias prove to facilitate settlement. We do find in the theory, however, a strong assumption of the importance of externality for the success of mediation. The successful mediator must intervene from *outside* the conflict situation.

The Insider-Partial

We suggest an additional mediator role (one that may be particular to more traditional societies) whose effectiveness depends neither on externality nor neutrality but on quite the opposite attributes, namely, internality and partiality. We further suggest, from our observations of Central American mediation, that the insider-partial mediator complements quite usefully those interveners who bring neutrality from outside the conflict situation.

The insider-partial is the "mediator from within the conflict" whose acceptability to the conflictants is rooted not in distance from the conflict or objectivity regarding the issues, but rather in connectedness and trusted relationships with the conflict parties. The trust comes partly from the fact that the mediators do not leave the postnegotiation situation. They are part of it and must live with the consequences of their work. They must continue to relate to conflictants who have trusted their commitment to a just and durable settlement. Such a mediator is more likely to develop out of more traditional cultural settings where primary, face-to-face relations continue to characterize political, economic, and social exchange, and where tradition has been less eroded by modernity.

In a recent ethnographic study, Lederach (1988) found that neutrality is not what Central Americans seek for help in resolving conflict; they look primarily for trust, *confianza*. In the *confianza* model (see Figure 3.2), authority to mediate is vested in the third party through a personal relationship with the disputant(s) rather than by a secondary role such as external intervener. This is what Weber (1947) called traditional authority.

Trust-based mediation assumes accumulated, sometimes intimate knowledge shared by helper and helped. One who can "deposit *confianza*" in another person knows that person well. They are connected in many ways, not just through a limited service performed. As Simmel wrote, "the

Figure 3.2 Confianza-based Model

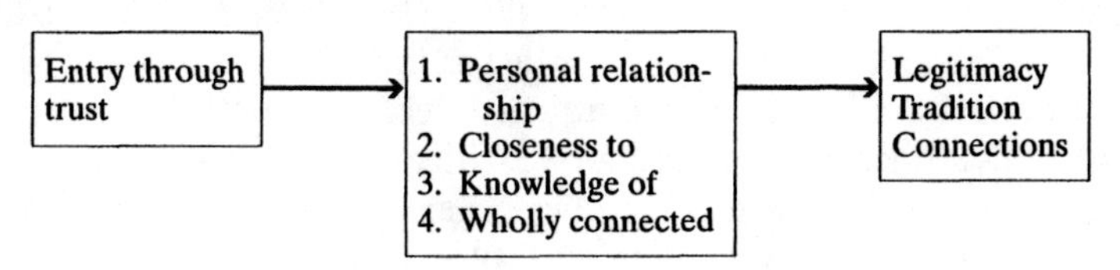

more we have in common with another as whole persons, the more easily will our totality be involved in every single relation to him" (1950: 44). In just that sense, the insider-partial does not relate with the conflictants simply through an intervention. Their trust relationship permits them to resolve the conflict together.

With respect to trust, the insider-partial is not the polar opposite of other models. Personal trust is always a concern in selecting any mediator; with insider-partials, however, it is the primary criterion for selection. They are recognized above all as having the trust of all sides. Unlike outsider-neutrals chosen for the absence of connection with disputants, insider-partials are selected precisely for positive connections and attributes, *for what they are and do:* they are *close to, known by, with and for each side*. This *confianza* ensures sincerity, openness, and revelation and is a channel through which negotiation is initiated and pursued.

We propose, then, to add the insider-partial to the taxonomy of types and roles of international mediators. Its potential for useful combination with outsider-neutrals and other types will, we trust, become apparent as we show how several of them were combined in Esquipulas mediation.

THE ESQUIPULAS PROCESS

Esquipulas is the most recent of a series of historical efforts to resolve interstate conflict and promote regional integration in Central America: the Central American Confederation, 1823–1838; the Central American Court of Justice, 1907–1917; a regional federation all but ratified in 1923; the Central American Common Market from 1962 onward. There have been counterforces as well: border conflicts such as the 1969 so-called Soccer War between El Salvador and Honduras; the Filibuster Wars of the nineteenth century; military governments that have favored national over regional identity. When the Sandinista movement overthrew the Somoza regime in 1979, such counterforces were holding in check the region's longstanding desire for self-determination.

The Sandinista revolution radically altered social and political conflict throughout Central America, most of all within Nicaragua itself. There, it moderated though did not eliminate class conflict, but it created two new conflicts. First, the Sandinistas' effort to integrate by force the Atlantic-coast peoples into a revolutionary state stimulated armed resistance in the east. Second, the Sandinistas' Marxist ideological approach to governance and nation-building encouraged defections from their own ranks. Many of these dissidents became, along with Somozista elements, the raw material for a U.S.-organized Contra insurgency after 1982. The more conservative elements in Nicaraguan society, led by the Catholic hierarchy and those of the upper class who had remained, came to oppose Sandinista policies and to give some support to the Contra movement.

The Nicaraguan revolution became increasingly militarized with the aid and involvement of the USSR and Cuba. The U.S.-sponsored military buildups in El Salvador and Honduras completed the prospect of a region headed toward the abyss. As the Contra activity expanded into Honduras and Costa Rica it inevitably drew those nations into the Nicaraguan conflict. This transformation of national conflicts into a regional superpower confrontation moved neighboring states such as Mexico to initiate formal peacemaking efforts.

Contadora

Contadora, begun in January 1983 by Panama, Mexico, Venezuela, and Colombia, was an experiment in collective mediation. Its goal was to detach Central American conflicts from larger U.S.-Soviet competition and to shift them from military to political and diplomatic levels. The Contadora Group, consulting with a Central America Group (presidents of Guatemala, El Salvador, Nicaragua, Costa Rica, Honduras) and a Contadora Support Group (Peru, Brazil, Argentina, Uruguay), had produced a draft treaty by 1986. The draft was a blueprint for demilitarizing Central American conflicts and resolving them through negotiation.

Contadora reached an impasse in mid-1986. Honduras, under pressure from the Reagan administration with its growing military presence there, declined to sign the treaty (Buvollen, 1989a). The United States had alternately ignored and criticized Contadora while pursuing its military options throughout the region. The U.S. was, therefore, simultaneously subverting the Contadora process diplomatically (Bagley, 1987) and intensifying the conflicts Contadora sought to moderate.

Although Contadora fell short of its objectives, viewed within the larger peace process it was considerably more productive than would appear. Contadora created bases on which Esquipulas could build. It provided a consultative history and framework, and a comprehensive and accurate diagnosis of the region's conflicts. Most important, perhaps, it was an example of Central American regional independence. Contadora happened not only without but *in spite of* U.S. policy.

Actually, we find much of Contadora in Esquipulas. Eight Contadora documents are acknowledged as precedents in the Esquipulas treaty

(Gomariz, 1988, p. 355). Contadora states have subsequently participated in both the International Verification and Support Commission and the UN Observer Group–Central America peacekeeping force. It appears to us, then, that Esquipulas was not a break with Contadora, as some (Robinson, 1988) may see it, but a continuation of it within an exclusively Central American framework.

Although Esquipulas built upon Contadora, it was also motivated by the latter's failures. One such stimulus was the refusal of Honduras to sign the Contadora Act, a failure that led to congressional resumption of military aid to the Contra insurgents. That alarming development motivated Oscar Arias Sanchez, newly elected president of Costa Rica, to make a new initiative. Arias had been involved in the final Contadora consultations; with a four-year term before him in the region's most stable political system, he had many of the resources needed by an international intermediary (Young, 1967).

Arias set to work simplifying negotiation objectives. Contadora's preoccupation with security issues had produced proposals too complex to work, and Arias set aside security as a temporarily insoluble problem. He circulated a simple draft agreement among his fellow presidents, Ortega excepted. His success at simplification is suggested by the comparative lengths of the "Acta de Contadora" (twenty-two pages) and the Esquipulas agreement (six pages).

The Time Path

By February 1987, Arias was receiving encouragement from his presidential counterparts. That was met over subsequent months with increasing opposition from the Reagan administration. Its release of the Wright-Reagan Plan two days before the Central America Group's summit meeting in August was perceived by the group as an attempt to undercut the peace process. Hopmann (1988) credits that perception with motivating the five presidents to sign the agreement; they were also urged to sign by certain members of the U.S. Congress. With the signing of Procedimiento para Establecer la Paz Firme y Duradera en Centroamerica (Gomariz, 1988:355–361), a framework was created for mediated negotiation both among the signatory governments and between them and their respective insurgent opponents.

The agreement set objectives and prescribed specific measures: *demilitarization* of conflict through cease-fires, refusal of support for and use of territory by insurgents; *national reconciliation* through negotiated settlements, amnesty for insurgents, repatriation of refugees; *democratization* of political systems through free and open elections, ending states of emergency, protection of human rights; *continuing regional consultation* through periodic summits and a parliament. Subsequent summits assessed interim progress, adjusted timetables, invited third-party participation, and renegotiated agreements. The San Jose meeting (1988), for example, led to a Sandinista cease-fire and negotiations with the Contras. The San Salvador summit (1989) produced agreement on Nicaraguan elections and Contra demobilization and repatriation. The Tela agreement (1989) firmed up the demobilization schedule and its supervision by the International Commission for Verification and Support. The Montelimar summit (1990) ratified and reinforced the new Nicaraguan transition and Contra demobilization agreements that guided the transfer of power from the Sandinistas and Contra disarmament.

By April 1990, Nicaragua, Guatemala, and El Salvador all had national reconciliation commissions in place and operating. In Nicaragua, the peace process had produced some striking precedents: an internationally supervised election and a peaceful transfer of power; the transformation of a revolutionary government into a reasonably loyal opposition; a procedure for disarming and reintegrating insurgents into civilian life. In Nicaragua, the Esquipulas process had been faithful to the intentions if not the implementation timetable of the agreement. Elsewhere in Central America, however, Esquipulas had produced no real peace.

Leaders in the Process

Three of the Esquipulas participants were responsible for getting it to work: Oscar Arias of Costa Rica through his orchestration and mediation; Vinicio Cerezo of Guatemala through his organizing and hosting of the initial summit, his insistence that Nicaragua be included as a full participant, and his subsequent role as its reliable supporter within the group; and Daniel Ortega of Nicaragua through his negotiating flexibility and important concessions at key points.

Arias was a central figure as a mediator-negotiator. Since Costa Rica was already in compliance with "Procedimiento," he had a special status in the group. He appeared to combine the exogenous and endogenous approaches to conflict management (Bercovitch, 1984). Arias's secure tenure in Costa Rica and his status as Nobel Laureate were resources to be drawn on. He used a number of obvious intermediary tactics (Robinson, 1988): early private confrontation of Ortega on the need for Nicaraguan flexibility; building momentum toward agreement to enlist a reluctant Honduras; using deadlines and timing of meetings to preclude U.S. subversion—all to produce the Esquipulas II agreement.

THE ESQUIPULAS STRUCTURE

Three principles determined the structure for implementing the agreement (Hopmann, 1988): simultaneity (eliminating the "who goes first" problem—a thorny one with respect to Contra demobilization and elections); calendarization ("who does what by which dates"); and transparency ("how do we know that they are doing it"). Commissions were created to apply those principles: a regionwide Commission for Verification and Support; a National Commission for Reconciliation in each nation; subnational Conciliation Commissions where necessary (see Figure 3.3). Commission members were selected for their moral leadership, for useful connections they had with the conflicting parties, and for their experience as intermediaries. They illustrated the connected, trusted insider-partial third party. These commissions came to use outsider-neutral mediators as well and were in turn used by them. We will next examine how the Esquipulas structure was used rather successfully in Nicaragua.

The National Reconciliation Commission

Because of its international and military impacts, the Contra-Sandinista conflict was the major concern of Esquipulas. Cardinal Obando y Bravo was chosen to head the Nicaraguan NRC. He was not selected for his

Figure 3.3 Esquipulas II Institutional Structure

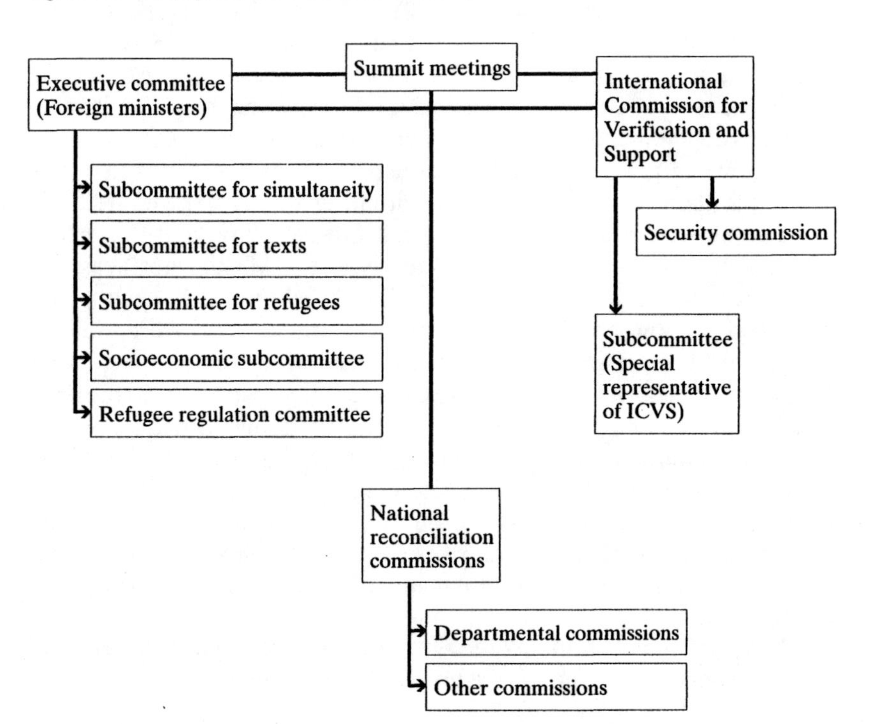

neutrality; his hostility toward the Sandinistas was well known. But his status as spiritual leader, his close connections with resistance elements, and his visibility as national symbol all suggested his usefulness as intermediary. The two sides met under Obando's auspices early in 1988. Several months of negotiations produced the Sapoa agreement and a subsequent government cease-fire, though direct talks were then broken off by the Contras and not resumed for over a year.

Obando's mediation became more instrumental as the 1990 national elections and Contra demobilization approached. Several sets of delicate negotiations were necessary, involving at various points the Contra commanders, the verification and support commission, the Sandinista government, the UN, the OAS, the UNO opposition, and after April 25, 1990, the Chamorro government. Throughout the difficult period from the March elections to the April transfer of power, Cardinal Obando was the most visible intermediary. It is not clear how active or directive his mediation was, but each time he intervened—Sapoa, Toncontin, transition negotiations—a major, durable agreement issued from the negotiation.

The Conciliation Commission

The second mediation effort involved the Sandinista government and the Atlantic-coast resistance. The Indians and Creoles had historically been isolated from the hispanicized Pacific coast. British and U.S. manipulation of ethnic divisions had encouraged that isolation (Hale, 1988; Brooks, 1989). The *costeños*, therefore, had been relatively unengaged in the anti-Somoza rebellion and hardly welcomed a revolutionary Nicaragua.

Sandinista attempts to integrate the east coast were met first with suspicion, then with resistance. The situation swiftly degenerated into armed conflict that sent 30,000 refugees into Honduras and Costa Rica and caused much destruction particularly in the Miskito northeast. By 1984, realizing its past errors, the Sandinista government began a two-track conciliation strategy. The first track initiated talks with Atlantic-coast leaders; these would subsequently result in a National Autonomy Commission (1984), local cease-fires, elected Peace and Autonomy commissions (1986), the drafting of a National Autonomy Law, and its ratification by a Multiethnic Assembly (1987) (Buvollen, 1989b; Sollis, 1989). This lengthy consultative process reflected the Atlantic coast's complex ethnicity, with six groups speaking four languages. Although these groups numbered only 300,000, a tenth of Nicaragua's population, their region represented well over a third of its land area and much of its natural resource base.

Essential in this autonomy-building process were certain well-regarded persons from the east who were sympathetic to the revolution, thus trusted by both the Sandinistas and the indigenous leaders (Freeland, 1989: 178). Such intermediaries as Myra Cunningham and Humberto Campbell sustained the dialogue to ultimate agreement. They are further examples of the insider-partials whose reservoir of trust and mutually recognized stature among conflictants, and crosscutting affiliations with both sides, are so substantial as to permit a mediating function.

The second track involved Sandinista negotiations with the leaders of the armed resistance who were in exile and who had joined to form YATAMA in 1987. Their objectives were the restoration of historical Indian traditions and territorial rights, not the multiethnic regional independence made possible by the Autonomy Law. Esquipulas provided a new mediating structure for the Sandinista-YATAMA conflict.

Whereas the Catholic church had an important mediating role in the Sandinista-Contra conflict, here the intermediary was the Moravian church. It is the primary church on the Atlantic coast just as Catholicism is dominant in the west. Rooted within the Miskitos, Ramas, Sumos, and Creoles, it had the trust of the various resistance leaders and was the logical intermediary. In the early 1980s the Moravian church, seen as antirevolutionary by the Sandinistas, had suffered greatly, losing pastors, churches, schools, and hospitals in the Sandinista-Indian war. From 1983 on, however, the Moravian Provincial Board and the Sandinista government had worked to improve relations. Church leaders had facilitated cease-fires and autonomy consultations. Board members had been schoolmates of key resistance leaders and had maintained those ties.

It was not surprising, therefore, that YATAMA asked Moravian leaders to mediate Sandinista-YATAMA negotiations. The government, too, accepted the Moravians in this role, while acknowledging that they were neither neutral nor impartial. As Interior Minister Tomas Borge put it, "They are more there than here." With some balance provided by appointees from the west, the team began mediating direct talks in January 1988. The Moravian Provincial Board, Gustavo Parajon of CEPAD (a Protestant relief organization) and a member of the National Reconciliation Commission, and John Paul Lederach of the Mennonite Central Committee (another relief and development agency) were named members of this Conciliation Commission.

Throughout 1988 the Commission mediated under serious constraints. The Oliver North/CIA Contra operatives were doing everything possible to inhibit a Sandinista-Indian agreement, since that would preclude a united Nicaraguan resistance. The mediators were kept on the move by CIA-funded kidnapping threats and assassination attempts against them as they went about their work. Competition among YATAMA leaders and Sandinista indecision also slowed progress, but by late 1988 agreement had been reached on more than half of the issues. Not until September 1989, however, was full agreement publicly acknowledged with the added intervention of former U.S. President Jimmy Carter.

The mediation of the Conciliation Commission reflected the *confianza*-inspired, insider-partial model discussed earlier. Its success depended not on neutrality or externality but on continuing relationships of trust that its members had with the conflictants. During face-to-face negotiation phases, Commission members lived side by side with YATAMA leaders. They ate and relaxed with both parties together. Their knowledge and connections were used by each side to explain its views and objectives to the other. The Commission, therefore, was much more connected to disputants than in neutrality-based mediation.

Its functions were broad rather than narrow. Its range of tasks stretched from arranging travel and daily schedules for disputants and resolving their family problems to negotiating a cease-fire in a war involving several national governments. Such a diverse mix is not beyond the scope of international third-party intervention (Pruitt and Rubin, 1986), but it suggests the multidimensional role of the insider-partial rather than the narrower specialized one of the outsider-neutral. The commissioners' legitimacy as mediators came not from their distance from the conflict but from their personal connections, which inspired the disputants' trust. That trust relationship with the conflict parties created safe negotiating space.

The Commission's legitimacy as third party also issued from the duration and depth of its functions. The outsider-neutral usually leaves a conflict soon after settlement. The insider-partial, the *confianza* model of mediation, implies a continuing mediator-disputant connection. The Moravians and CEPAD have continued to work with both sides in peace development ever since the 1988 cease-fire.

The Commission's multiple functions were carried out at different levels of the conflict. Members worked on Peace and Autonomy commissions, thus connecting with that process at the local level. They accompanied exiled leaders to their home villages as part of the reconciliation process. At the national level, the Commission mediated the Sandinista-YATAMA negotiation. Internationally, it worked with Nicaraguan refugees in Honduras and Costa Rica and brought east-coast exiles together from three nations to form the YATAMA negotiating team. Given these multiple and continuing conciliation functions at several levels, Commission mediators were generalists rather than specialists. Their effectiveness depended equally on *who they were* in relation to the conflictants (not who they were not) and *what they did* (not what they did not do).

Insider-partial mediation had produced a tentative settlement. But final and public agreement was facilitated by an outsider-neutral, Jimmy Carter, who, as chair of the Council of Freely Elected Heads of State, had come to Nicaragua to monitor the 1990 elections for fairness and legitimacy. He offered to mediate any remaining Sandinista-YATAMA differences, maintaining that Indian leaders had to be free to return to participate in the electoral campaign.

Carter asked that YATAMA be offered the same conditions for political reintegration extended to the Contras—renounce armed struggle, participate in the political system, encourage demobilization of all armed insurgents. The sides agreed publicly to conditions earlier arrived at and within a week of a Carter-Borge meeting, Brooklyn Rivera and other YATAMA leaders were returning to Nicaragua. Carter made good use of his leverage: the Sandinistas very much wanted his certification of the elections. Timing was also working for him. The pressures of the impending elections and their high visibility in the world produced a flexibility among the disputants that was absent a year earlier. Carter went on to serve other useful third-party functions, as a monitor and conciliator during the elections themselves, and in the difficult postelection transition period.

In the resolution of the Sandinista-YATAMA conflict we have seen how insider-partial and outsider-neutral intermediaries were used at different times and in different settings. The autonomy conciliation relied heavily on those intermediaries who were trusted by both sides because they belonged to both. Within Esquipulas, the Conciliation Commission pursued the Sandinista-YATAMA conflict with considerable success as "mediators from within" who had the trust of both sides. Finally, the Carter intervention broke the impasse, permitting YATAMA leaders to return, thus furthering the democratization and demilitarization goals of Esquipulas. These disparate approaches to mediation were mutually complementary. All of them required considerable trust in the mediators. The evenhanded external mediator was combined with the trusted intermediaries engaged in long-term peacemaking within Nicaragua to moderate the conflict.

A second set of outsider-neutrals should be mentioned here. These were the mediating agencies structured into the conflict through the International Commission of Verification and Support, provided for in the Esquipulas agreement but not actually created until the Tela summit of August 1989. This commission carried out the repatriation, disarming, and resettlement of Contra troops. Represented on the ICVS were the Organization of American States, the Contadora groups, and the UN Observer Group–Central America with its contingent of 800 Spanish and Venezuelan peacekeeping troops. Structured into Esquipulas to validate and monitor its achievements, then, were three international governmental organizations with a major concern for the plan's success: the UN, the OAS, and the Contadora Group. By June 1990, the Commission had disarmed 11,000 of 15,000 insurgents and guaranteed a peaceful Sandinista-to-opposition transfer of power, surely one of history's most successful peacekeeping operations.

THE ESQUIPULAS CONTEXT

We have presented Esquipulas mediation both as a process over time and in terms of the intermediary structures developed to implement it. A third perspective for understanding it is through its broader conflict environment. That context was created largely by actors not directly involved in the mediation.

Certainly Reagan's Contra option rapidly lost momentum in the waning of his second term. Civil wars in Central America quickly lost their external supporters as the Reagan-Gorbachev friendship began to thaw the Cold War. Decisions in Washington and Moscow to end military aid to the Nicaraguan conflictants did much to reinforce the efforts of Esquipulas mediators.

When Reagan left office in 1989, his Central America policy team went with him. That group had labored mightily to sink Esquipulas and discredit Oscar Arias, who mistrusted Assistant Secretary of State Elliott Abrams. It was reported by a key Costa Rican official that Arias had postponed an Esquipulas summit meeting until Abrams had left office.

The U.S. Congress influenced the mediation context both in its encouragement of Contadora through Jim Wright, Christopher Dodd, and others, and by opening space for the Arias initiatives through its Iran-Contra investigations in the summer of 1986. Precisely when Contadora had stalled, those revelations exposed the deep divisions in congressional opinion over Reagan Central America policies—divisions that renewed the regional search for alternatives. This also permitted a progressive decoupling of the Sandinista-YATAMA conflict from the Contra war, a separation that made both easier to resolve. Senator Kennedy, at the request of Indian rights organizations, pressured the Sandinistas to be more flexible on the rights of the indigenous peoples. The American Indian Movement's involvement was influential, though ambiguous in its consequences, for settling the conflict between the Sandinistas and the Atlantic-coast peoples.

Arias's Nobel Peace Prize gave Esquipulas new legitimacy. It heartened the mediators, renewed support in the U.S. Congress for negotiated settlement, and further engaged European governments and publics in the peace process. The award punctuated the substantial support for both Nicaraguan development and Esquipulas that was already coming from Europe.

The United Nations came to influence the Esquipulas context more and more toward negotiated settlement. The General Assembly resolution of June 27, 1989, stimulated agreement at the Tela summit on a Joint Plan for the Voluntary Demobilization, Repatriation and Relocation of the Nicaraguan Resistance. Subsequent UN funding and staffing of the UNOG-Central America and its peacekeeping contingent proved invaluable in disarming and reintegrating Nicaraguan insurgents. Its third-party presence must be given much credit for the peaceful transfer of power in Nicaragua in 1990.

Citizen volunteers from North America and Europe were important shapers of the mediation context. They worked from both ends of the problem, at home and in the field. In the United States, peace activists influenced government policy directly toward political and diplomatic settlement and away from military confrontation. The Central America peace lobby in the U.S., through such groups as Friendship Cities, Witness for Peace, Sanctuary, Pledge of Resistance, and CISPES, helped build public and congressional support for Esquipulas.

In Central America, such peace-movement organizations provided a "sympathetic third party" presence that worked to moderate conflict. Thousands of people visited and lived in Nicaragua, El Salvador, and Guatemala as volunteer generalists, technical experts, human rights escorts, and representatives of municipal governments and labor unions. This citizen third-party presence moderated conflict, producing a more supportive mediation environment. It encouraged flexibility of Central American governments, who wished to appear reasonable and nonviolent. It reduced violence through its on-site reporting of military and paramilitary action. It represented to Central Americans a larger citizen movement in North America and Europe that was pressing for policy changes and sending direct assistance to alleviate suffering. The reaction to the Contra killing of U.S. volunteer Benjamin Linder in 1987 suggested the importance of such a presence for restraining militarization.

Many of these persons were working in Nicaragua under the auspices of nongovernmental organizations (NGOs). These NGOs had a longstanding presence in the region, responding to conflict in the usual ways of lobbying for policy changes and providing civilian war relief. But we saw emerging in the Esquipulas context a broader, more active NGO role in peacemaking, notably mediation by Protestant and Catholic representatives, and secular organizations such as the Carter Center in Atlanta. The Moravian Church, CEPAD, and the Mennonite Central Committee provided mediators and sites. They channeled resources for the negotiation from a mediation support network including the World Council of Churches. The Moravian church in Nicaragua has been still more broadly engaged in *conflict transformation* (Lederach, 1990)—the continuous involvement of sympathetic third parties to move a conflict from latent to overt and negotiation stages. That is a long-term effort involving empowerment of weaker parties, trust-building, conflict skills development, and other requisites for transforming a conflict situation into sustainable peace.

THEORETICAL CONSIDERATIONS AND PRACTICAL IMPLICATIONS

By mid-1990, Esquipulas had been only partially successful in moving the region toward stable peace. In El Salvador and Guatemala, civil conflict and state repression continued to undermine economies and kill thousands, though there were preliminary insurgent-government negotiations under way in both cases. Critics of Esquipulas will point out that Nicaragua has been the focus for change; conflict-producing conditions in other participating states have received little attention at Esquipulas meetings, and the principle of simultaneity has not been applied in that respect.

The Nicaraguan conflicts, on the other hand, appeared to be well on their way toward successful management. An end to military confrontation, disarming and reintegration of insurgents, the end of conscription and major reductions in military forces, a classic pluralist election and peaceful transfer of power, an autonomy process for integrating Atlantic and Pacific regions—all of those achievements were reached within or with the help of Esquipulas. It may be that a conflict management model had to be developed in Nicaragua before other Esquipulas states with more deep-rooted problems involving social conflict and state violence could open to the process. Time and events will tell.

Our study of Esquipulas raises some theoretical and practical issues. Should the conceptualization of mediator roles be broadened to embrace developing-world variants such as the insider-partial? Should identification and selection of mediators be done more systematically, with greater care for drawing on and creatively mixing the external and internal conflict moderation resources available? Should more attention be given by international mediators to modifying the wider context so as to make it more supportive of their intervention?

Expanding the Mediator Concept

Our study suggests that the field would do well to agree on a simple, inclusive definition of mediation, differentiating the mediator roles as research and practice reveal them. We prefer to define mediation simply as third-party-facilitated negotiation, and the mediator as one "who attempts to help the principals reach a voluntary agreement" (Pruitt and Rubin, 1986:166). Within such a simple, inclusive definition a hundred flowers can bloom, so to speak. Esquipulas has produced some variations on the basic mediation theme that we have not found in the literature.

We have suggested the concept of the *insider-partial* to reflect a type very visible in Nicaraguan mediation. We distinguished that from the *outsider-neutral* concept characterizing mediation in North America, and from international mediator roles that generally regard third parties as necessarily coming from outside the conflict situation. We have shown how the insider-partial and outsider-neutral polar opposites interacted synergistically in Nicaraguan mediation. It may be, however, that externality and neutrality are dimensions, or continua, along which every mediator falls. Those dimensions may be independent of one another rather than interdependent as the types we suggest imply.

If the outsider-neutral and insider-partial types are valid, however, each bringing different strengths to the same conflict, as did Jimmy Carter and the Conciliation Commission, what practical consequences might issue from teaming them up as counterparts in a mediation? They might not work together physically, but would consult, divide up functions, coordinate interventions, and the like. If these are distinct types, each of which performs different but equally important functions in mediated negotiation, that would influence the mediator selection process. In any event, it would seem useful to explore the insider-partial concept further. Although we have presented it here as a region-specific, culture-determined model, it might have equally useful functions in the postindustrial societies of the world.

Esquipulas suggests other additions to the range of mediator roles. We noted the way Oscar Arias appeared to act as both mediator and negotiator. He, too, was internal to the conflict situation, had the trust of all parties, yet had a status apart. The *mediator-negotiator* of Esquipulas appears to have some precedents in the Kissinger of the Yom Kippur War negotiation (Rubin, 1981) and the Walesa (1987) of Polish Solidarity, both of whom seem to have played such a dual role. If it is not a new genre, should it at least be included in the range of mediator-types? Would there be a place as well for the *mediator-legitimizer* characterized by Obando y Bravo, whose role went much beyond providing good offices? The full weight of the church's moral authority in his person appears to have legitimated such negotiation and guaranteed the implementation of its outcomes.

One question raised by such a discussion is whether mediator selection in such cases should not be more conscious and deliberate than it normally is, according to mediator functions required and persons and agencies available. If, for example, the Carter and Conciliation Commission interventions had been coordinated, each performing different, complementary functions, a year of time might have been saved. We are suggesting that the selection of mediators could and should be a more systematic, and informed, process.

Modifying the Mediation Context

Our study has suggested the importance of the *mediation context*—the events, persons, and attitudes influencing the mediation from a distance. Time and again in Esquipulas, negotiation was rescued from an impasse by the transformation of a context. A striking example was the agreement of August 1989 between the Sandinista government and the United National Opposition for free and open elections. It was reached in a televised marathon negotiation reminiscent of that which legitimated Polish Solidarity in 1980 (Wehr, 1985). The Sandinista-UNO accord triggered the breakthrough three days later for the Tela agreement on Contra demobilization; the context had been transformed to permit this.

Both supportive and obstructive forces in the mediation context, while not controllable by mediators, are amenable to their influence. If the larger environment were seen as more integral to mediation success, third-party interveners could map that context to identify key influentials, a preliminary step to creating more support for negotiated settlement. Could mediators have a more direct influence on mass communicators, for example, who frame the issues, characterize the actors, present the options, and largely determine whether a context encourages or discourages mediated settlement? The mass media were exceptionally influential in the context of Nicaraguan mediation (Chomsky, 1987). Should a mediation team include someone with exclusive responsibility for mapping the context for ways to render it more supportive of intervention?

An important mediation-supportive element in the Esquipulas context was the presence of *conflict moderators,* the sympathetic third parties described earlier. Conflict moderation is the third party's most important function. It is a more realistic goal than permanent resolution, which is rarely possible (Touval, 1982). Does the Esquipulas experience show the conflict-moderating sympathetic third parties to be so useful in the mediation context that a conscious effort should be made to include them as a desirable component of international third-party interventions?

Mediation from Within the Conflict

Esquipulas has revealed to us how rich may be the indigenous resources for conflict moderation and negotiated settlement in developing areas of the world. The insider-partial, the mediator-negotiator, the mediator-legitimizer, the sympathetic third party are conflict management roles that are probably useful beyond Central America as well. The effective combining of such local resources with external third parties in Esquipulas can be seen as a contribution to the theory and practice of international third-party intervention. We suspect that international mediation would be more effective were the various external and internal mediators and the moderators within the context to be systematically identified and enlisted: a deliberate citizen volunteer presence, a mixed team of outsider-neutrals and insider-partials, a resident *conflict transformation* group working on a deep-seated conflict situation.

It remains to be seen whether the Esquipulas innovation in conflict management will produce positive results in other Central American states as it has in Nicaragua. Continuing involvement of the United Nations and other international interveners will help determine those results. Thus far, however, Esquipulas represents a major step forward in regional conflict management, a model well worth the attention of scholars and practitioners alike.

NOTE

The authors acknowledge the useful comments of Jacob Bercovitch, Wenche Hauge, and Raino Malnes in the preparation of this chapter. This research was supported by the Council for Research and Creative Work, and Conflict and Peace Studies at the University of Colorado. Reader comments are welcome and should be sent to: Paul Wehr, Sociology 327, University of Colorado, Boulder, CO 80309, USA, or John Paul Lederach, Eastern Mennonite College, Harrisonburg, VA 22801, USA.

REFERENCES

Bagley, B. (1987). "The Failure of Diplomacy." In B. Bagley, ed., *Contadora and the Diplomacy of Peace in Central America,* vol. 1. Boulder, Colo.: Westview, 181–211.

Bercovitch, J. (1984). *Social Conflict and Third Strategies of Conflict Resolution.* Boulder, Colo.: Westview.

Brooks, D. (1989). "US Marines, Miskitos and the Hunt for Sandino: The Rico Coco Patrol in 1928." *Journal of Latin American Studies* 21, 2: 311–342.

Buvollen, H. P. (1989a). "Low-Intensity Warfare and the Peace Plan in Central America." *Bulletin of Peace Proposals* 20, 3: 319–334.

Buvollen, H. P. (1989b). "Regional Autonomy in Nicaragua: A New Approach to the Indigenous Question in Latin America." *Alternatives* 14: 123–132.

Chomsky, N. (1987). *On Power and Ideology: The Managua Lectures.* Boston: South End Press.

Freeland, J. (1989). "Nicaragua's Atlantic Coast." *Third World Quarterly* 10, 4: 166–190.

Goffman, E. (1959). *The Presentation of Self in Everyday Life.* Garden City, N.Y.: Anchor Doubleday.

Gomariz, E., ed. (1988). *Balance de Una Esperanza: Esquipulas II Un Ano Después.* San José, Costa Rica: FLACSO.

Hale, C. (1988). "Relaciones Interétnicas y la Estructura de Clases en la Costa Atlantica de Nicaragua." *Estudios Sociales Centoramericanos* 48, 4: 71–91.

Hopmann, P. T. (1988). "Negotiating Peace in Central America." *Negotiation Journal* 4, 4: 361–380.

Lederach, J. P. (1988). "Of Nets, Nails and Problemas: A Folk Vision of Conflict in Central America." Unpublished doctoral dissertation in sociology. University of Colorado, Boulder.

Lederach, J. P. (1990). "Conflict Transformation: The Case for Peace Advocacy." Unpublished paper. Mennonite Central Committee, Akron, Penn.

Moore, C. (1986). *The Mediation Process*. San Francisco: Jossey-Bass.

Pruitt, D, and Rubin, J. (1986). *Social Conflict*. New York: Random House.

Robinson, L. (1988). "Peace in Central America." *Foreign Affairs* 66, 3: 591–613.

Rubin, J. (1981). *Dynamics of Third-Party Intervention: Kissinger in the Middle East*. New York: Praeger.

Simmel, G. (1950). *The Sociology of Georg Simmel*. New York: Free Press.

Sollis, P. (1989). "The Atlantic Coast of Nicaragua: Development and Autonomy." *Journal of Latin American Studies* 21, 3: 481–520.

Touval, S. (1982). *The Peace Brokers: Mediators in the Arab-Israeli Conflict 1948–1979*. Princeton, N.J.: Princeton University Press.

Walesa, L. (1987). *A Way of Hope*. New York: Henry Holt.

Weber, M. (1947). *The Theory of Social and Economic Organization*. New York: Oxford University Press.

Wehr, P. (1985). "Conflict and Restraint: Poland 1980–1982." In P. Wallensteen, J. Galtung, and C. Portales, eds., *Global Militarism*. Boulder, Colo.: Westview, 191–218.

Yarrow, C. H. M. (1978). *Quaker Experiences in International Conciliation*. New Haven: Yale University Press.

Young, O. (1967). *The Intermediaries: Third Parties in International Crises*. Princeton, N.J.: Princeton University Press.

CHAPTER FOUR

The UN Secretary-General and the Mediation of International Disputes

Kjell Skjelsbæk and Gunnar Fermann

Approaching its half-centennial, the United Nations has once more come into vogue. The relationship between the United States and the Russian Federation, which inherited the permanent membership of the Security Council from the Soviet Union, has improved dramatically since the second half of the 1980s. The United States and other major powers now participate more actively in many aspects of the work of the world organization;[1] they are more eager to cooperate with one another under its umbrella. The decade ended with a joint U.S.-Soviet draft resolution in the General Assembly committing everyone to "work to strengthen further the role and effectiveness of the United Nations."[2] During the 1990–1991 Gulf crisis, they cooperated diplomatically and to some extent practically to make the UN sanctions against Iraq effective. In an unprecedented move, the Soviet Union supported the SC Resolution 678 initiated by the United States authorizing the use of force ("use all necessary means") to end the Iraqi occupation of Kuwait.

There has been a parallel enhancement of the role of the Secretary-General in peaceful settlement of disputes. Over the past few years, he has contributed significantly to the cease-fire between Iran and Iraq, the withdrawal of Soviet forces from Afghanistan, the successful decolonization of Namibia, the glimmer of hope for a settlement in the dispute over Western Sahara, and the fragile peace process in Kampuchea that includes the establishment of the largest peacekeeping force since the UN force in the Congo. Although his good-offices mission during the 1990–1991 Gulf crisis was accepted by President Saddam Hussein of Iraq, these efforts were not sufficient to secure a negotiated withdrawal of Iraqi forces from Kuwait. However, a peacekeeping mission along the Iran-Iraq border directed by the Secretary-General's office remains an indispensable stabilizing element in the region. For years he has chaired the negotiations on a new constitution for the divided island of Cyprus. He is engaged in talks on a new UN peacekeeping mission in Western Sahara, and in more informal consultations about the use of UN observers in Angola, Haiti, El Salvador and, once again, Afghanistan. Aided by special representatives, the Secretary-General is deeply involved in the efforts to end the hostilities and atrocities in Bosnia and in supervising the peace process in Kampuchea toward general elections in 1993.

The mediating function of the Secretary-General of the United Nations is both unique and complicated. In this article, we shall analyze both its potential and its limitations as well as the prospects for mediation by the Secretary-General in the post–Cold War era. We begin with some theoretical reflections on the nature of mediation.

THIRD-PARTY MEDIATION

There is a rich literature on mediation.[3] For the purposes of this chapter, mediation will be defined as efforts by third parties to prevent the eruption or escalation of destructive conflict behavior and to facilitate a settlement that makes renewed destructive behavior unlikely. The concept encompasses narrower terms such as "good offices" and "conciliation." On the other hand, it excludes conflict prevention or conflict suppression by means of force. The essence of mediation is persuasion, not coercion. Mediation is often presented as a form of "peacemaking" (Mitchell, 1981: 280).

Mediation is in principle voluntary in international disputes as well as in the rare instances when the parties to a convention have agreed in advance to settle possible disagreements by means of arbitration (institutionalized mediation as opposed to ad hoc arrangements). Would-be mediators, whether governments, international bodies, or prominent individuals, may offer their services at the risk of being rejected by one or more of the disputants. It is usually the weaker party that first accepts the services of an intermediary. The stronger may hope to win, or at least to prevail, and consequently regards offers of mediation as detrimental to its interests.

Hence, the problem of timing is crucial. Early offers of mediation could make the intermediary unpopular with one or more parties to a particular dispute and ruin its chances of playing a useful role at a later stage. Acceptance by one party and not by the other(s) conjures up an impression of partiality. There may be a genuine trade-off between the likelihood that a mediator will continue to be perceived as impartial and the extensiveness or decisiveness of the initiatives that he or she undertakes (Young, 1967:271). Finally, if the offer comes too late the situation may have deteriorated to a point where hostile attitudes and acts have made mediation almost impossible. A situation of generally recognized stalemate or a state of mutual exhaustion makes the acceptance of mediation more likely. Mitchell notes that:

> many students of intermediary activity, both analysts and practitioners, have argued that . . . structural considerations really determine whether any intermediary activity will even begin, let alone succeed, and that intermediaries make little contribution to bringing about an agreement. More often, the parties to the conflict themselves decide, either independently or tacitly, that they wish to arrange a compromise solution, and when this stage is reached, they look around for a convenient third party to act as a go-between and legitimiser of their activity. (Mitchell, 1981:281)

Mitchell's statement ignores the importance of premediation contacts.[4] A potential mediator may probe the attitudes of the parties to a dispute in order to determine whether or when a suggestion for mediation should be made. In this process, he or she may be able to correct misperceptions and transmit information without injecting substantive ideas or proposals of his or her own. If this service is appreciated by the parties, they may gradually accept a more active and independent role of the intermediary and move imperceptibly from the stage of premediation to mediation.

Even if the parties to a dispute have considered third-party mediation, this may not take place unless a qualified intermediary acceptable to all is available. Disagreement about the suitability of a potential mediator could easily become part of the dispute. Acceptability to all relevant parties is a sine qua non in international mediation. Independence and impartiality are in turn the keys to acceptability. An intermediary who is dependent on at least one of the parties to a dispute, and hence susceptible to its influence, is unlikely to be trusted by the others. A relatively powerless third party depends more on its perceived neutrality than does an already involved but powerful party. The latter may threaten or pay the parties to accept a settlement that otherwise would have been rejected. A powerful third party may use its resources to balance an asymmetrical power relationship between the adversaries. The status of the mediator is also important: in general, the higher its status the more likely it is to succeed. A high-status mediator has more authority and its efforts are less easily rejected by parties skeptical about mediation. The status of an individual is a combination of the status of the agency he or she represents, his or her office or position in that agency, and his or her personal reputation.

Adequate information about the parties and the conflict is another decisive factor in mediation. A good mediator should know the history of the conflicts he or she deals with. Regular briefings on the day-to-day developments are necessary, particularly in time of crisis. Previous personal contacts with the most important decisionmakers of the parties to a dispute make it easier to establish a rapport and formulate appropriate messages to them.

In this chapter, we shall look at the mediation function of the UN Secretary-General. Much of his work in this area is confidential; consequently it is impossible to study in detail the methods and tactics the different incumbents have used. However, we can research some of the structural conditions of their work and the resources and instruments at their disposal.

THE LEGAL BASIS

The Charter of the United Nations, adopted by the founding member governments at the San Francisco conference in 1945, accords considerably higher status and more responsibility to the Secretary-General than did the Covenant of the League of Nations. Schwebel (1952:4–5) summarizes the relevant stipulations of the Covenant as follows:

> The clauses which concern the Secretary-General imply only a tenuous political role. The Secretary-General shall "act in that capacity at all meetings of the Assembly and of the Council," in case of war or threat of war "shall on the request of any Member of the League forthwith summon a meeting of the Council," and shall "make all necessary arrangements for a full investigation and consideration" of a dispute submitted to the Council which any party to the dispute sees likely to lead to a rupture. The Secretary-General shall be appointed by the Council with the approval of a majority of the Assembly; he in turn shall appoint the staff subject to the Council's approval.

Article 7 of the Charter of the United Nations establishes the Secretariat as a principal organ on a par with the Security Council and the General Assembly. It is reasonable to interpret the Secretariat as meaning the Secretary-General. It is upon the Secretary-General, not upon the Secretariat, that the charter confers specific functions. All staff members are appointed by and subordinate to him.

The Secretary-General himself is appointed by the General Assembly upon the recommendation of the Security Council (Article 97). Thus any of the five permanent members of the council can veto a candidate it does not favor. This was a controversial point in San Francisco, but the Great Powers successfully maintained that the value of a Secretary-General who did not enjoy the confidence of the permanent members would be limited. All six incumbents of the office of the Secretary-General of the UN have been appointed as a result of difficult compromises among the five permanent members. The decisions were subsequently rubber-stamped by the full council and by the General Assembly.

The charter contains no provisions regarding the length of the Secretary-General's term of office. The Preparatory Commission[5] recommended a term of five years, which was accepted by the General Assembly. Neither are there any provisions for the removal of an unwanted incumbent. This highly significant omission made it possible for Trygve Lie and Dag Hammarskjöld to remain in office even after they had incurred the wrath of the USSR.

According to Article 98, "the Secretary-General shall act in that capacity in all meetings" of the General Assembly and the three councils of the UN, and "perform such other functions as are entrusted to him by these organs."

However, it is Article 99 that most clearly sets out the political function of the Secretary-General. He "may bring to the attention of the Security Council any matter which in his opinion may threaten international peace and security."[6] This article has been explicitly invoked only a few times, but its importance is far greater than this number indicates. According to Urquhart (1985:258), the article "gives the Secretary-General the basis for political judgement, and even action, in his own right." It is noteworthy that the article uses the broader term "matter" and not "situation or dispute." The Secretary-General may place on the provisional agenda of the Security Council any matter, not just an open conflict. By implication, the Secretary-General has the authority to investigate difficult situations or simmering conflicts and determine whether they constitute a threat to international peace. It is generally accepted that his role should be more active than that of an analyst. The Preparatory Commission commented on it as follows: "The Secretary-General may have an important role to play as a mediator and as an informal adviser of many Governments, and will undoubtedly be called upon from time to time, in the exercise of his administrative duties, to take decisions which may justly be called political."[7]

The purpose of Article 100 is to ensure the international and impartial character of the Secretary-General and his staff. They "shall not seek or receive instructions from any government or from any authority external to the organization." Staff must be appointed by the Secretary-General, according to Article 101, which also emphasizes the need for competence. The Secretary-General must, in addition, pay due regard to "the importance of recruiting the staff on as wide a geographical basis as possible." However, major and minor powers have often exerted influence on the Secretary-General's hiring and firing of staff. According to Pérez de Cuéllar (1988:72), few governments "refrain from trying to bring pressure to bear in favour of their own particular interests, especially on the personnel side."

SIX INCUMBENTS

As may be expected, the six Secretaries-General differ considerably in background, training, temperament, intellectual style, and ambition. Trygve Lie was foreign minister of Norway when he unexpectedly emerged as a compromise candidate recommended by the Security Council to the first General Assembly in 1946. He started his term before the East-West conflict imperiled the very existence of the United Nations Organization, and his ambitions were high. A sympathetic writer thinks that "Lie acted on Article 99 in a statesmanlike way, mostly in the framework of UN 'parliamentary' public diplomacy" (Alexandrowicz, 1966:310–311). Others have been far more critical.[8] Lie kept a high political profile; he irritated Washington at times, particularly over the issue of Chinese representation in the UN after 1949, and he antagonized Moscow during the Korean War.

The North Korean attack on South Korea in 1950 precipitated a situation that demonstrated the limits of the independent role of the Secretary-General. Lie came down hard in defense of the charter principles, which he was convinced had been seriously undermined by North Korea. He said as much in an opening statement to the Security Council, proclaiming it to be the "clear duty of the Security Council to take steps necessary to reestablish peace" in Korea.[9] This statement marked the end of his acceptability to the Soviet Union and the end of his active role as Secretary-General. He was boycotted by the USSR, which threatened to veto his candidacy for a second term. The United States, on the other hand, declared its willingness to veto any other candidate than Lie. As the Security Council was deadlocked, the General Assembly by an overwhelming majority extended Lie's term by three years. His confidence with the USSR and other socialist governments could not be restored, however, and in October 1952 he announced his decision to resign.

The permanent members of the council now wanted a less forceful and ambitious successor. They expected that their choice, Dag Hammarskjöld of Sweden, would function as a quiet and unobtrusive civil servant.[10] However, Hammarskjöld became the architect of a new conception, that of "combined public and private multilateral diplomacy," which he put into practice with the utmost skill and ingenuity (Alexandrowicz, 1966:311). The international situation was also more propitious. Stalin had died, the newly elected Eisenhower administration in Washington had set a new tone, and the war in Korea had come to an end.

In the following years Hammarskjöld's quiet diplomacy, although not approved by all governments, resulted in many successes and enhanced the prestige of his office. He was increasingly convinced that in the political field the UN should concentrate on preventive rather than corrective action. But in the end he too fell out with the Soviets. In 1960 he recommended, and the Security Council accepted, the establishment of a UN peacekeeping operation in the Congo (ONUC). The story is too complicated to be retold here. ONUC found itself in the midst of a civil war with foreign (Belgian) intervention; Hammarskjöld was accused of providing inadequate support to one of the Congolese factions headed by Premier Lumumba and supported by the USSR. The Security Council was once more deadlocked by disagreement between the permanent members and unable to give specific guidance to the Secretary-General on how to proceed in the Congo. Hammarskjöld's response to this situation was remarkable:

> I believe that it is in keeping with the philosophy of the Charter that the Secretary-General should be expected to act also without such guidance, should this appear to him necessary in order to help filling any vacuum [*sic*] that may appear in the system which the Charter and traditional diplomacy provide for the safeguarding of peace and security.[11]

Instead of terminating ONUC he continued the operation, guided by his interpretation of the principles of the charter. None of his successors has claimed such an independent moral basis for the office. Although the majority of the General Assembly gave Hammarskjöld a vote of confidence in the fall of 1960, the vitriolic attacks on him by representatives of the USSR put him in a precarious position. The Soviet leader Nikita Khrushchev proposed that the office of the Secretary-General be reorganized and staffed by three secretaries of equal rank and responsibility, one from a member of the Eastern bloc, one from a Western country, and one from a neutral nation. This reform, or course, would have severely impaired the political functions, including the mediation and good-offices missions, of the chief executive officer(s) of the UN. The so-called troika proposal never received much support outside the East European caucus, but it was a strong indication of Soviet dissatisfaction with Hammarskjöld. His untimely death in September 1961 may have saved him from troubles that could have been as difficult as those that befell his predecessor. One of Hammarskjöld's biographers sums up his achievement as follows:

> How far Hammarskjöld succeeded in these infinitely ambitious aims is still hard to judge. Certainly he gave the Secretary-Generalship and the Secretariat—and to some extent the United Nations itself—a new status. He provided the most dynamic and striking leadership an international organization ever had, and he personified the ideals of the Charter in action in a way that made a profound impression on hundreds of millions of people all over the world. In the end he carried this implicit challenge to national sovereignty further than some of the more powerful states were prepared to tolerate. In doing this he displayed a certain overconfidence born of the successes of previous years—an overconfi-

> dence that disturbed many governments in addition to those which actively opposed him. (Urquhart, 1972:595–596)

U Thant came to the Secretary-General's office at a catastrophic moment in the history of the United Nations. He was a devout Buddhist from Burma, apparently without great personal ambitions but with a strong moral commitment.[12] U Thant continued the quiet-diplomacy tradition of Hammarskjöld, but he was reluctant to put forward challenging theories about the significance of his office. He managed to complete the controversial operation in the Congo, a considerable achievement. However, he came under severe and mostly unfair criticism when he felt compelled to accept President Nasser's demand for a withdrawal of the first UN peacekeeping force in the Sinai in 1967.[13] U Thant may not have been as brilliant as Hammarskjöld, but he was both courageous and skillful. He left the organization at the end of his second term in 1971 without having become very controversial, and yet he basically salvaged the prestige, independence, and effectiveness of his office.

U Thant came from one of the newly independent countries that joined the United Nations in great numbers from the late 1950s and significantly changed both the composition and agenda of the organization. It is therefore surprising that the next Secretary-General would again be a European. Kurt Waldheim had served as Austria's foreign minister. Waldheim was less inclined than his predecessors to offend the major powers. By all accounts, he was constantly concerned about his reappointment even for a third term. However, he was also ambitious on behalf of the organization and worked hard to contribute to a settlement of the conflicts in Cyprus, the Middle East, Southern Africa, and elsewhere.[14]

Javier Pérez de Cuéllar of Peru was the first UN Secretary-General from Latin America. Unlike Waldheim he did not seem to enjoy publicity, but followed his predecessors' tradition of offering the service of his office for peaceful settlement of disputes. His achievements are remarkable, including mediating efforts that contributed to the termination of the war between Iraq and Iran, the conclusion of the Geneva Agreements leading to the withdrawal of Soviet forces from Afghanistan, and the emergence of Namibia as an independent state. During his second term, the criticism of the UN leveled off and the organization enjoyed a process of revitalization.

Boutros Boutros-Ghali of Egypt was appointed sixth Secretary-General by the General Assembly on December 3, 1991, following a unanimous recommendation for the post by the Security Council.[15] Generally accepted and specifically favored for the post by the Arab world, the Organization of African Unity, France, and China, Boutros-Ghali is the first Arab and African holding the position of chief executive of the United Nations. For many years the *éminence grise* of Egyptian foreign policy,

Boutros-Ghali played a major role in negotiating the Camp David Accords leading to the peace treaty between Egypt and Israel. Fluent in Arabic, English, and French, the current Secretary-General has committed himself to institutional reform in order to strengthen the problem-solving capacity of an overstretched organization. Having embarked on as many peacekeeping missions in the past four years as took place in the previous forty, Boutros-Ghali seems reluctant to commit the organization to engage in further conflict-management missions unless member states take action to strengthen the UN's financial base. Partly for this reason, the Secretary-General was skeptical of the May 1992 decision of the Security Council to send peacekeepers to Bosnia. He also favored mediation by "countries of the region or regional organizations" in the conflict in Nagorno-Karabakh, rather than committing the UN itself (*UN Chronicle* June 1992:37). Thus, to maintain the credibility of the United Nations in the field of "international peace and security" in the post–Cold War era, the Secretary-General seems to have changed his position from urging the Security Council to take action to restraining its new aptness to utilize the already overstretched resources of the organization.

What lessons can be learned from this brief exposition? In light of the basic requirement that in order to function effectively a mediator must be perceived as neutral and impartial toward the parties and the conflict, the Secretary-General should avoid a high political profile that may put his neutrality in jeopardy. By taking a clear and openly expressed political stand on the North Korean attack on South Korea in 1950, Trygve Lie became a "lame duck" during his last two years as Secretary-General. The difficulty of retaining confidence as mediator while playing an activist role is also demonstrated by Dag Hammarskjöld's management of the Congo operation. By alienating the Soviet camp, he ruined the basis for continuing the "quiet diplomacy" he initially adopted as his political methodology.

If the Secretary-General is to act successfully as a mediator, he has to keep himself above the conflict and not become part of it by making controversial statements. At the other extreme of the spectrum, however, there is another challenge to the mediating role of the Secretary-General that should not be ignored: to the extent that the "quiet diplomacy" propagated by Hammarskjöld should degenerate into political servility toward the big powers, it may erode his credibility as a mediator among the not-so-big powers of the Third World and elsewhere. Concern for reelection provided a disincentive for Kurt Waldheim to take positions that might have weakened his standing with the big powers. Arguably, this preoccupation tended to reduce his credibility as a mediator.

Perhaps the optimal code of conduct for a Secretary-General who emphasizes the importance of his mediating role is to be found in an interpretation of the concept of "quiet activist diplomacy," which involves the active seeking of politically feasible solutions, as well as informing the parties about his views on problem-solving strategies, in such a way as will not harm the political prestige of member states. In order to achieve politically feasible solutions in his mediation, the Secretary-General should, in other words, be innovative and strong in opinion, yet tempered in the way he communicates his views to the parties and even more so when issuing statements to the public. We believe the mediating success of the early Hammarskjöld, U Thant, and Pérez de Cuéllar can be attributed to a diplomatic methodology that incorporated this combination of characteristics.

Having looked first at the juridical basis and then at the historical development of the office of the Secretary-General, we now turn to a more systematic analysis of its role as mediator. It is very difficult, if not impossible, to measure the influence of the Secretary-General in specific situations. However, we may arrive at a better understanding of his role by identifying the assets or resources that he can mobilize. This will be done in the next section, where we also note some failures and successes. We then proceed to a discussion of how these resources are put into effect; that is, which methods, techniques, and instruments are employed by the Secretary-General. Finally, some restraining factors will be analyzed.

ASSETS AND RESOURCES

Moral Standing: Impartiality

The ability of the Secretary-General to reward or punish is limited indeed. The physical resources at his disposal are very small and arguably of less importance than the moral and political status of his office. His authority rests to a considerable extent on the ideals of the charter and the fact that these ideals are formally accepted by all members of the world's most universal intergovernmental organization, whose servant and spokesman he is. He is supposed to expound these ideas in his public statements and be an embodiment of them in his diplomatic activities. The incumbent is also expected generally to conform to the highest moral standards. This explains the consternation caused by the disclosure of Waldheim's deliberate falsehoods about his past.

The problem is that many member governments regularly and seriously violate the principles of the charter and react negatively when their policies are exposed and criticized by other governments or by the Secretary-General. Trygve Lie met his fate when he declared in the Security Council that the North Korean attack on South Korea in 1950 was a violation of the charter. His successor faced a similar situation in 1956 when France and Britain intervened militarily in Egypt to gain control of the

Suez Canal. Hammarskjöld, more subtle than Lie, rebuked the two governments in an opening statement in the Security Council, but also pointed out the dilemma of his office:

> The principles of the Charter are, by far, greater than the Organization in which they are embodied, and the aims which they are to safeguard are holier than the policies of any single nation or people. As a servant of the Organization the Secretary-General has the duty to maintain his usefulness by avoiding public stands on conflicts between Member nations unless and until such an action might help to resolve the conflict. However, the discretion and impartiality thus imposed on the Secretary-General by the character of his immediate task may not generate into a policy of expediency.[16]

In such situations, the Secretary-General is presented with different options. He may expound the principles of the charter or he may abstain from public political statements and remain impartial. The first alternative may earn him the praise of a majority of the member governments, but possibly at the cost of jeopardizing his role as a potential mediator. By choosing the other avenue, he risks criticism for lack of moral courage and consistency; this, in turn, could weaken the principles of the charter and the moral basis of his office, but on the other hand he would not have ruined his possibilities of playing a constructive third-party role in the conflict at hand. The Secretary-General's freedom of choice is largely determined by the general international climate and by the sensitivity of the governments involved. All incumbents have had the courage to criticize publicly certain aspects of the policies of major and minor powers. Nevertheless, there has been a clear trend toward greater emphasis on the Secretary-General's usefulness as an honest broker and mediator, even in situations where one party seems more guilty than others. In August 1990, when the Persian Gulf crisis began, Pérez de Cuéllar did not join the Security Council in condemning the occupation of Kuwait by Iraq. This undoubtedly made it easier for him to communicate with the Iraqi government.

There is a certain division of labor between the principal organs of the United Nations in this respect. Their handling of the Cyprus conflict will serve as an illustration. After the Turkish intervention in 1974 effectively divided the island into two parts, one Greek Cypriot and the other Turkish Cypriot, the General Assembly repeatedly adopted, despite Turkish opposition, resolutions demanding a settlement of the conflict by a return to the status quo ante. The Security Council, though acknowledging the resolutions of the General Assembly, chose a more pragmatic approach that included calls for a negotiated settlement. An intermittent process of negotiations under the auspices of the Secretary-General was started. Both Waldheim and Pérez de Cuéllar have presented settlement plans in these talks, but unfortunately they have been rejected by one party or another. In presenting the various proposals, the Secretary-General has taken into account the changed power relationship on the island and avoided the unrealistic demands of the General Assembly. As a result, he has been generally accepted as an impartial outsider.

The Middle East conflict is another example of an issue that has been dealt with in a different manner by different organs of the United Nations. Israel is constantly the target of criticism by the deliberative organs, particularly the General Assembly. Successive Secretaries-General have been reluctant to associate themselves with the crusade against Israel and have remained on speaking terms with various Israeli governments. This impartiality has made it possible to conduct several peacekeeping operations along Israeli borders and to undertake relief work for Palestinian refugees in the territories controlled by Israel.

One scholar concludes that the link between UN resolutions relating to a specific situation, and the good offices of the Secretary-General in connection with the same matter, is a very delicate one. "It may be safely submitted, however, that an ideal peacemaking mandate for the Secretary-General with regard to a specific conflict is limited to a general statement of the objectives that the negotiations are expected to achieve, while preserving the Secretary-General's freedom of action that a third party normally requires" (Cordovez, 1987:166).

Support from Member Governments

As explained above, the Secretary-General is in reality elected by the five permanent members of the Security Council. There are often many candidates; at least eleven were considered in 1981 when Pérez de Cuéllar was finally appointed.[17] The successful candidate is not necessarily the first choice of any of the permanent members. On the other hand, he does not appear offensive to any of them and may even enjoy a good measure of confidence. As history shows, this confidence is a precondition for satisfactory performance. It is particularly important when the Secretary-General offers his services in conflicts in which the major powers are directly involved. During the Cuban missile crisis in 1962, both the United States and the USSR reacted favorably to an appeal by U Thant for urgent negotiations. They also welcomed his trip to Cuba and thanked him afterward in an unprecedented joint letter signed by Ambassadors Stevenson and Kuznetsov (Thant, 1977:ch. 8; Nassif, 1988:ch. 3).[18]

There may also be situations, however, when action by the Secretary-General is discouraged or rendered ineffective by lack of support. During the summer and fall of 1971, U Thant worked desperately to get the major powers involved in the crisis that developed on the Indian subcontinent. A bloody strife took place in East Pakistan between the Awami

League, demanding independence, and the Pakistani army, which was dominated by West Pakistanis. India was covertly supplying the rebels with arms, and a war between India and Pakistan seemed imminent. However, the interests of the five permanent members were divergent. The USSR generally supported India, whereas China and the United States favored Pakistan; neither they nor France and Britain wanted the Security Council to discuss the issue. U Thant established informal contacts with the leaders of both India and Pakistan, but to no avail. In December, India attacked the Pakistani army in East Pakistan; the Security Council remained immobilized. U Thant's silent diplomacy had produced no results, but he made a passionate address to the General Assembly when the matter was transferred to that organ under the Uniting for Peace resolution.[19]

The notion of a constituency for the Secretary-General has been discussed by several authors.[20] Rovine (1970:433ff.) compares the first three incumbents and notes that Hammarskjöld was sympathetic to, and wanted to rely on support from, the newly independent nations of Africa and Asia. During the Congo crisis this support was equivocal, however. In U Thant the new nations got a more genuine representative; unlike his predecessors he had experienced colonial administration. His relationship to this caucus, which was courted by East and West for its voting strength, may have made it easier for him to speak his mind about U.S. participation in the second Indo-China war and about the Soviet invasion of Czechoslovakia in 1968. Waldheim had no natural constituency of any significance; this may be one reason why he carefully avoided antagonizing any of the major groups. Pérez de Cuéllar was the first Secretary-General from Latin America, a region of great political diversity; he does not seem to have sought a constituency. Britain had no problem accepting him as mediator in its conflict with Argentina in 1982 over the Falklands/Malvinas (Parsons, 1983:172–174).

The present Secretary-General, Boutros Boutros-Ghali, was among the Organization of African Unity's candidates for the post, preferred by most Arab countries, and actively supported by France in the Security Council. There is, however, little in his behavior to indicate that Boutros-Ghali seeks a particular constituency. For instance, he has yet to appoint a French citizen to one of the thirty-two top-level posts as under- and assistant secretary-general, although France was among the fiercest sponsors of his candidacy.

The gist of the matter seems to be that the influence of the Secretary-General depends first and foremost on his ability to remain acceptable to all, and in particular to all the major powers. If he espouses the concerns of one geographical or ideological group at the expense of others, his reputation for principled impartiality will suffer. The prudent policy of the Secretary-General seems to be to avoid strong identification with any particular constituency.

Organizational Position

As noted, the Secretary-General is a principal organ of the United Nations and may take independent initiatives. But he is also, according to Article 98, a servant of the General Assembly and the three councils established by the charter. Thus, in theory the relationship between the Secretary-General and the other organs could be one of dependence, interplay, or leadership. We shall look at each of these possibilities in some detail and give examples.

He may be told to carry out tasks in the diplomatic field that he would not have performed on his own initiative. Waldheim's role in the conflict in East Timor in 1974–1975 may serve as an example. When Indonesia invaded the former Portuguese colony, the Security Council, after much foot-dragging, requested the Secretary-General "to send urgently a special representative to East Timor for the purpose of making on-the-spot assessment of the present situation and of establishing contact with all the parties . . . in order to ensure the implementation of the present resolution."[21] The resolution called on Indonesia to withdraw all its forces without delay. Waldheim appointed V. Winspeare Guicciardi his special representative, and Guicciardi traveled to the territory with a small team. But many important governments, China being a notable exception, sympathized with Indonesia. The Western powers were worried about the possibility of East Timor becoming "the Cuba of the Indian Ocean."[22] The mission of the special representative of the Secretary-General was not supposed to succeed as stated, but to serve as a fig leaf. Waldheim was reported to have been reluctant to inject his office into this situation, but he could not refuse (Crawford and Dayanidhi, 1976:26). In his memoirs, one sentence covers the whole affair (Waldheim, 1985:95).

Interplay between the Secretary-General and the Security Council is a more normal situation. U Thant, Waldheim, and Pérez de Cuéllar have all used their good offices in the Cyprus conflict and chaired the negotiations between representatives of the Greek Cypriot and the Turkish Cypriot communities. It appears that the permanent members of the council, particularly the United States, keep the Secretary-General reasonably well informed about their pertinent bilateral contacts with the parties to this conflict. As mentioned above, Pérez de Cuéllar mediated in the Falklands/Malvinas conflict with the full support of the council. His several good-offices missions during the Iran-Iraq War illustrate the same point.

The major powers may delegate tasks to the Secretary-General, but in general they do not want him to exercise leadership. Lie and Hammarskjöld occasionally tried to do this, mostly with meager results and sometimes with ruinous consequences. The USSR in particular resented any weakening of the pivotal position of the Security Council and often opposed the delegation of power to the Secretary-General. However, in a major article in *Pravda* in September 1987 Mikhail Gorbachev changed this policy.

As we have seen, members of the council do not always have complete confidence in the initiatives and actions of the Secretary-General. Over the years the USSR made several suggestions to involve the council itself more directly in operational activities and to make the Secretary-General a mere servant of the council. For example, it tendered the idea that a subsidiary organ of the council should play a major role in setting up and directing peacekeeping operations, including the selection of force commanders and national contingents (Rikhye, 1983:180ff.). In some instances the USSR has proposed the establishment of fact-finding commissions appointed by the council. These proposals were, however, stillborn. The Security Council is a complicated organ of fifteen members that is not well suited to organizing activities on a day-to-day basis. It has to rely on an executive, that is, the Secretary-General, to whom organizational imperatives give a certain latitude of independent initiative and responsibility.

Personal Skills of the Secretary-General and His Staff

In the absence of the power of sanctions, the importance of the personal qualifications and skills of the Secretary-General and his immediate staff is obvious. All six incumbents had considerable relevant experience when they took office. They had held high positions in their respective national governments, and with the obvious exception of Lie had also worked in national missions of their countries to the UN and/or served in the Secretariat.

Some authors stress the importance of the different personalities of the Secretaries General. The list of desirable traits of character is indeed a long one. The Secretary-General must have a quick and yet profound mind and be able to work long hours. He should have a vision of the future of the organization, including the role of his own office, and at the same time should be able to take a pragmatic and practical approach to organizational, financial, and diplomatic matters. In this job, compassion is as pertinent as the ability to conceal emotions.

Some traits of character may have been more befitting than others in different phases of the history of the organization. Lie's forthright style may have been refreshing in the period of great expectations just after the founding of the organization. His success as a mediator was limited, however, and with the advent of the Cold War his outspokenness created serious problems, particularly regarding the USSR. Waldheim's low profile may have been more suitable in a period of intense East-West rivalry, although many found him too cautious.

At each election of a Secretary-General, there were other qualified and possibly more capable candidates. The permanent members of the Security Council are not likely to prefer strong and independent-minded personalities. Sir Brian Urquhart, who has worked closely with all the Secretaries-General, expresses his disappointment with the priorities of the major powers in their selection of the top civil servant of the UN:

> The Waldheim episode is above all an indictment of the way in which governments, and especially the great powers, select the world's leading international civil servant. Although good men *have* been selected, looking for the person with the qualities best suited to this infinitely demanding and important job seems to hold a very low priority for governments. Rather, political differences dictate a search for a candidate who will not exert any troubling degree of leadership, commitment, originality, or independence. Waldheim was an energetic mediocrity. In fact he did rather better as Secretary-General than I had anticipated and demonstrated determination and even, on occasion, courage, but lacked the qualities of vision, integrity, inspiration, and leadership that the United Nations so desperately needs. (Urquhart, 1987:227–228)

It is unlikely that Hammarskjöld would have been appointed if his character had been well known in advance. And yet the ability to work with and retain the confidence of the most powerful of the member governments is an indispensable qualification in this job. All 179 member governments are, in actual fact, the Secretary-General's employers.

It is the very small Department of Special Political Affairs that has provided most of the assistance to the Secretary-General's mediating and peacekeeping functions. Public knowledge about the personalities and workings of this important unit is sketchy, although the autobiography of Urquhart (1987), who for several years served as one of the two heads of the department, provides a number of interesting insights. In 1988, Pérez de Cuéllar decided to change the name of this unit to the Office of Special Political Affairs (OSPA) and to have it headed by a single undersecretary-general. The current incumbent, Marrack Goulding, is responsible for all peacekeeping operations (Jonah, 1989:83). The Secretary-General relies primarily on his executive office for assistance in the mediating and good-offices functions. Extraordinary diplomatic skills and loyalty are required of the persons in both units.

Where the United Nations is involved in complex or prolonged conflicts or in conflicts threatening to escalate, the Secretary-General may appoint a special representative to serve as a mediator. This was the case in Kampuchea, where the Japanese Yasushi Akashi was placed in charge of the United Nations Transitional Authority in Cambodia (UNTAC) attempting to secure the continuous support of the four political factions for the elections held in May 1993. In the former Yugoslavia, the envoy of the United Nations, former U.S. secretary of state Cyrus Vance, contributed to the negotiation of a cease-fire (heavily violated throughout 1993) in Croatia that included the establishment of the United Nations Protection Force in Yugoslavia (UNPROFOR). Currently, UN envoy Thorvald Stoltenberg (appointed UN mediator after the resignation of Vance) and European Community mediator Lord Owen are attempting to build support for a peace plan to end the hostilities in Bosnia-Herzegovina.

Soviet representation in the Department of Special Political Affairs has been a delicate issue. In the Preparatory Commission, the major powers agreed on a scheme for sharing the positions of several deputies to the Secretary-General. Despite the wording of Article 100 of the charter, Trygve Lie was politically obliged to appoint Assistant Secretaries-General in accordance with this plan. A Soviet citizen, Arkady Sobolev, was thus made Assistant Secretary-General for Security Council Affairs (Lie, 1954:46; Schwebel 1952:30–32, 58). (The title was later changed to Undersecretary-General.) There is still a Soviet citizen in this position; however, since Soviet members of the Secretariat regularly reported to and received instructions from Moscow, the position was never given much political clout by the successive Secretaries-General. The Department of Special Political Affairs was created in part to provide the Secretary-General with a small but reliable staff that could handle sensitive diplomatic issues. Urquhart had a Soviet assistant who served as a useful link to the Soviet mission, but it was understood that he would not be privy to confidential information (Urquhart, 1987:352–353).

Position in the Diplomatic Network

Irrespective of personal qualifications, the Secretaries-General benefit from the central location of their office. Heads of state, heads of government, and foreign ministers regularly visit the UN headquarters in New York, often to address the General Assembly. Paying a visit to the Secretary-General is frequently part of their program. Hence the Secretary-General has firsthand knowledge of most of the political leaders of the world. Many of these calls are more than courtesy; they are used to raise issues, transmit information, and air proposals relevant to international conflicts and other problems. The Secretary-General can be used as a channel between parties who prefer not to communicate directly. Links can be established in a discrete manner. It is particularly important that the Secretary-General is able to receive as visitors representatives of nonrecognized or disputed entities, for instance, the Turkish Federated Republic of Northern Cyprus or the Palestinian Liberation Organization.

Cooperation between the Security Council and Secretary-General is a central element in UN efforts for international peace and security. The council maintains a high degree of readiness and an emergency meeting can be summoned at a few hours' notice. This also means that the Secretary-General has the opportunity, virtually at all times, to contact the permanent representatives in New York of the governments of all the major powers. As a rule, he prefers to know the attitudes of these governments before taking significant diplomatic initiatives on his own. He may also want to express confidentially his own views on situations where the interests of these governments are involved.

FUNCTIONS AND METHODS

Calling on the Security Council

Article 99 of the charter has already been mentioned several times. It gives the Secretary-General the right to place any matter that in his opinion may threaten the maintenance of international peace and security on the provisional agenda of the Security Council. By implication, he may also request the president of the council to call a meeting. If the Secretary-General lets it be publicly known that he has put an item on the agenda and/or asked for a meeting of the council, it would be politically difficult for the council not to comply. This gives the Secretary-General some political leverage. Crises may develop without the members of the council being able or willing to address the matter, and the Secretary-General has the possibility of exposing their unwillingness.

Article 99, however, is a double-edged weapon. The major powers do not necessarily like to have their occasional lethargy exposed to possible international disdain, and a Secretary-General who puts them in an unpleasant situation risks losing their confidence and support. As mentioned above, in 1971 U Thant unsuccessfully appealed to the major powers to take up the conflict on the Indian subcontinent in the Security Council. "After four months of this futile exercise, I distributed a confidential memorandum to the Council members warning them that the conflict could all too easily expand" (Thant, 1977:23). He later made the memorandum public. Yet the council did not meet for another four months—after the outbreak of an international war between India and Pakistan—and even then it was unable to act.

The council's handling of the Iraqi attack on Iran on September 21, 1980, provides a more recent illustration of its occasional apathy. Waldheim's appeal on September 22 to both parties to end the hostilities was the first official UN reaction. One day later he requested an informal meeting of the Security Council, which resulted in a statement by its president. A formal meeting was finally called on the initiative of two of the nonpermanent members, Mexico and Norway. After some bickering, the council adopted a rather powerless resolution that did not condemn the invasion or demand a withdrawal of forces to international boundaries.[23]

There are many other situations where the Secretary-General might have formally invoked Article 99, but having considered the likely consequences chose to abstain. Diego Cordovez, one of Pérez de Cuéllar's closest associates, observed that "the real strength of Article 99 lies in the interpretation whereby this article can provide formal authority for informal action" (Cordovez, 1987:167).

The new collegial working relations among the members of the Security Council have opened new possibilities for the Secretary-General as well. The permanent members nowadays hold their own meetings and the Secretary-General consults them.[24] Since 1987, the foreign ministers of the permanent members have had at the invitation of the Secretary-General an annual luncheon to review recent developments. Such informal meetings may provide a basis for initiatives by both the Secretary-General and the council.

Good Offices, Mediation, and Arbitration

The Secretaries-General have spent much of their time as honest brokers in international conflicts, both on their own initiative and at the request of the Security Council. A study of Waldheim asserts that "a good deal of his most fruitful activity will take place behind the scenes" (James, 1983: 94). However instrumental a Secretary-General may have been in working toward a settlement, more often than not he may remain without public credit for his role. "The essence of quiet diplomacy is the art of avoiding the limelight when necessary" (Cordovez, 1987:169). It is, therefore, impossible to provide an adequate account of this kind of activity and we shall confine ourselves to a discussion of different kinds and styles of involvement.

At this point, a brief comment on terminology is required. The definition of mediation in this article is broad indeed and does not distinguish between passive and more active forms of third-party involvement. The more modest role of an intermediary is merely to transmit messages between parties that find him or her a convenient channel of communication. On the next rung of the ladder, the intermediary may encourage exchange of information. His or her involvement becomes more important if he or she also attempts to explain and interpret the messages to the receiving party in order to remove misunderstandings, improve confidence, and soften possible negative reactions. The intermediary may also propose procedures for continued exchanges and negotiations. The term "good offices" covers these functions.

In the UN jargon, the term "mediation" is sometimes defined more strictly than in this article. It is reserved for intercessions by an intermediary who, with the implicit or explicit consent of the parties, makes not only procedural but also substantive proposals for a settlement of disputes. Many authors use the two terms "good offices" and "mediation" almost interchangeably.[25] The choice of term is unimportant, however, if one realizes that they may cover a wide variety of intercessions.

As discussed above, the office of the Secretary-General is well placed to serve as a channel of communication, particularly when direct channels between adversaries are blocked or nonexistent. The Secretary-General and his representatives maintained contacts with the belligerents during the Iran-Iraq War and the Falkland/Malvinas War, and currently are doing so in the former Yugoslavia, where UN envoy Cyrus Vance communicates with both de jure and de facto parties to the ethnic conflicts. One of the advantages of the office of the Secretary-General is that contact with him does not imply diplomatic recognition by any of the member governments of the United Nations. He may transmit messages between governments that do not have diplomatic relations and between political factions that do not recognize one another.

Hammarskjöld's contacts with the People's Republic of China in 1954 are a celebrated case. At that time, the Peking government was not a member of the UN; China's seat was occupied by the government in Taipei, and the United States did not recognize the former government. However, the People's Republic of China had imprisoned a U.S. air crew that had been shot down while dropping leaflets over North Korea. Hammarskjöld traveled to Peking and managed to have the airmen released a few months later. This move was much appreciated by the United States, which until 1971 chose not to have direct contacts with Peking (Urquhart, 1972:96–131).

The Secretary-General may also communicate with nongovernmental actors. The armistice between Israeli and PLO forces in Lebanon in 1983 was negotiated with two third parties, the United States and the UN; neither the PLO nor Israel would speak directly with the other. The United States also refused to have open and direct relations with the PLO, but neither Israel nor the United States had objections to UN contacts with this organization (Cobban, 1983:95–96, 111–112). The United States and the UN coordinated their diplomacy, which resulted in a limited but important cease-fire agreement.

The UN and the Secretary-General may also refuse contacts with nongovernmental entities. The predominantly Christian South Lebanon Army (SLA) wants to be recognized by the United Nations Interim Force in Lebanon (UNIFIL) as a genuine indigenous militia like the Shi'ite AMAL, and wishes to establish liaison with the UN force. However, the SLA is paid for and supplied by Israel, which also to a considerable extent directs its operations. The UN has therefore turned down Israeli and SLA proposals for liaison with the latter and considers Israel responsible for SLA policies and military actions.[26]

There are also several examples of mediation in the strict sense of the term. Making substantive proposals is a risky business, particularly if they are publicized. If at least one of the parties considers the proposals biased, the exercise is likely to fail, as happened in Cyprus in 1965. Security Council Resolution 184 of March 4, 1964, which established the United Nations Force in Cyprus (UNFICYP), also provided for a mediator to be appointed by the Secretary-General. The mediator was supposed to submit a report containing elements of a proposal for a political solution to the Cyprus conflict. This mediation effort was unsuccessful.[27] From 1967 to 1974 the special representative of the Secretary-General in Cyprus chaired negotiations between representatives of the two main communities. Formally, the special representative was not supposed to inject his own ideas for a settlement, but he played a very constructive role nevertheless. These negotiations almost produced an agreement in 1973, when the progress was stopped as a result of the policies of the Greek junta. After the crisis of 1974, negotiations started again with the Secretary-General himself as chairman. During the last ten years he has regularly produced memoranda for consideration by the parties, often based on prior and separate discussions with each of them. These documents are in all but form proposals for a settlement.

The Secretary-General's office has been directly involved in a mediating function in a large number of conflicts. His efforts in the Middle East are particularly important. Count Folke Bernadotte, Dr. Ralph Bunche, and Ambassador Gunnar Jarring have represented the Secretary-General in this region.[28]

Also interesting are some more recent examples of mediation. Undersecretary-General Diego Cordovez, personal representative of the Secretary-General, played a vital role during the negotiations in Geneva between the governments of Afghanistan and Pakistan. They came to a successful end in 1988, permitting the subsequent withdrawal of Soviet forces from Afghanistan. The Secretary-General has also been involved in negotiations between Morocco and the Polisario about a cease-fire and election as steps toward a solution of the conflict in Western Sahara.

In the dispute between Libya and Malta about the continental shelf between the two states, Pérez de Cuéllar succeeded in convincing the governments to take their issue to the International Court of Justice. The court passed its verdict in 1985, ending the dispute (Cordovez, 1987:17–171).

The Secretary-General is not usually involved in arbitration. However, in the dispute between Guyana and Venezuela, the parties bestowed on him the authority to decide on the means of a settlement should their bilateral negotiations prove inconclusive. In the dispute between France and New Zealand resulting from the sinking of the *Rainbow Warrior*, the parties eventually agreed that the solution proposed by the Secretary-General would be binding (Franck, 1988:81–82).

More often than not the Secretary-General is not the only third party working for the settlement of a dispute. During the Iran-Iraq War, he and his special representative Olof Palme used their good offices. Representatives of the Non-Aligned Movement and the Muslim League also tried to prevail on the parties to accept a cease-fire. Currently, UN envoy Cyrus Vance cooperates with the European Community mediator, Lord Owen, to end the hostilities in Bosnia-Herzegovina.

During the Falkland/Malvinas crisis in 1982, U.S. secretary of state Alexander Haig mediated first between Argentina and Britain in order to avert war. Both the president of the Security Council and Secretary-General Pérez de Cuéllar maintained that they should do nothing that might inhibit Haig's efforts, which ended in failure. The President of Peru also made an abortive attempt to find a compromise. From then on Pérez de Cuéllar worked "in an orderly and systematic way towards the elaboration of an agreement." He was able to report considerable progress, but not enough to prevent war (Parsons, 1983:172–174).

As already mentioned, the Secretary-General and his representatives were engaged in mediation in the Middle East for many years, but since the October War of 1973 the UN has played a secondary role. The peace conference in Geneva after the war, in which both superpowers and the belligerents (except Syria) participated, was nominally chaired by Kurt Waldheim, but U.S. secretary of state Henry Kissinger took the diplomatic initiative in an effort to reduce Soviet influence in the area. His successful mediation resulted in military disengagement agreements between Israel and Egypt and between Israel and Syria. The 1978 peace treaty between Israel and Egypt was negotiated with the help of President Jimmy Carter, and the United States has retained the diplomatic initiative in this region, keeping the UN on the sidelines (Fermann, 1988).

In 1965, U Thant engaged in shuttle diplomacy between Rawalpindi and New Delhi. Pakistan and India were at war, and the Secretary-General tried to convince the leaders of the two countries to accept the cease-fire ordered by the Security Council. They agreed, but the cease-fire was not holding. The conflict was settled in response to a Soviet initiative: at the conclusion of a series of meetings in Tashkent that were mediated by Prime Minister Alexei Kosygin, the president of Pakistan and the prime minister of India signed an agreement to establish peaceful and normal relations.[29]

One inference from these examples is that the major powers often engage in mediation of so-called regional conflicts. In many instances, they can be more effective than the Secretary-General because they can, implicitly or explicitly, threaten punishment or promise rewards to the parties to the dispute. The Secretary-General cannot apply positive or negative sanctions; his main assets are skill, moral authority, and impartiality, which work as substitutes for power based on enforcement. The major powers do not necessarily base their mediation on strict impartiality; they often work for settlements that also suit their own interests.

Peacekeeping

The Charter of the United Nations prescribes different methods for the settlement of disputes. There is, however, no specific provision for peacekeeping, although this kind of conflict management has become one of the UN's main contributions to international peace and security and has attracted considerable public attention.[30] From 1948 to 1988, the UN launched ten observation missions composed of unarmed military officers, and eight peacekeeping forces consisting mainly of lightly armed infantry battalions.[31] The upsurge of peacekeeping during the last four years has nearly doubled the number of operations. Thus, by January 1993 more than 50,000 UN soldiers as well as observers and police forces from sixty-seven troop-contributing countries were in service. At the time of this writing, the observer force UNMOGIP reports violations of the cease-fire agreement between India and Pakistan in Kashmir. Another such force, UNTSO, operates in Southern Lebanon, on the Golan, and in Sinai. There are peacekeeping forces in Cyprus (UNFI-CYP), on the Golan (UNDOF), and in Southern Lebanon (UNIFIL). UNTAG has completed its mission in Namibia, which became an independent country without much bloodshed; UNAVEM has monitored the withdrawal of Cuban troops from Angola and the September 1992 elections there. UNIIMOG helps ensure the uneasy truce between Iran and Iraq. In 1989, the symbolic observer corps UNGOMAP ceased its monitoring of the withdrawal of foreign, mainly Soviet, troops from Afghanistan. ONUCA has assisted in the disarmament of the Contras in Central America and is now monitoring the Central American agreement banning clandestine aid for foreign guerrilla troops; ONUVEN verified the February 1990 elections in Nicaragua. In Croatia, UNPRO-FOR observes the fragile cease-fire between Croatian government forces and Serbian forces controlling two enclaves. In Kampuchea, the second-largest UN peacekeeping force ever (UNTAC) is engaged in a nation-building process and preparing for general elections in May 1993. Since May 1992, UNOSOM has been engaged in monitoring the heavily violated cease-fire between the warring factions in Mogadishu, Somalia.

In each case, the Secretary-General has played or is playing a pivotal role. He organizes the force, writes its terms of reference, appoints the commander, negotiates the necessary agreements with the parties including the host countries, and handles numerous smaller and larger diplomatic problems connected with the mission. Reports are regularly submitted to the Security Council.

Peacekeeping is not mediation or good-offices missions in the strict sense of these terms, but it is nevertheless a closely related function of the United Nations and the Secretary-General.

In some cases, in the midst of crises peacekeeping missions have been launched to stabilize a critical situation and buy time for negotiation of a lasting settlement. The deployment of UNEF II between Egyptian and Israeli forces in 1973 is perhaps the best example; this force bought time for negotiations about a peace treaty between the two nations (Fermann, 1988). The deployment of UNEF(I) in 1956 and UNFICYP in 1974 also belongs in this category.

In other instances, peacekeeping missions have been part of a settlement that has already been negotiated; UNTAG and UNAVEM are good examples. As mentioned, the Secretary-General plays a pivotal role in setting up and running peacekeeping operations, subject to the approval of the Security Council. This position strengthens his hand as a mediator in negotiations about political settlements in which a peacekeeping mission may become necessary.

Finally, the peacekeeping function of the United Nations is essentially political, not military. Although peacekeeping forces are lightly armed, they can use their weapons only in self-defense. During crises in the field, they rely more on persuasion and negotiations than on the use of firepower. In principle, disputes should be settled at the lowest possible level, but when attempts at finding a local solution fail, the force commander may become directly involved. Even more difficult situations have to be handled by the Office of Special Political Affairs and the Secretary-General, such as happens relatively often in the fluid and tense situation in southern Lebanon. Mediation at this level may encompass both the practical difficulties in the field and wider political issues. The UN-sponsored negotiations in 1984–1985 between Israel and Lebanon are an example; they took place in UNIFIL's headquarters and touched upon the problem of the reestablishment of the authority of the Lebanese government in the area vacated by Israeli withdrawal (Skogmo, 1989: 68–69, 124–127). Assisting the government of Lebanon in reestablishing its authority and confirming Israeli withdrawal were included in UNIFIL's mandate.

CURRENT CHANGES AND FUTURE ROLE

The office of the Secretary-General is a unique institution in international politics. As the chief executive of the world's most universal and representative political organization, no other international civil servant enjoys a higher status in the eyes of governments. But the Secretary-General also confronts enormous and often conflicting expectations. Meeting his successor at Idlewild Airport in 1953, Lie described the task to Hammarskjöld as "the most impossible job on earth" (Lie, 1954:417).

There is a tendency to forget the meager and uncertain basis on which the Secretary-General's role in the area of peaceful settlement of disputes had to be built. The text of the charter is not particularly explicit with respect to what he can do (Cordovez, 1987:162–163); yet it is equally brief and nonspecific about the limitations of his functions. The main legal limitation on his office is that it is not a policymaking organ; all UN resolutions are mandatory for him (Elaraby, 1987:177, 182).

The Cold War and the consequent failure to implement properly the collective security system of the charter had conflicting effects on the evolution of the Secretary-General's role. On the one hand, the debilitation of the collective security machinery led to the development of alternative diplomatic action by the successive incumbents of this office. On the other hand, it had a moderating effect on the creative capacity of the chief executive (Cordovez, 1987:163).

The Cold War has come to an end. The cooperation between the permanent members of the Security Council has significantly strengthened and activated this organ and enhanced the image of the United Nations as a whole. There is a corollary change in the role of the Secretary-General in degree, though not in essence. The potential scope of mediation by the Secretary-General depends very much on what he is permitted to do by the major powers. Since they are more able to take collective initiatives, one might think that there would be less room left for him. However, this assumption is belied by the Secretary-General's increased activity and by his considerable number of successful endeavors in international diplomacy—a development for which there are several reasons.

First, the Security Council needs an executive. Mediation can rarely be performed by a committee, although there are exceptions to this rule. The peace plan for Kampuchea was worked out by the five permanent members of the council, but the agreement was specified and supplemented by the Secretary-General and his staff in negotiations with the parties to the conflict. In most cases, negotiations with a single mediator are technically easier. The main weakness of the Secretary-General is that he cannot apply sanctions, but the members of the Security Council can strengthen his position by endorsing his endeavors and by exerting bilateral pressure on the parties to a dispute.

Second, the Secretary-General is often able to monitor and perform good-offices missions in disputes that the deliberative organs of the United Nations do not handle effectively. For a variety of reasons members of the Security Council or the General Assembly may be opposed to placing a particular dispute on the agendas of these organs, leaving the ground to the Secretary-General alone. However, the new working style of the council makes it easier for him to test the waters and decide for himself whether, or at which stage, he should try to involve it in attempts to head off an incipient conflict or bring a violent dispute to termination.

Third, in some cases the deliberative organs produce acrimonious debates and biased resolutions rather than constructive proposals for a settlement. In such situations, the Secretary-General "has to improvise, and may sometimes feel compelled to suggest means other than those which have been envisaged by the Security Council [and the General Assembly] in [their] original discussions of the matter" (Pérez de Cuéllar, 1988:67).

We should not, however, be too optimistic about an enhanced role for the Secretary-General in the post–Cold War era. The mediating role of the Secretary-General may be restricted by at least three developments that affect his credibility as a mediator.

First, because of the combination of an increased demand for UN intervention and a lack of sound financial basis for UN activities in the field of "international peace and security," the resources of the UN Secretariat are becoming overstretched. Although since the late 1980s the Security Council has increasingly been able to agree upon resolutions, the political consensus established among former rivals has yet to translate into a corresponding willingness to strengthen the Secretariat's ability to act on the growing number of missions authorized by the Security Council. If not counteracted, this incongruency will undermine the Secretariat's ability to implement efficiently the resolutions of the Security Council and may place the reputation of the United Nations in jeopardy.

Second, as noted earlier, acceptability to all relevant parties is a sine qua non in international mediation; independence and impartiality are, in turn, the keys to acceptability. It can be argued, however, that the new activism of the Security Council may threaten the credibility of the Secretary-General as mediator: in conflicts where the Security Council authorizes the use of force and thus becomes a party to a conflict, the impartiality of the Secretary-General as a mediator may be brought into question. The Security Council is becoming increasingly willing to authorize the use of force under chapter VII of the charter and to intervene in civil-war conflicts with reference to humanitarian law (Wallensteen, 1992). One should not be surprised that the parties to conflicts that attract the forceful attention of the Security Council do not accept the impartiality of a Secretary-General so closely linked to it.

Third, the moral standing of the UN and the Secretary-General may be seriously affected by the narrow limits set on the mediating efforts of the Secretary-General by realpolitical constellations. Thus, in the Balkans UN mediating envoys have been delegated the unwelcome function of mediating peace plans that, by implication, reward acts of "ethnic cleansing" and violations of "territorial integrity," as well as the use of military force to achieve political goals. Instead of organizing and authorizing the use of force in self-defense to safeguard Bosnian sovereignty, as envisaged in the charter, the UN finds itself forced to adjust its peacekeeping operations and reinstruct its mediators according to the evolving offensives of the aggressors. Such a situation is intolerable in the long run, and may harm the reputation of the UN and the mediating role of the Secretariat to the extent that in addition to the Bosnian Republic itself the organization becomes a major victim of the Balkans war. There are instances when even the Secretary-General should decline to mediate; because of the wounds it inflicts on the Secretary-General's mediating reputation and the precedent it sets for future efforts, the Bosnian nightmare may be such a case.

Nevertheless, cooperation between the Security Council and the Secretary-General on the basis of the relative advantages to both is the key to a more potent role for the United Nations in the area of peaceful settlement of disputes. Although the Security Council may be considered the more powerful organ, it is also to a greater extent subject to the vicissitudes of international politics. The performance of the office of the Secretary-General is more low-key; but as the world's most reputable intermediary it remains an essential and stabilizing element.

The first version of this article was written by Kjell Skjelsbæk while he was at the Norwegian Institute of International Affairs (NUPI) and published in *Journal of Peace Research* 1, 1991. It arose out of a project on international peacekeeping, funded by the Ford Foundation at NUPI. Kjell Skjelsbæk died on June 20, 1991. At the request of Jacob Bercovitch, Nils Petter Gleditsch, the editor of *JPR,* agreed to have the article revised for this volume. Under a grant from the Norwegian Ministry of Foreign Affairs to the International Peace Research Institute, Oslo (PRIO), Gunnar Fermann of the Fridjtof Nansen Institute has revised and updated the article to early 1993. Fermann served from 1985 to 1988 as a research assistant to Skjelsbæk in the Ford/NUPI project. We are grateful to Kari Skjelsbæk for her permission to revise and publish this article. —*Ed.*

NOTES

1. Still, the United States and the Russian Federation were by September 1992 responsible for nearly three-quarters of the $1.6 billion debt of unpaid contributions to the United Nations.

2. It was adopted as General Assembly Resolution 44/21 of November 15, 1989.

3. Wall's (1981) survey of the theoretical and empirical literature in English is somewhat dated, but nevertheless very useful.

4. He discusses them later in the same publication (299ff.).

5. The Preparatory Commission served from the conclusion of the San Francisco conference in October 1945 to the first General Assembly in February 1946.

6. The first Secretary-General of the League of Nations, Sir Eric Drummond, once remarked that he wished that Article 99 had been at his disposal. It would have made his office much more potent (Schwebel, 1952:11).

7. As cited in Urquhart (1985:258).

8. There are many studies of Lie's term as Secretary-General. His autobiography (Lie, 1954) was published soon after his retirement. Gordenker (1967) and Rovine (1970) both provide a historical outline and some assessment of the first Secretary-General. Urquhart (1987), who for some time worked closely with Lie but had an uneasy relationship with him, gives a critical closeup of Lie's diplomatic and administrative style. A recent study by Barros (1990) provides much interesting information, but is not based on Lie's private papers, and in addition Barros has not understood Lie's role in Norwegian politics before his service in the United Nations.

9. From Lie's speech to the Security Council on June 25, 1950, as cited in Rovine (1970:238).

10. By far the most comprehensive and authoritative study of Hammarskjöld has been written by Urquhart (1972).

11. United Nations General Assembly *Official Records,* 825th meeting, par. 86, as given in Goodrich (1974:479).

12. U Thant's autobiography (1977) contains an interesting introduction to his religious and ethical thoughts. There is no general study by others of U Thant's long service in the United Nations. However, a new book by one of his staff provides interesting insights and makes public some of his private documents from the Cuban missile crisis in 1962 and from the withdrawal of UNEF in 1967 (Nassif, 1988).

13. Urquhart is indignant about Western and Israeli criticism of U Thant and his closest associate, Undersecretary-General Ralph Bunche. He writes that "in a situation where the West simply did not want to, or could not, face up to the truth, U Thant provided a perfect scapegoat. . . . Neither Britain nor the United States, for example, took the situation to the Security Council. They knew all too well that nothing could be done and therefore wished to take no responsibility" (Urquhart, 1987:213).

14. Waldheim seems to be remembered these days mostly because of his lying about his position in the Wehrmacht during World War II. While accepting this as a serious blemish on his record as Secretary-General, one should not forget his contributions to the United Nations.

15. SC Resolution 720 (1991), November 21, and GA Resolution 46/21, December 3, 1991.

16. United Nations Security Council *Official Records,* 11th year, 751st meeting, p. 2, as given by Rovine (1970:287).

17. See Urquhart (1987:332). Nine names remained after Salim Salim of Tanzania and Waldheim had been prevailed upon to withdraw theirs.

18. Young (1967:287–288), while commending U Thant's initiative, is critical of his proposals for a settlement. Young thinks that U Thant was unable to assess accurately what his proposals' effect would be on the military balance.

19. The Secretary-General was able to exert influence mainly by organizing humanitarian aid. In an "unusual and unprecedented form of activity for the United Nations," U Thant had initiated two of the largest operations in the history of the organization without any supporting resolution from the United Nations organ (United Nations Press Release SG/1763/Iha 93, November 17, 1971).

20. The strength derived from catering to the needs of a constituency is strongly underlined by Cox (1969). Albert Thomas, the first director of the ILO, is the prototype of a successful Secretary-General in Cox's analysis.

21. United Nations Security Council Resolution 384 of December 22, 1975.

22. Phrase used by an anonymous UN official describing the Western concerns.

23. A description of the pitiful role of the UN at the beginning of the Iran-Iraq War is found in Eknes (1989:11–12).

24. United Nations Security Council *Official Records,* Supplement, S/15830.

25. *Webster's Third New International Dictionary* (1986) gives the following definition of good offices: "services as a mediator especially between belligerent and disputing states."

26. A discussion of the UN policy with respect to the SLA is found in Skogmo (1989:35–36 and 74, note 20).

27. The Turkish Cypriot leadership rejected the report as unbalanced and refused to cooperate with the mediator. No successor was appointed.

28. Touval (1982) has made a good survey of their mediation efforts in the Middle East.

29. Personal accounts of the Secretary-General's role in this conflict are found in Thant (1977:99–115) and Urquhart (1987:202–207).

30. The judicial status of the peacekeeping institution is discussed by Seyersted (1962:125–147).

31. A list of these operations and their main characteristics is found in Skjelsbæk (1989: 256–257). In Fermann (1992a), eleven peacekeeping forces are analyzed focusing on the conditions for effective peacekeeping.

REFERENCES

Alexandrowicz, C. H. (1966). "The Secretary-General of the United Nations." In R. Falk and S. Mendlowitz, eds., *The Strategy of World Order.* Vol. 2. New York: World Law Fund, 304–325.

Barros, J. (1990). *Trygve Lie and the Cold War: The UN Secretary-General Pursues Peace, 1946–1953.* Dekalb: Northern Illinois University Press.

Cobban, H. (1983). *The Palestinian Liberation Organization.* Cambridge: Cambridge University Press.

Cordovez, D. (1987). "Strengthening the United Nations Diplomacy for Peace: The Role of the Secretary-General." In UNITAR, ed., *The United Nations and the Maintenance of International Peace and Security.* Dordrecht, Netherlands: Nijhoff.

Cox, R. W. (1969). "The Executive Head: An Essay on Leadership in International Organization." *International Organization* 23, 2: 205–230.

Crawford, R., and Dayanidhi, P. (1976). *East Timor: A Study of Decolonization.* New York: Ralph Bunche Institute of United Nations Affairs, City University of New York. (photocopied)

Eknes, A. (1989). *From Scandal to Success: The United Nations and the Iran-Iraq War 1980–1988.* Working Paper no. 406. Oslo: Norwegian Institute of International Affairs.

Elaraby, N. (1987). "The Office of the Secretary-General and the Maintenance of International Peace and Security." In UNITAR, *United Nations,* 177–209.

Fermann, G. (1988). *United Nations Emergency Force II—1973–80: Instrument for Negotiated Conflict Resolution.* Report no. 120. Oslo: Norwegian Institute of International Affairs. (Norwegian)

Fermann, G. (1992a). *International Peacekeeping 1956–1990: Comparative Analysis.* Defense Study no. 5. Oslo: Institute for Defense Studies. (Norwegian)

Fermann, G. (1992b). *Bibliography on International Peacekeeping.* Dordrecht, Netherlands: Nijhoff.

Franck, T. M. (1988). "The Good Offices Function of the UN Secretary-General." In A. Roberts and B. Kingsbury, eds., *United Nations, Divided World: The UN's Role in International Relations*. Oxford: Clarendon, 79–94.

Goodrich, L. M. (1974). Review of Brian Urquhart's *Hammarskjöld* (New York: Knopf, 1972). *International Organization* 28, 3: 467–483.

Gordenker, L. (1967). *The UN Secretary-General and the Maintenance of Peace.* New York: Columbia University Press.

James, A. (1983). "Kurt Waldheim: Diplomats' Diplomat." *Yearbook of World Affairs,* vol. 37, 81–96.

Jonah, J. (1989). "The Management of U.N. Peacekeeping." In I. J. Rikhye and K. Skjelsbæk, eds., *The United Nations and Peacekeeping.* London: Macmillan, 75–90.

Lie, T. (1954). *In the Cause of Peace*. London: Macmillan.

Mitchell, C. R. (1981). *Peacemaking and the Consultant's Role*. Westmead, U.K.: Gower.

Nassif, R. (1988). *U Thant in New York, 1961–1971: A Portrait of the Third UN Secretary-General*. London: Hurst.

Parsons, Sir A. (1983). "The Falkland Crisis in the United Nations, 31 March–14 June 1982." *International Affairs* 59, 2: 169–178.

Pérez de Cuéllar, J. (1988). "The Role of the UN Secretary-General." In A. Roberts and B. Kingsbury, eds., *United Nations, Divided World: The UN's Role in International Relations.* Oxford: Clarendon Press, 61–77.

Rikhye, I. J. (1983). *The Theory and Practice of Peacekeeping*. London: Hurst.

Rovine, A. W. (1970). *The First Fifty Years: The Secretary-General in World Politics 1920–1970.* Leyden: Sijthoff.

Schwebel, S. M. (1952). *The Secretary-General of the United Nations: His Political Powers and Practice.* Cambridge: Harvard University Press.

Seyersted, F. (1962). "Can the United Nations Establish Military Forces and Perform Other Acts Without Specific Basis in the Charter?" *Österreichische Zeitschrift fur Öffentliches Recht* 12: 125–147.

Skjelsbæk, K. (1989). "United Nations Peacekeeping and the Facilitation of Withdrawal." *Bulletin of Peace Proposals* 20, 3: 253–264.

Skogmo, B. (1989). *UNIFIL: International Peacekeeping in Lebanon, 1978–1988.* Boulder, Colo.: Lynne Rienner.

Thant, U (1977). *View From the UN.* London: David & Charles.

Touval, S. (1982). *The Peace Brokers: Mediators in the Arab-Israeli Conflict, 1948–1979.* Princeton, N.J.: Princeton University Press.

Urquhart, B. (1972). *Hammarskjöld.* New York: Knopf.

Urquhart, B. (1985). "The Role of the Secretary-General." *Aussenpolitik* 36, 3: 257–263.

Urquhart, B. (1987). *A Life in Peace and War.* New York: Harper & Row.

Waldheim, K. (1985). *In the Eye of the Storm: The Memoirs of Kurt Waldheim.* London: Weidenfeld & Nicolson.

Wall, J. A., Jr. (1981). "Mediation: An Analysis, Review and Proposed Research." *Journal of Conflict Resolution* 25, 1: 157–180.

Wallensteen, P. (1992). "The Security Council in Armed Conflicts 1986–91." In B. Heldt, ed., *States in Armed Conflict 1990–91*. Report No. 35. Uppsala, Sweden: Uppsala University, Department of Peace and Conflict Research, 11–28.

Young, O. R. (1967). *The Intermediaries: Third Parties in International Crisis.* Princeton, N.J.: Princeton University Press.

Part Two

CULTURE AND INTERNATIONAL MEDIATION

CHAPTER FIVE

Cultural Aspects of International Mediation

Raymond Cohen

Recent research presents international mediation as a complex process subject to many overlapping influences. At the international level, influences cited include past relations between the rivals and distribution of power. At the state level, regime type and degree of internal cohesion are mentioned. Mediator characteristics include features of personality, degree of impartiality, and choice of directive or nondirective approaches (Bercovitch and Lamare, 1993:9–11). If culture is mentioned at all, it tends to be viewed, like personality, as yet another independent variable affecting the behavioral dependent variable. All this is solidly in the social science tradition of causal analysis.

There is, however, another tradition parallel to the behaviorist approach to the study of negotiation and mediation current in political science. For many years now, ethnographers have been less interested in correlating regularities of conflict resolution across cultures than in analyzing in depth culturally specific forms of behavior (see Nader and Todd, 1978). Within this tradition, researchers, conscious of the difficulties of describing let alone explaining behavior in a value-free way, focus on interpretation—on revealing the meaning of unfamiliar and ambiguous actions in given cultural settings—rather than on assigning causes to determinate effects. "Cultural analysis is not causal analysis," argue Avruch and Black, but "the searching out of meanings in . . . systems of symbols" (Avruch and Black, 1993:133, 134). "What is happening here and what does it mean?" is the question, not "What are the correlates of this class of phenomena?"

From an ethnographic perspective, disputants look less like competitors in a strategic interaction, rationally choosing among strategic and tactical moves, than performers in a stylized enactment in which the roles and plays are culturally constructed (see Gulliver, 1979:ch. 7). North American mediators are expected to be impartial, trained professionals. Their job is not to preach, but to provide such services for the protagonists as assisting communication and inventing alternative options. In the international arena, their role is infused with a Christian moral imperative: "blessed are the peacemakers." In contrast, the Middle Eastern *wasta* has an ascriptive, not professional role, and is chosen from among local notables. He—for women do not qualify—is expected to separate the adversaries, scrupulously protect their honor, and restore equilibrium between them, if necessary by preferring the claims of the weaker party. His strongest appeal is not to ethics but to the good of the community. Although culture does not predetermine behavior in detail, it does assign meaning, establish norms, and define roles.

As long as conflict and its resolution remain governed by common knowledge—assumptions and meanings shared by both participants and observers—culture can be largely ignored as a pertinent factor. This is not because culture is absent but because it is understood. Rules of the game construct the game, but players and commentators rarely refer to those rules in order to explain outcomes. If actors are all playing by the same rules, then it is clearly not the rules that account for variance in performance. It is a very different matter, however, if contestants play by different rules; that is, operate on the basis of dissonant assumptions or systematically violate the rules as the other side understands them. The starting point of this chapter is the observation that in international disputes the "rules" cannot simply be taken as common knowledge, and that significant cultural differences between rivals may exacerbate conflict and complicate its resolution. This premise, first suggested in the intercultural communication literature, is supported by studies of Egyptian-Israeli relations and U.S. diplomacy (Ting-Toomey, 1985; Cohen, 1990, 1991; Avruch and Black, 1991).

It should immediately be made clear that many traditional international disputes do not involve a clash of cultures. We shall call these "Model T" conflicts. Familiar factors such as divergent interests, opposing ideologies, competing ambitions, and historical antagonisms are sufficient to explain such conflicts. Groups and states in continuous and prolonged contact tend, moreover, to develop shared diplomatic conventions to facilitate unimpeded communication (see Little, 1987:594–596). In these cases, cross-cultural differences hardly hinder conflict resolution. Within regions such as Latin America, the Arab world, and the North Atlantic and West European security community, common diplomatic forms and practices of conflict resolution, based on shared civilizational assumptions and norms, have emerged from long histories of interaction. It is suggestive that since the Second World War the incidence of interstate armed conflict has been particularly low in the Americas and Western Europe. In the Middle East, the major international disputes have engaged Arabs and non-Arabs—Israel to the west, and Iran to the east. But in disputes across cultures and regions—henceforth, "Model C" conflicts—familiar obstacles to conflict settlement may be compounded by both communication and negotiation dissonances. Lacking shared conventions, disputants may define the situation differently, misunderstand each other's signals, and misinterpret bargaining moves.

THE NATURE OF CULTURE

To explain the source of these difficulties, it is well to start with a brief discussion of the nature of culture itself. An enormous body of literature on the subject has accumulated over the past one hundred years. Indeed, a whole discipline, that of ethnography, is devoted to its study. For present purposes, the most useful (but not the only) characterization of culture views it as the system of meaning and value shared by a community, informing its way of life and enabling it to make sense of the world. Members of a group acquire their signification system through a complex process of learning, or acculturation, permitting intelligible communication and interaction—linguistic, nonverbal, ritualistic, and symbolic—between them. Without culture there could be no communal life. Kluckhohn provides a classic formulation: "Culture consists in patterned ways of thinking, feeling and reaction, acquired and transmitted mainly by symbols, constituting the distinctive achievements of human groups, including their embodiment in artifacts; the essential core of culture consists of traditional (i.e. historically derived and selected) ideas and especially their attached values" (1951:86).

Although culture may seem abstract and hard to operationalize, it has been extensively examined by measuring and comparing the incidence of behavioral, attitudinal, and semantic traits across societies. *The Journal of Cross-Cultural Psychology* has over the years produced considerable evidence of the differential incidence of behavioral characteristics among separate national groups. Hofstede (1980) has demonstrated how work-related behavior and attitudes across cultures can be identified and compared along a limited number of critical dimensions. In a particularly interesting project, Szalay and Deese (1978) developed verbal association tests to reveal cross-cultural differences in the modal meaning of concepts in key domains such as sense of self, the family, the wider community, education, and government.

From characterizing culture as a shared body of meaning, it is but a short step to realizing that a boundary that contains may also be a barrier that excludes. This insight, implicit in the thought of such anthropologists as Sapir and Whorf, was first given coherent and systematic expression by Hall. Hall's basic thesis is that it may not be possible "to bypass language and culture and to refer back to experience in order to reach another human being." Such a belief, he suggests, assumes that all human beings, subject to the same experience, receive the same sense data. Looking into the human use of space, movement, and gesture, Hall's research across cultures indicated that "people from different cultures not only speak different languages but, what is possibly more important, *inhabit different sensory worlds.* Selective screening of sensory data admits some things while filtering out others, so that *experience as it is perceived* through one set of culturally patterned sensory screens is quite different from experience perceived through another" (1969:2; emphasis in original). Simply put: culture constructs reality; different cultures construct reality differently; communication across cultures pits different constructions of reality against each other.

Building on the work of Hall, many studies have emerged that are concerned with mapping and suggesting solutions to problems involved in cross-cultural contact (Stening, 1979). Practitioners working in such diverse fields as medicine, social work, education, and business have made insightful contributions; the study of intercultural communication difficulties is not simply an academic exercise but is of considerable practical relevance and application. For example, Weingarten (1992:105–132), chair of family medicine at Tel Aviv University and for twenty years a general practitioner in a Yemenite township in Israel, attests to the way in which culture constructs the presentation of illness, description of pain, expectation of right treatment, and appropriate setting for care. Failing to understand these differences, Western-trained doctors often are unable to function effectively or communicate intelligibly with their non-Western patients.

Do cross-cultural dissonances affect international mediation? There are two contending points of view. One school of thought argues that the problem exists simply in the eye of the beholder, a result of stereotyping and the confusion of individual personality traits with amorphous cultural tendencies (Rubin and Sander, 1991). The implication is that mediation is a universal activity conducted according to generally held assumptions and conventions. Thus, differences in negotiating behavior can be satisfactorily explained by variations in contextual and psychological factors without resorting to cross-cultural differences.

The opposing view asserts the salience of such antinomies and the need for culturally sensitive, Model C mediators to bridge the gap between cultures. It does not deny that within given cultural traditions circumstances, personality, and other individual variations are key influences. But it cautions against uncritically accepting the validity of this assumption in cross-cultural encounters. It also notes that modal personality traits, the independent variable in some studies, tend to vary across cultures (Segall, Dasen, Berry, and Poortinga, 1990). A comparative analysis of even a few cross-cultural mediations can raise questions about the universality of such "self-evident" and very Western negotiating conventions as reciprocity, avoidance of deliberate mendacity, or the finality of agreements reached. On the contrary, this position suggests that it might be wise to assume that until proven otherwise cross-cultural dissonance may potentially creep in as a source of difficulties.

International diplomacy, as an institution, has developed a number of solutions to the problem of intercultural negotiation. One classic answer was the emergence of a diplomatic corps, a kind of "epistemic community" of trained envoys, whose expertise lay in the area of communication and negotiation across cultures and who shared assumptions about the nature and functioning of the international system, work methods, and the desirable goals of diplomacy. As interdependence has grown, however, international negotiation has come to be increasingly conducted by many people who are not trained diplomats and have domestic political, professional, or military backgrounds. This is not necessarily detrimental. In technical negotiations, it may be helpful to rely on professionals with common epistemic skills in their area of expertise, whether air transport, trade, nuclear energy, water resources, or arms control. Another diplomatic solution to the problem of intelligibility is provided within regimes. One of the constituent and defining features of regimes is the establishment of rules of good-faith negotiation—general principles set up to govern the subsequent "rolling negotiations" that are a prominent feature of such entities. The European Community, for example, has evolved a set of metarules known as "the community spirit" (Wallace, 1990).

In negotiations for the resolution of protracted conflict, however, these solutions are often unavailable. Political and military figures, rather than diplomatic experts, loom large. Elected representatives, reflecting all the prejudices and predispositions of their constituents, tend to become centrally involved. Public opinion is vociferously and emotively engaged, downgrading the discreet discussions between experts that are a vital feature of the working of epistemic communities and regimes. Metarules of negotiation are by definition hard to attain, since the issue under dispute is invariably one-off and even minimal trust is hard to establish. The iterated game solution proposed by Axelrod (1984) for the "evolution of cooperation" in the prisoners' dilemma can hardly apply if failure of the negotiation will preclude there being a "next time" and the anticipated sucker's payoff is national disaster. In these circumstances, the tendency is for cross-cultural discrepancies to be exacerbated.

Hence the particular need for a mediator. Alongside the classic tactics described in mediation literature (for example, Bercovitch, 1992:104–105; Bercovitch and Wells, 1993:8–9), I argue that the Model C mediator can perform three specifically cross-cultural roles: the interpreter, decoding and explaining the parties' culturally encoded messages and enabling them to communicate intelligibly; the buffer, helping to protect high face-salient disputants from painful and unwelcome confrontation; and the coordinator, synchronizing the discordant negotiating conventions of the rivals and enabling coordinated solutions to emerge at each of the various stages of the talks.

THE MEDIATOR AS INTERPRETER: BRIDGING THE INTERCULTURAL COMMUNICATION GAP

The complicating effect of cross-cultural dissonances on communication has been extensively studied and documented (Condon and Yousef, 1975; Gudykunst and Kim, 1984; Singer, 1987). Negotiation and conflict resolution may be hindered by the failure of adversaries to exchange messages freely and intelligibly (Cohen, 1987; Avruch and Black, 1991:37–38). Different cultures may attach subtly discrepant meanings to apparently identical concepts, raising the possibility of serious confusion. Communication fundamentally involves the exchange of symbols. An idea is encoded by a speaker and transmitted to an interlocutor who must then decode the message. An idea itself cannot be directly transferred from one mind to another. The meaning attached to a symbol, whether gesture, stylized performance, or utterance, is culturally acquired. Individuals no more invent their own signification systems than they invent their own language. They acquire them from the surrounding culture—representational systems in which meanings are shared. As long as certain semantic and syntactic rules are maintained, the response elicited by the message will be isomorphic with the intention. However, in communication across representational systems it cannot be assumed that the symbol in question, embedded as it is in a given social context of beliefs, values, and assumptions, will necessarily evoke the same resonances in the interlocutor as in the speaker (see Szalay, 1981).

Of course, the simpler (more primitive) the concept, the less likely is cross-cultural confusion. Words attached to basic objects such as foot, sun, and tree are easily translated without loss or distortion of meaning. However, more complex terms such as justice, soul, sovereignty, or leader are embedded within overall signification systems and possess special associations that may only be conveyed with difficulty, if at all. Within a conflict resolution context, one may observe the variety of connotations and meanings attached to terms such as concession, agreement, fairness, compromise, and mediator.

For example, in a commercial, contract-based culture such as the United States, "concession" is a neutral term, part of a normal process of "give-and-take" in a jointly beneficial negotiation. Concessions may be wise or foolish, depending on circumstances. If anything, "to concede a point" may have connotations of open-mindedness and generosity. However, in Arabic, a language spoken by a high face-salience culture, *tanazol,* concession by one of the parties, implies retreat and abandonment of a right. To remove this negative connotation, one has to use the term *musawama,* implying mutual concession, the process of reaching a compromise or a fair or "middle solution," *hal wassat.* Assuming that language reflects and constructs behavior, it follows that in negotiation among Arabs concessions, to be acceptable, must be reciprocal or mutually contingent. In these circumstances, they are not thought of as "concessions" at all but as coordinated actions in the search for a settlement. The best way to achieve this state of joint and therefore honorable contingency is through the aid of a mediator.

Like most negotiating words, in English "mediator" has neutral, aseptic, professional associations. In other cultures, however, it evokes rich associations and covers a multiplicity of roles. Throughout the Arab world, the wasta is a major figure in the resolution of conflict. Chosen from the ranks of respected local notables, the wasta mediates in local disputes over property or honor, acts to separate rival clans in a feud and to terminate violence, organizes the reconciliation ceremony of the *sulkha,* negotiates compensation, helps to arrange marriages, intervenes with the authorities, and in general is instrumental in preserving the harmony of the collective, face-to-face society of the village.

In Hebrew, the concept of mediator encompasses related but subtly different associations. Jewish communities in the Diaspora were neither village societies in the accepted sense nor organized on a clan basis. Jews were excluded from citizenship and land ownership, and were often employed as artisans and traders in small towns. Their common denominators were religion and the shared fate of a vulnerable minority. Social cohesion was maintained by external pressures and autonomous courts granted by host rulers. Where Arabic has the one word, wasta, Hebrew has several different terms because Jewish culture distinguished between a number of separate mediatory roles. *Shadkhan* is a mediator in the arrangement of marriages. *Metavekh* is a mediator in the sense of broker or middleman in commercial transactions. (The word also refers to a go-between in diplomatic missions.) Connotations of conciliation, however, are reserved for the *borer,* an individual—often a rabbi—who acts as arbitrator rather than intermediary, presenting an impartial settlement to the parties. Finally, *shtadlan* (literally "interceder") was the traditional go-between acting on behalf of the Diaspora Jewish community at the court of the *poritz,* the local nobleman upon whose benevolence the Jews of Christian Europe depended for their survival and sustenance. (This is the precursor of AIPAC, the uniquely effective American Jewish lobby.) Thus the institution of the mediator evolved in Jewish culture to meet special environmental and social needs.

It can readily be observed that "mediator," in the current American sense of facilitator in the resolution of conflict, is not a familiar concept in either Israeli or Arab cultures. That is not to say that the meaning cannot be changed; for example, many Jews are active in mediation work in the United States. However, attempts to import alternative dispute resolution (ADR) techniques into Israel have not been successful; Israelis still prefer to take disputes either to litigation or arbitration (Matz, 1991).

Conceptual antinomies of this kind may hinder communication within negotiating settings; a different semantic problem arises from colloquialisms and euphemisms. The notorious "we shall bury you" remark by Nikita Khrushchev is a case in point. Understood as a threat by the United States, it was merely a folksy way of predicting that communism would outlast capitalism.

A more subtle linguistic problem arises between low- and high-context cultures. The former, of which the United States is a paradigm example, use language in a very direct, unadorned, and explicit way. The latter, which include traditional, collectivist, honor-based cultures, are meticulous about protecting the face of interlocutors and prefer to communicate elliptically and nonverbally (Ting-Toomey, 1985; Ting-Toomey and Cole, 1990; Cohen, 1991:25–27, 116–130). In the 1969 negotiations between Japan and the United States on the perennial issue of the trade imbalance, President Nixon asked Japanese Prime Minister Sato to exercise export restraint. Sato, who probably could not have implemented this request given the Japanese system, answered with the evasive reply "*zensho shimasu.*" Literally the term means "I will do my best," which is how Nixon understood it. In fact, it is a polite way of avoiding any commitment, preferred to the explicit negative. Thinking he had obtained Sato's consent to his proposal, Nixon was subsequently furious when nothing happened (Haberman, 1988). There are numerous examples of such cross-cultural, linguistic misunderstandings (for example, Fisher, 1980:59–66).

In theory, one might expect a competent interpreter to avoid the worst cross-cultural pitfalls. Alternatively, interlocutors might resort to a shared lingua franca, like Latin in the Middle Ages. In practice, both interpretation and use of a common language often fail to convey underlying cultural resonances (Glenn, 1966). Interlocutors may not even be aware of the problem. It is for these reasons that the Model C mediator is needed. Sick explains the mediatory role of Algeria in the U.S.-Iranian negotiations for the release of the embassy hostages:

> Ultimately, the role of the Algerians was to stand as a cool screen between two angry adversaries. Iran was burning with revolutionary and religious passion in the wake of the seemingly miraculous overthrow of the monarchy, while the United States seethed with righteous wrath at Iran's flouting of international law and elementary human rights. Direct conversation was impossible under these circumstances, and a translator or interpreter was required to permit each party to listen to what the other had to say. (1985:32–33)

On several occasions, Algerian "interpretation" proved invaluable. In November 1980, Algerian officials sensitive to Iranian buzzwords checked over American draft proposals and suggested simple, nonsubstantive changes in the text that would avoid unnecessarily complicating matters. At the same time, the Algerians were able to offer their best judgment about the acceptability of the text as a whole. The Algerians advised that as it stood, the American response was too general in nature and failed to address what they viewed as vital Iranian requirements. Out of this exchange emerged the original and very constructive idea of adding proposed presidential draft orders on various matters as appendages to the main paper (Sick, 1985:31).

Algerian interpretation of Iranian needs demonstrated its worth on another occasion in December 1980. In devising a mechanism to deal with the numerous financial claims against Iran before the U.S. courts, the U.S. team discussed the transfer of claims from the courts to a mutually agreed settlement procedure. However, the team erroneously projected their preconceptions onto the other side, and the idea was dropped on the grounds that Iran would view it as inimical to its interests. Algeria's Model C reading of Iranian thinking was very different. In its view, Iran's problem was not so much to protect its tangible, financial assets as to find a cosmetically attractive face-saving formula that would stand up to Majlis (Iranian parliament) scrutiny. Seen in this light, the materially inferior settlement procedure would appeal to Teheran by enabling the Iranians to pretend that there were no outstanding claims against Iran and that its assets had been transferred out of direct U.S. control. The Algerians proved absolutely correct in their thinking, even though in the final analysis the arrangement placed billions of dollars outside Iranian reach while fully protecting U.S. creditors (Sick, 1985:35, 49).

THE MEDIATOR AS BUFFER: PROTECTING THE FACE OF ADVERSARIES

There can be few international actors indifferent to issues of face, defined as "the projected image of one's self (or one's national identity or image) in a public negotiation situation" (Ting-Toomey and Cole, 1990:78–79). Some of the most awkward problems in negotiation involve intangible factors such as the fear of loss of reputation or the search for honor. As Brown points out: "In some instances, protecting against loss of face becomes so central an issue that it swamps the importance of the tangible issues at stake and generates intense conflicts that can impede progress toward agreement" (1977:275). Despite the widespread presence of prestige elements in international conflict, the meaning and salience of face vary considerably across cultures. This fact has important implications for mediation.

In an enlightening account, Ting-Toomey (1988) draws a distinction between the attitude of individualistic, low-context cultures toward face, and that of collectivistic, high-context cultures. In a nutshell, she argues that the former, which include societies such as Australia, Germany, and the United States, are particularly concerned with autonomy and personal integrity. It is all-important to be true to oneself, to be "taken as I am." Laying stress on the development and integrity of the self, members of individualistic cultures look inward for moral guidance (conscience) and are unlikely to be swayed by public disapproval from doing what they believe to be right. Conflicts, seen as the legitimate struggle of competing interests, are handled either in a problem-solving manner, minimizing subjective desires and needs ("separating the people from the problem" in the famous formulation by Fisher and Ury, 1983), or through adversarial techniques of open confrontation. Debate, challenge and refutation, and controversy carry no threat to the ego. Provided one preserves one's personal integrity, there is no shame in disagreement or nonconformity. Articulations are low-context and direct, placing relatively little emphasis on euphemism, allusion, or nonverbal gesture. What has to be said is stated honestly and without embellishment.

High-context, collectivistic cultures—China, Korea, and Japan are cited by Ting-Toomey—are underpinned by a quite different concept of the self. In emphasizing the community above all else, such cultures define individuals not as autonomous entities capable of self-reliance and personal realization but as links in interlocking chains of relationships. To dissociate oneself from the collectivity is a contradiction in terms under such conditions, for self-approbation derives from one's satisfactory fulfillment of the obligations and expectations imposed by group membership. Shame, the prospect of loss of face in the eyes of the community, is the guide to moral choice. Conflict is handled by the avoidance of confrontation, and no virtue at all is seen in publicly airing differences. Anything likely to disturb harmony and generate group disapproval is shunned. Consensus, the reconciliation of disagreement even at the cost of abstract justice, is preferred to the disruptive victory of one point of view over another. Communication is high-context and indirect, preferring allusions and contextual hints to blunt and potentially hurtful articulations.

Different conceptions of face lie at the very heart of the individualistic-collectivistic dichotomy. In individualistic cultures, Ting-Toomey reasons, stress is on negative face—defending one's personal self-esteem and preserving the inviolability of one's individual space. There is less perceived need for positive face, the appreciation and approval of others: and consequently there is no special concern with others' need for approbation and possible exposure to embarrassment. Individualistic cultures resting on individual rights, freedom of choice, and resort to conscience do not assume that interpersonal friction will threaten the fabric of society. Collectivistic cultures present a quite different picture. To concern with saving one's own face is added an acute preoccupation with the need to give face and to avoid at all costs damaging others' self-esteem. When communal harmony and cohesion cannot be taken for granted (for reasons such as clan cleavages and the risk of endemic feuding), the sensitive anticipation of the needs of others overrides the individualistic consciousness of one's private needs. Honoring face, and above all not threatening face, become categorical imperatives.

At the risk of simplification, I shall refer for purposes of convenience to individualistic cultures as possessing low face-salience, and to collectivistic cultures as possessing high face-salience.

Within any given culture, appropriate mechanisms of conflict resolution, including mediation, are cultivated to meet its particular requirements. For instance, in the Kabyle society of North Africa mediators are chosen from the clans of saints (*marabouts*): they may attempt to restore balance between the aggrieved parties by showing preference to the face needs of a weaker supplicant, may adopt a tone of moral rebuke, and have the prestige to impose a settlement (Bourdieu, 1965:196–197). This is clearly very different from the situation in North America, where mediation is a profession rather than a role defined and conferred by custom. Objectivity is stressed, along with the avoidance of moralizing and the consent of the parties. Many other culture-specific patterns of mediation exist (Nader and Todd, 1978:10). If mediation occurs within the normative and psychological boundaries of a culture, an acceptable solution will possess predictable, possibly even stylized features.

Intervening between Egypt and Saudi Arabia in the Yemen crisis of 1963, Ellsworth Bunker was obliged to act in conformity with the requirements of the Arab wasta (mediator) role, ubiquitous throughout the Middle East and familiar in inter-Arab conflict resolution (Al-Kadhem, 1976:22–25). The Yemen civil war had become a supreme issue of *sharaf*—honor in a peculiarly elevated Arabic sense meaning purity of soul, nobility, and ethical righteousness—for both King Faisal and President Nasser (McMullen, 1980:3). Acting with great tact and wide discretion as the prestigious personal representative of President Kennedy, Bunker patiently shuttled between Arab capitals, constructing a settlement based on the principles of symmetry, mutual disengagement, and the introduction of a neutral third force between the two parties. Sensitive points were left verbal rather than written; open pressure was never exercised (though presidential authority was invoked). Personalized, ad hominem arguments played a prominent and persuasive function. The requirements of maintaining honor were always paramount. All this was in perfect conformity with wasta traditions (see Ammar, 1954:57–59).

Special problems arise, however, when the mediator is obliged to span the gap between collectivistic and individualistic disputants. In these circumstances, the mediator cannot assume that the two parties will understand each other's psychological needs. Given their differing conceptions of face, the indispensable task of a third party is to protect the high face-salience party against the unintentional, but still potentially fatal, face-threatening behavior of its low face-salience opponent. Mediation in the Arab-Israeli conflict has had to pay particular attention to this factor. Looking back on his own contribution to Egyptian-Israeli peace, former president Carter observed that one of the constraints on Middle Eastern leaders "is that they don't want to put forward a proposal to the other adversary and be rebuffed. It's a deep embarrassment and a loss of face if you make a proposal and you have it rejected publicly" (*Jerusalem Post,* 1985:5).

Conversely, compromise positions that could never be proposed by Egypt might be acceptable if they were known to be the wish of the mediator. This point was crucial at the September 1978 Camp David summit, hosted by President Carter, between President Sadat of Egypt and Prime Minister Begin of Israel. Sadat's opening position, which reiterated familiar, hard-line Egyptian demands, was utterly unacceptable to Israel but had to be stated for the record. The far-reaching modifications of that position necessary for agreement could only emanate from an esteemed third party—the president of the United States (Carter, 1982:365). A similar consideration arose in the Algeria-mediated negotiations between the United States and Iran for the release of U.S. hostages. The final package, involving a complex list of agreements by the parties, came in the form of a declaration by the government of Algeria. Although it was out of the question for Iran to enter an agreement with the Great Satan, Iran did find it possible to make promises to a trusted coreligionist (Sick, 1985:42–43).

THE MEDIATOR AS COORDINATOR: SYNCHRONIZING DISSONANT NEGOTIATING CONVENTIONS

Different connotations of terms such as concession, compromise, and mediator hint at a third major problem that impedes conflict resolution across cultures: disputants' discordant bargaining conventions. Conventions provide solutions to coordination problems (Lewis, 1969; Stein, 1982:127; Snidal, 1985:932). In situations of interdependent choice, cooperation in the form of the synchronization of separately performed actions depends on the ability of actors to rely on congruent expectations of behavior (Cohen, 1981:14–16). An obvious example of an unintended outcome arising from uncoordinated behavior is a collision at a road junction in the absence of a traffic light. To obviate road accidents, societies agree on certain conventions about the right of way and the meaning of certain signs and signals. When conventions are infringed, serious consequences arise because the very possibility of orderly communal behavior is called into question (Cohen, 1979: 178).

International negotiation, as game theorists have realized, is a case of interdependent decisionmaking (Brams, 1990). For mutually desired outcomes to occur, expectations have to be synchronized and behavior coordinated by reliance on common conventions. Diplomacy, the peaceful management of relations between states, would not be possible without the existence of an elaborate formal and informal code of communication and conduct (Cohen, 1987). Some aspects of diplomatic negotiation are regulated by explicit rules about the status and immunities of diplomatic agents and the significance of various kinds of diplomatic instruments and documents. However, essential features of the actual to-and-fro of negotiation rest on tacit assumptions about what is and is not done. Many of these assumptions do not vary across cultures. Some researchers have discerned the existence of a kind of universal diplomatic culture (Zartman and Berman, 1982:224–229). Good faith, for instance, even if not always observed, has to be assumed for negotiation to be possible at all. Other fundamental expectations, however, derive from culturally specific, not universal, patterns of negotiating behavior. When unconsciously assumed procedures diverge, interlocutors tend to react first with puzzlement and then with annoyance. It becomes impossible to achieve that complex synchronization of interlocking moves and meanings required to navigate through the various negotiating stages to ultimate agreement.

Of all cultural features, the concept of time is among the most insidious. It is ever-present, unconscious, and formative (Hall, 1973). It shapes two subjective features of negotiating behavior: timing, the judgment of the right moment for the performance of a given action; and tempo, the sense of the appropriate rate of progress or transition from one move to the next. In the absence of shared conventions, cross-cultural differences in assumptions about time can raise the problem of coordination in acute form and can further constitute a recurrent source of negotiating confusion.

Trouble may therefore start even before the commencement of formal negotiations. Recent writing has emphasized the importance of choosing the "ripe moment" in a conflict to launch talks (Zartman, 1986). Developing the idea, Haass defines "ripeness" as the existence of "circumstances conducive for negotiated progress or even solution." Correct assessment of ripeness is important to the immediate rivals and to potential mediators (Haass, 1990:6–7, 145). Judgment of ripeness, however, rests not only on the objective assessment of hard facts but on culture-bound value assumptions about the right and proper, or honorable, time to act. For cultures prone to making decisions on the basis of a pragmatic, cost-benefit analysis of gain and loss, vulnerability and the prospect of defeat are the right times to enter negotiations for settlement of a conflict. Within the materialist world view, the need to "cut one's losses" provides sufficient justification. But for high face-salience cultures such shameful circumstances may actually preclude fruitful negotiation.

A case in point is the Haig mediatory mission following the Argentinean invasion of the Falkland Islands in 1982. As the British armada steamed across the Atlantic toward the coast of South America, it seemed reasonable to suppose that the military junta would become increasingly inclined to settle. Presenting a fair proposal to the Argentinean government, U.S. secretary of state Haig believed it "inconceivable . . . that any rational government could reject these terms." Surely it made infinitely more sense to cut a deal with the Royal Navy while it was still far away and Argentinean troops were unbloodied than to await the British arrival. The junta thought otherwise. Indeed, the closer British warships sailed, the more intransigent the Argentinean leadership became (Haig, 1984:286, 293). For them, the prospect of defeat in battle was preferable to dishonor. Anglo-Saxon material common sense, in this instance, did not coincide with the imperative requirements of Argentinean *machismo* and *dignidad*. Secretary Haig graphically describes the combination of grandiloquence, bravado, and fascination with death displayed by members of the junta (280, 288). His account corroborates Gillin's analysis of the individual in Latin American society and the conclusion that in the Latin American ethos "pragmatic and technological approaches do not, in themselves, constitute what might be called a first-order appeal" (1955:498; also see Stokes, 1952). In the final analysis, Argentinean pride actually precluded a compromise agreement; no coordinated solution was attainable.

With hindsight, we can also view the stalemate in Egyptian-Israeli relations following the 1967 war as a result of very different assumptions about ripeness. The ill-fated mission of UN mediator Gunnar Jarring foundered on (among other things) an asymmetry of perceived readiness. It was not until after the 1973 war that a convergence of expectations occurred. The Israelis, for their part, were convinced by 1968 that "the hour is ripe for the creative adventure of peace." But for the Arabs "the hour was not 'ripe' at all" (Eban, 1978:457). Full peaceful relations, a condition of withdrawal for a strong and victorious Israel, were out of the question for a defeated and humiliated Egypt. Analyzing Jarring's failure, Egyptian Foreign Minister Mahmoud Riad explained just why this was so:

> in any quarrel between two persons, any third party seeking to separate them would naturally pull the weaker one away. In the dispute with Israel, we were still the weaker party. Our problem was that if we took one step backwards, we would fall into an abyss—therefore any attempt to push us backwards would never achieve the desired peace. (Riad, 1981:80)

Both Haig and Jarring, then, failed in their mediatory missions because they were unable to construct mechanisms to overcome an asymmetry of ripeness between the adversaries.

For the Model C mediator to succeed he or she must find an answer to the synchronization riddle, not only at the initiation stage but also in the middle and end games of a mediation. At all stages, cross-cultural differences of timing and tempo are equally felt. In the 1979 Lancaster House conference on Rhodesia/Zimbabwe, British foreign secretary Lord Carrington faced a tough problem of coordination. The two antagonists needed a settlement; dividing them, however, was a cultural barrier. On the one side was the largely white Smith-Muzorewa delegation representing the illegal Rhodesian regime. Organized with a clear chain of responsibility and preoccupied with constitutional details, its approach, in the Anglo-Saxon tradition, was practical and its tempo brisk and businesslike. On the other side was the all-black Patriotic Front led by Robert Mugabe and his longtime rival Joshua Nkomo. Its discontinuous, sluggish tempo was dictated by the need for consensus, strong attachment to abstract but cherished principles (such as land ownership), and high face-salience. At times it displayed ambivalence about the very process of negotiation, dreaming of a glorious military entry into Salisbury. Left to themselves the two delegations would have locked into angry immobility, as had happened so often in the past, and probably would have abandoned the talks altogether.

Lord Carrington's patrician solution was high-handedly to impose his own tempo on the talks. This device was only possible because of the special constitutional and political circumstances of the time: Britain, as the legitimate sovereign power, was able to bestow or withhold its benediction on the successor regime. From beginning to end, Lord Carrington, working always with his own draft proposals, presented ultimatum after ultimatum. Decisions were demanded from the Patriotic Front within draconian time limits—sometimes as little as two days, and once by the following day. On one occasion, the conference was menacingly adjourned. In a tour de force at the very end, interim Governor Lord Soames was sent off to Salisbury to begin implementing the settlement even before the Patriotic Front had given their consent (Davidow, 1984:62, 63, 80, 86).

Lord Carrington's strategy has rightly been referred to as dominant or directive third-party mediation (Davidow, 1984:115–121). It is the very antithesis of the conciliatory intercession of Haig and Jarring, which necessitated "running from one side of the table to the other with proposals and counter-proposals." Carrington presented a text, revised it in the light of the adversaries' reactions, then presented his draft on a "take it or leave it" basis. Invariably the Rhodesian government delegation would quickly accept, whereas the Patriotic Front, after dragging its heels, submitted time after time to Carrington's ultimatums. Mugabe deeply resented this approach, finding it "baffling and, in a way, repugnant" (Charlton, 1990:79). Nkomo went so far as to accuse the British foreign secretary of "arrogance tinged with racism" (Davidow, 1984:80). The Victorian atmosphere orchestrated by the British Foreign Office under Lord Carrington was not accidental. The impressive Lancaster House setting, the dictatorial colonial script, the lordly presence of the foreign secretary himself, and the dispatch of a colonial governor were all intended to evoke Britain's imperial heritage and legitimacy in the matter, playing on the rivals' stereotyped but powerful perceptions of the British role. Whereas the Rhodesian whites could find comfort in the dependable authority of a Conservative government of their own kith and kin led by the sturdy Margaret Thatcher, the Popular Front blacks were confronted by familiar colonial symbols. Arrogant Lord Carrington may have been, but he was also prestigious and decisive. Mugabe and Nkomo obviously loathed this reminder of British imperialism. However, with the "no-nonsense, school-masterish, almost district commissioner approach of Lord Carrington" they knew where they stood (Bendahmane and McDonald, 1986:175).

At Camp David in 1978, President Carter faced a rather different problem of synchronization. He needed to harmonize the utterly incompatible needs of a high-context, traditionalist, high face-salience Egypt with those of an ultra-low-context, low face-salience, Westernized Israel. It is hard to imagine two more contrasting leaders than Begin and Sadat; as Bercovitch points out, "Interaction and debate between two such culturally divergent personalities with contrasting negotiating styles was possible only through the key link of a mediator" (1986:52). For all their idiosyncrasies, their leadership and negotiating styles were unmistakably rooted in their respective cultures. President Sadat of Egypt moved in a lofty realm of sweeping "general principles and broad strategic concepts" (Carter, 1982:355). The *rais* (leader, president) of a paternalist and authoritarian society, he was not subject to democratic controls and could disregard, if he wished, the advice of other members of his delegation, officials he had personally appointed. He often compared his role to that of father of a family or village elder. Begin, on the other hand, was every inch the Talmudic scholar and Polish-Jewish lawyer, engrossed in nitpicking detail and special pleading. "When he was feeling pressed, the Israeli leader invariably shifted to a discussion of minutiae or semantics" (Carter, 1982:356). As a democratically elected prime minister in the Western sense and leader of the majority party, his authority in the Israeli delegation was that of a first among equals; he could neither ignore nor override the views of his colleagues or of the Israeli parliament.

President Carter acknowledges that his mediating technique was shaped by these differences. As past experience had demonstrated, Sadat was allergic to Begin's tenacious and argumentative point-by-point debating technique, whereas Begin was equally mystified by Sadat's philosophical and intuitive expositions. The successful outcome of the Camp David conference, then, was contingent on Carter's ability to reconcile such antinomies. Imposition of a settlement in the Carrington style was out of the question; colonialist techniques could not work with the proud Egyptians and contentious Israelis. Nor was the passivity and limited initiative of a go-between in the Jarring mold a feasible option. Carter's solution was to combine two very different mediatory strategies: with the Israelis he displayed the energy, acumen, and drafting ingenuity of a high-powered lawyer; with President Sadat he played the part of the political patron, protective and deeply caring but occasionally sternly authoritative, reminding his client of hard truths.

> I would draft a proposal I considered reasonable, take it to Sadat for quick approval or slight modification, and then spend hours or days working on the same point with the Israeli delegation. Sometimes, in the end, the change of a word or a phrase would satisfy Begin, and I would merely inform Sadat. I was never far from a good dictionary and thesaurus, and on occasion the American and Israeli delegations would all be clustered around one of these books, eagerly searching for acceptable synonyms. . . . The Egyptians were never involved in these kinds of discussions with me. (Carter, 1982:356)

Carter's treatment of Sadat was based on a very personal intimacy that was established in their first meeting at the White House, a relationship of friends but also of patron and client. "There was an easy and natural friendship between us from the first moment I knew Anwar Sadat. We trusted each other. Each of us began to learn about the other's family members, hometown, earlier life, and private plans and ambitions, as though we were tying ourselves together for a lifetime" (Carter, 1982:284). At Camp David, Carter drew on this warm rapport in his role of mediator. When necessary he called in past and future political debts. At a key point in the talks, with Sadat threatening to walk out, Carter gravely warned the rais of the consequences: "his action would harm the relationship between Egypt and the United States, he would be violating his personal promise to me, and the onus for failure would be on him . . . I was deadly serious, and he knew it." Such a walkout would damage Egypt's international standing and entail the public admission that Sadat's enemies in the Arab world had been right to condemn his visit to Jerusalem (Carter, 1982:392). Here, too, Carter might have added: "The Israelis were never involved in these kinds of discussions with me."[1]

CONCLUSIONS

Gulliver (1979:211–212) noted some years ago the tendency of the English-language literature on mediation to rest on "strong cultural stereotypes and subjective dogmatic assumptions." One preconception is that "mediators are or should be merely catalysts or that they are and should be impartial or neutral." Looking beyond the Western experience to practices in other cultures (particularly African) reveals a much richer range of roles and methods than one might have imagined.

It follows from my analysis that the cross-cultural study of mediation is not only educative in itself, but also essential for third-party intervention in international settings. For every Jimmy Carter or Lord Carrington adopting, by accident or design, a style of mediation suited to the needs and role expectations of the parties, one suspects that there is a Gunnar Jarring or Alexander Haig who fails to do so.

Model C, cross-cultural mediation adds three distinctive functions—interpretation, face-protection, and coordination—to the conventional range of third-party tasks grouped under the headings of communication, formulation, and manipulation (Bercovitch, 1992:104–105; Bercovitch and Wells, 1993:8–9). Whereas the latter Model T activities are present in all negotiations and are only performed by the mediator because the disputants cannot do the job themselves, Model C functions absolutely require a third party interposing itself between the rivals in order to harmonize their dissonances. The Model C mediator is indispensable where antagonists are separated by fundamental, unconscious antinomies relating to the use of language, significance attached to face, and conventions regulating the business of negotiation. Not all Model C functions need be performed at one and the same time. The Algerian mediation was largely involved in problems of face-saving and interpretation. Lord Carrington was mostly engaged in coordinating—by imposition—the dissonant tempos of the parties. At Camp David, however, all elements were present.

Beyond instrumental tasks, a major element in the success of the mediators was their ability to design a role appropriate to the problem and acceptable to their clients. The Algerian delegation in 1980 and Ellsworth Bunker in 1963 both excelled in the role of the self-effacing wasta in the Middle Eastern tradition. Whereas Algeria adopted a nondirective strategy, Bunker acted in a more directive manner, as befitted the rank of his principal. The mediation performances of Carter and Carrington are particularly significant. Between Egypt and Israel and between Rhodesian whites and Zimbabwean blacks, there was no single appropriate role. The solution was to relate differently to each of the parties. Carter adopted a role that was part patron, part lawyer; Carrington was part family friend, part district commissioner. The difficulty involved in implementing this kind of dual performance is suggested by some aspects of Haig's 1982 Falklands failure. Acting out, almost exclusively, the part of mediator in the pragmatic, inductive, unemotive Anglo-Saxon tradition, Haig's mission became bogged down in detailed and elaborate legal formulations that missed altogether the Argentinean junta's deductive, declamatory, principled needs.

We tend to overlook the special features of Model C mediation because we are not used to thinking cross-culturally. Mediation theory, like game theory, assumes that players in a bargaining game play by the same rules. However, they may not even be playing the same game. The assumption of common knowledge is legitimate when one is examining mediation within a given society, but it is seriously misleading when the mediator is obliged to span cultures, as is increasingly the case in international relations. The cross-cultural approach recommends that we drop the ethnocentric supposition, incongruous in a multicultural world, that our own preconceptions and way of life are universally relevant and valid. In the study of mediation, we should start out by examining three things: the cultural meanings of key concepts; traditional assumptions about mediatory roles; and the conventions governing mediation and negotiation in the societies in question. Rather than treating culture as a secondary influence on players' performance within the game, it deserves to be recognized for what it is: the metasystem of signification that assigns meaning to the game in the first place.

NOTE

1. The dramatic face-to-face meeting at which Carter persuaded Sadat to stay on at Camp David corresponded to one of the main devices in traditional Egyptian village conflict resolution: the *mulakah,* or getting together, according to which the mediator takes the aggrieved party to one side and appeals to him to "consider the Arabs, or the people, or his kinsfolk." The encounter is strictly private and confidential and intended to avoid any personal embarrassment or retreat in public. See Ammar (1954).

REFERENCES

Al-Kadhem, S. J. (1976). "The Role of the League of Arab States in Settling Inter-Arab Disputes." *Revue Egyptienne de Droit International* 32: 1–31.

Ammar, H. (1954). *Growing Up in an Egyptian Village.* London: Routledge & Kegan Paul.

Avruch, K., and Black, P. W. (1991). "The Culture Question and Conflict Resolution." *Peace and Change* 16: 22–45.

Avruch, K., and Black, P. W. (1993). "Conflict Resolution in Intercultural Settings: Problems and Prospects." In D. Sandole and H. van der Merwe, eds., *Conflict Resolution Theory and Practice: Integration and Application.* Manchester, U.K.: Manchester University Press.

Axelrod, R. (1984). *The Evolution of Cooperation.* New York: Basic Books.

Bendahmane, D. B., and McDonald, J. W., eds. (1986). *Perspectives on Negotiation.* Washington, D.C.: Foreign Service Institute.

Bercovitch, J. (1986). "A Case Study of Mediation as a Method of International Conflict Resolution: The Camp David Experience." *Review of International Studies* 12: 43–65.
Bercovitch, J. (1992). "Mediators and Mediation Strategies in International Relations." *Negotiation Journal* 8: 99–112.
Bercovitch, J., and Lamare, J. (1993). "Correlates of Effective Mediation in International Disputes: Theoretical Issues and Empirical Evidence." Paper presented at the annual meeting of the American Political Science Association. Washington, D.C., September 1–4: 9–11.
Bercovitch, J., and Wells, R. (1993). "Evaluating Mediation Strategies: A Theoretical and Empirical Analysis." *Peace and Change* 18: 3–25.
Bourdieu, P. (1965). "The Sentiment of Honor in Kabyle Society." In J. G. Peristiany, ed., *Honour and Shame: The Values of Mediterranean Society*. London: Weidenfeld & Nicolson, 191–241.
Brams, S. J. (1990). *Negotiation Games*. New York: Routledge.
Brown, B. (1977). "Face-Saving and Face-Restoration in Negotiation." In D. Druckman, ed., *Negotiation: Social-Psychological Perspectives*. Beverly Hills, Calif.: Sage.
Carter, J. (1982). *Keeping Faith: Memoirs of a President*. New York: Bantam Books.
Charlton, M. (1990). *The Last Colony in Africa: Diplomacy and the Independence of Rhodesia*. Oxford: Blackwell.
Cohen, R. (1979). *Threat Perception in International Crisis*. Madison: Wisconsin University Press.
Cohen, R. (1981). *International Politics: The Rules of the Game*. London: Longman.
Cohen, R. (1987). *Theatre of Power*. London: Longman.
Cohen, R. (1987). "International Communication: An Intercultural Approach." *Cooperation and Conflict* 22: 63–80.
Cohen, R. (1990). *Culture and Conflict in Egyptian-Israeli Relations: A Dialogue of the Deaf*. Bloomington: Indiana University Press.
Cohen, R. (1991). *Negotiating Across Cultures*. Washington, D.C.: United States Institute of Peace Press.
Condon, J. C. and Yousef, F. S. (1975). *An Introduction to Intercultural Communication*. New York: Bobbs-Merrill.
Davidow, J. (1984). *A Peace in Southern Africa: The Lancaster House Conference on Rhodesia, 1979*. Boulder, Colo.: Westview.
Eban, A. (1978). *An Autobiography*. London: Futura.
Fisher, G. (1980). *International Negotiation: A Cross-Cultural Perspective*. Yarmouth, U.K.: Intercultural Press.
Fisher, R. and Ury, W. (1983). *Getting to Yes*. New York: Penguin.
Gillin, J. (1955). "Ethos Components in Modern Latin American Culture." *American Anthropologist* 57: 488–500.
Glenn, E. (1966). "Meaning and Behavior: Communication and Culture." *Journal of Communication* 16.
Gudykunst, W. B., and Kim, Y. Y. (1984). *Communicating With Strangers*. Oxford: Pergamon.
Gulliver, P. H. (1979). *Disputes and Negotiations: A Cross-Cultural Perspective*. New York: Academic Press.
Haass, R. N. (1990). *Conflicts Unending*. New Haven: Yale University Press.
Haberman, C. (1988). "Japanese Have a Way (Out) With Words." *International Herald Tribune*, March 26–27.
Haig, A. M. (1984). *Caveat*. London: Weidenfeld & Nicolson.
Hall, E. T. (1969). *The Hidden Dimension*. New York: Anchor Books.
Hall, E.T. (1973). *The Silent Language*. New York: Anchor Books.

Hofstede, G. (1980). *Culture's Consequences.* Beverly Hills, Calif.: Sage.

Jerusalem Post, 1985. Wolf Blitzer interviews Jimmy Carter. March 29: 5.

Kluckhohn, C. (1951). "The Study of Culture." In D. Lerner and H. D. Lasswell, eds., *The Policy Sciences*. Stanford: Stanford University Press.

Kratochwil, F. V. (1989). *Rules, Norms, and Decisions*. Cambridge: Cambridge University Press.

Lewis, D. (1969). *Convention: A Philosophical Study*. Cambridge: Harvard University Press.

Little, W. (1987). "International Conflict in Latin America." *International Affairs* 62: 589–601.

Matz, D. (1991). "ADR and Life in Israel." *Negotiation Journal* 7: 11–16.

Mazrui, A. (1967). "The Monarchical Tendency in African Political Culture." *British Journal of Sociology* 18: 231–250.

McMullen, C. J. (1980). *Resolution of the Yemen Crisis, 1963*. Washington, D.C.: Institute for the Study of Diplomacy.

Moore, C. H. (1977). "Clientelist Ideology and Political Change: Fictitious Networks in Egypt and Tunisia." In E. Gellner and J. Waterbury, eds., *Patrons and Clients in Mediterranean Societies*. London: Duckworth, 255–273.

Moser, L. J. (1986). "Cross-Cultural Dimensions: U.S.-Japan." In D. P. Bendahmane and L. J. Moser, eds., *Toward a Better Understanding: U.S.-Japan Relations*. Washington, D.C.: Foreign Service Institute.

Nader, L., and Todd, H. F., eds. (1978). *The Disputing Process: Law in Ten Societies*. New York: Columbia University Press.

Riad, M. (1981). *The Struggle for Peace in the Middle East.* London: Quartet Books.

Rubin, J. Z., and Sander, F.E.A. (1991). "Culture, Negotiation, and the Eye of the Beholder." *Negotiation Journal* 7: 249–254.

Segall, M. H., Dasen, P. R., Berry, J. W., and Poortinga, Y. (1990). *Human Behavior in Global Perspective: An Introduction to Cross-Cultural Psychology*. New York: Pergamon.

Sick, G. (1985). "The Partial Negotiator: Algeria and the U.S. Hostages in Iran." In S. Touval and I. W. Zartman, eds., *International Mediation in Theory and Practice*. Boulder, Colo.: Westview, 21–66.

Singer, M. R. (1987). *Intercultural Communication: A Perceptual Approach*. Englewood Cliffs, N.J.: Prentice-Hall.

Snidal, D. (1985). "Coordination Versus Prisoners' Dilemma: Implications for International Cooperation and Regimes." *American Political Science Review* 79: 923–942.

Solomon, R. H. (1985). *Chinese Political Negotiating Behavior: A Briefing Analysis*. Santa Monica, Calif.: Rand Corporation.

Stein, A. A. (1982). "Coordination and Collaboration: Regimes in an Anarchic World." *International Organization* 36: 115–140.

Stening, B. W. (1979). "Problems in Cross-Cultural Contact: A Literature Review." *International Journal of Intercultural Relations* 3: 269–313.

Stokes, W. S. (1952). "Violence as a Power Factor in Latin American Politics." *Western Political Quarterly* 5: 445–466.

Szalay, L. B. (1981). "Intercultural Communication: A Process Model." *International Journal of Intercultural Relations* 5: 133–146.

Szalay, L.B., and Deese, J. (1978). *Subjective Meaning and Culture: An Assessment Through Word Associations*. New York: Halsted.

Ting-Toomey, S. (1985). "Toward a Theory of Conflict and Culture." In W. B. Gudykunst, L. P. Stewart, and S. Ting-Toomey, eds., *Communication, Culture, and Organizational Processes. International and Intercultural Communication Annual* 11. Beverly Hills, Calif.: Sage.

Ting-Toomey, S. (1988). "Intercultural Conflict Styles: A Face-Negotiation Theory." In Y. Kim and W. Gudykunst, eds., *Theories in Intercultural Communication*. Beverly Hills, Calif.: Sage.

Ting-Toomey, S., and Cole, M. (1990). "Intergroup Diplomatic Communication: A Face-Negotiation Perspective." In F. Korzenny and S. Ting-Toomey, eds., *Communicating for Peace: Diplomacy and Negotiation. International and Intercultural Communication Annual* 14. Beverly Hills, Calif.: Sage.

Vance, C. (1983). *Hard Choices*. New York: Simon & Shuster.

Wallace, H. (1990). "Making Multilateral Negotiations Work." In W. Wallace, ed., *The Dynamic of European Integration*. London: Pinter.

Weingarten, M. (1992). *Changing Health and Changing Culture: The Yemenite Jews in Israel*. Westport, Conn.: Praeger.

Zartman, I. W. (1986). "Ripening Conflict, Ripe Moment, Formula, and Mediation." In Bendahmane and McDonald, *Perspectives on Negotiation*.

Zartman, I.W., and Berman, M. (1982). *The Practical Negotiator*. New Haven: Yale University Press.

Chapter Six

The Limits of Mediation: Lessons from the Syria-Israel Experience, 1974–1994

Brian Mandell

The signing of the Gaza-Jericho agreement by Israeli and Palestinian officials on May 4, 1994, together with the signing of the Israel-Jordan peace treaty on October 26, 1994, has fueled expectations about a similar breakthrough in Syrian-Israeli relations. Indeed, early hopes that Syria and Israel would soon produce a new agreement appeared justified in the wake of the Geneva Summit between U.S. President Bill Clinton and Syrian President Hafez Assad in January 1994, the exploratory efforts of U.S. Secretary of State Warren Christopher in shuttle diplomacy in May and July 1994, and President Clinton's trip to Damascus on October 27, 1994.

Unfortunately none of these peacemaking initiatives, undertaken against a backdrop of some two years of Syria-Israel bilateral talks in Washington, have proved capable of moving the parties beyond their current deadlock. Sensing that time is running out for a more fruitful dialogue, both Damascus and Jerusalem have called publicly for active, high-level U.S. mediation efforts. They fear peace will not be possible without vigorous U.S. involvement. Such pleas for outside assistance serve as a sobering reminder that conflicts within the same regional subsystem may not be susceptible to positive spillover from peacemaking efforts elsewhere, even when ripe moments for active mediation and the formulation of new agreements are readily apparent.

This chapter aims to explain the limits of mediation in the development of conflict-management norms. It argues that new conflict-management practices fostered by U.S. mediation efforts in the initial Syria-Israel disengagement agreement of May 31, 1974, were insufficient for creating new norms, and thus precluded further expansion of the domain of politicomilitary cooperation between the two sides. Although mediation facilitated a triadic negotiation process and successfully altered the short-term decision calculus of the parties regarding the futility of armed conflict, such intervention neither fostered additional policy coordination, strengthened collective expectations about stability, nor engendered shared understandings for durable, peaceful development.

Syria and Israel achieved an initial agreement in 1974, and although they have complied with it for the past twenty years their inability to build on this earlier success remains troubling. This "arrested development" in peacebuilding suggests that rather than evolving in a cumulative, linear fashion, new conflict-management norms develop sporadically as adversaries continue to weigh the costs and benefits associated with a more comprehensive adjustment of mutual expectations (Mandell and Tomlin, 1991). In the Arab-Israeli context, the extent to which the mediator is unable to influence the disputants' calculus of the value of extended cooperation and to embed incentives for further risk taking increases the chances for backsliding and conflict escalation and the liklihood that the transition to a new normative order of conflict management will be stalled.

Assuming that active U.S. mediation will continue to be needed to produce a Syria-Israel peace treaty, scholars and practitioners of third-party intervention must reconceptualize mediator roles and strategies to identify the ways in which third parties can generate and sustain the momentum necessary for the normative transformation of intractable conflicts. This chapter takes a preliminary step toward meeting this challenge by exploring four aspects of the Syria-Israel conflict (and drawing on lessons gained from the Egyptian-Israel experience). First, we look at the mediation strategies that provided the initial disengagement agreement between Syria and Israel in May 1974. Second, we examine the short- and longer-term impact of the U.S.-mediated May 1974 accord on the Syria-Israel normative order of conflict management, including the agreement's impact on U.S. willingness to sustain mediation efforts. Third, we identify barriers to normative transformation. Finally, by way of conclusion, we consider the development of new influence strategies the United States might employ as a third party to sustain "transformation momentum" in the resolution of protracted regional conflicts.

THE SYRIA-ISRAEL CONFLICT, OCTOBER 1973–MAY 1974: THE ANATOMY OF MEDIATION

Neither Israel nor Syria was anxious to engage in peacemaking at the end of the 1973 October War. Although Israel could claim battlefield victory and had its forces positioned closer to Damascus than at any time since 1967, it was fearful about the fate of its POWs. At the same time, Syria had little incentive to remove the threat of renewed hostilities with Israel, wanting both to garner some political victory from the war and to avoid isolation in the Arab world. The disputants needed an agreement to disengage their forces from forward positions, but neither side demonstrated any initial willingness to make concessions.

A number of formidable obstacles—political, military, and psychological—prevented the early creation of a negotiating dynamic. Egypt and Israel had set up such a dynamic in the immediate aftermath of hostilities; in effect, they had been negotiating with each other indirectly since the War of Attrition in 1971, and they had already begun to talk about including mutual arms restraint in a possible interim agreement between the two sides. But Syria and Israel had never engaged in such a dialogue. Ingrained mutual suspicion and mistrust prevented a mediated negotiation. Syria not only refused to recognize or negotiate with Israel but also rejected diplomatic overtures from the United States. Although Egyptian President Anwar Sadat had made a conscious effort from the outset of the October War to enlist U.S. mediation assistance, President Assad of Syria had developed no such diplomatic strategy. A prominent member of the radical Arab camp, Syria perceived no particular value in seeking help from a biased intermediary to resolve the conflict.

Ideological, domestic, and territorial constraints also hindered the development of flexibility and exploratory risk taking. Assad's leadership was not as secure as that of his Egyptian counterpart. Constrained both by the ideology of the ruling Ba'ath party and by his armed forces, Assad could not afford to make Sadat's unilateral, grand gestures. Assad had to build a consensus carefully for each step he took toward a potential disengagement agreement. Nor was Israel flexible in its attitude toward Syria. The governing Labor coalition in Israel was fragile, and public opinion was far more skeptical of an agreement with Syria than of one with Egypt. Domestic opposition to Syria was particularly intense because of Syria's alleged mistreatment of Israeli POWs. Finally, the limited strategic space of the Golan Heights, in comparison with the Sinai peninsula, made the thought of Israeli compromise with Syria far more problematic.

U.S. Secretary of State Henry Kissinger also seemed uninterested in peacemaking between Syria and Israel. Kissinger appeared to have attached more importance to an Egyptian-Israeli agreement than to a Syria-Israel accord. At best, he calculated that although the Egypt-Israel agreement was more important in the long term to U.S. Middle East policy, a Syrian-Israeli accord was needed in the short term to lift the oil embargo and to preserve the diplomatic gains just made with Egypt and Israel. Without an agreement between Israel and Syria, another round of hostilities was likely. And Egypt would be hard pressed to avoid the fray if war broke out. The U.S. mediator, while continuing to exclude the Soviet Union from the peacemaking process, was left to fashion incentives for a disengagement agreement in an atmosphere of mutual mistrust.

Kissinger won approval from both sides to proceed with disengagement negotiations under U.S. auspices after an impasse about Syria's handling of Israeli POWs was broken and Israel was subsequently willing to put forward initial proposals. Then Kissinger, who had initially been amenable to hearing the views of Syrian and Israeli representatives in Washington as well as those of other Arab foreign ministers, refused to engage the parties seriously until the Arab oil embargo was lifted. This major U.S. foreign policy goal was satisfied on March 18, 1974. After consultation with the Soviets about unilateral U.S. efforts, Kissinger was then ready to press the parties for an agreement.

From late March 1974, when Kissinger began his efforts, he realized that Syrian-Israeli disengagement would be significantly more difficult to negotiate than Egyptian-Israeli disengagement had been. Egypt and Israel (who signed the so-called Sinai I accord on January 18, 1974) had both had strong incentives to reach an agreement quickly and had almost concluded one even before Kissinger intervened, shuttling between Aswan and Jerusalem. Syria and Israel, however, remained far apart with no zone of agreement, even after preliminary efforts. The problem was exacerbated by Assad's continuous need to build consensus for policy decisions and by strains in Israel within Prime Minister Golda Meir's government, which ultimately collapsed on April 10, 1974.

Damascus nevertheless agreed in early May to the concept of reciprocal force reductions on either side of a UN buffer zone, and Israel showed some flexibility about withdrawal west of the lines of October 6, 1973 (Kissinger, 1982). The rudiments of a deal seemed in sight. But even this degree of movement proved insufficient for sustaining the momentum of negotiations. As a tactical ploy, Kissinger considered recessing the negotiations until each party further considered its position and fully appreciated the indispensable role played by the United States.

Each side, heavily constrained by domestic considerations, appeared unwilling to take the necessary risks to reach an agreement. The secretary of state believed failure could be avoided only by restructuring the presentation of the issues. He had to interject a substantive proposal, with Israeli approval, about the location of the disengagement line. Syria's acceptance of the U.S. proposal cleared the way for a discussion of the issues of limited-forces zones and the role of the United Nations in a buffer zone. To circumvent problems about the proposed buffer zone, Kissinger synthesized two ideas already on the table. In his memoirs, he recalls:

> With respect to the U.N. presence, a concept was emerging that combined the structure of the U.N. Emergency Force in Egypt with the nomenclature that had been traditional on the Golan since 1967. Assad did not want a *force* but was willing to accept *observers*. Golda rejected observers and insisted on a force. What could be more natural than to create a hybrid called the United Nations Disengagement Observer Force [UNDOF] whose function or charter no one could possibly deduce from its title. (Kissinger, 1982:1093–1094)

Finally, to surmount obstacles about limited-forces zones Kissinger used a procedure he had already established in the Egypt-Israel agreement: mutually acceptable limitations of forces would be conveyed as Syrian and Israeli responses to an American proposal on force limitations.

With the military and technical issues resolved, other problems remained: the final placement of the Syrian forward line, and assurances for Israel that terrorist raids originating from Syrian territory would not be permitted. Once Israel agreed to U.S. assurances about the cease-fire along with a one-kilometer extension of the Syrian forward line, Syrian and Israeli military representatives signed the disengagement agreement in Geneva on May 31, 1974. The language of the agreement carefully reflected the adversaries' relations and their expectations about the future. "This is not a peace agreement," it states. By contrast, the Egypt-Israel agreement of January 1974 states: "This agreement is not regarded by Egypt and Israel as a final peace agreement. It constitutes a first step toward a final, just and durable peace" (Kissinger, 1982:1251).

Despite the difficult and protracted bargaining, Israel and Syria both gained from the agreement. For Israel, the new accord stabilized the Golan front, placed a UN buffer zone between the opposing forces, and allowed general demobilization and a return to normalcy. In addition, the new agreement strengthened U.S.-Israel ties and buttressed the disengagement agreement with Egypt. For its part, Syria believed it had secured the first Israeli withdrawal in a broader process that would culminate in a full Israeli evacuation of the Golan Heights. Assad could argue, in the context of inter-Arab relations, that Syria had avoided direct negotiations with Israel by working through the U.S. mediator and the Egyptian working group of the Geneva Conference. Equally important, Assad proved Syria no longer had to rely exclusively on Moscow to gain concessions from Israel.

Pressing and Compensation: The Mediator as Manipulator

In many ways, the Syrian-Israeli disengagement negotiations proved to be a more significant test of the skills and strategies of the U.S. mediator than the Sinai I accord had been, given the nature of the issues at stake and the absence of any history of formal rule making for more effective conflict management (except for the Armistice Agreement of 1949). Strategic concerns compelled the United States to exercise its diplomatic leverage with Israel and Syria. On the Israeli side, Kissinger combined incentives and pressures to ensure continued participation by Israel's leaders in the peace process. Before the start of the May 1974 shuttle, he compensated Israel for its risk-taking efforts by converting to a grant $1 billion of a $2.2 billion U.S. loan to Israel. He pressed Israel hard for concessions in the wake of this gesture, warning Israeli leaders of the consequences of failure: the resumption of the oil embargo; the possibility of an Egyptian-Syrian alliance against Israel if U.S. influence in Cairo waned; and an increase in Soviet influence in the region. The most effective element in this strategy was Kissinger's manipulation of the so-called Egyptian factor. By intimating that Egypt would be compelled to rejoin the struggle if inter-Arab pressures increased, the United States impressed on Israel the need to keep up the momentum of the disengagement process on all fronts.

In addition, Kissinger threatened to blame Israel for any breakdown in negotiations that occurred, and threatened as well to withdraw completely from the peacemaking process. Reminding Israel of its nonagreement alternatives, he repeatedly stressed to the Israeli cabinet the degree to which U.S. mediation shielded Israel from less favorable negotiating forums where pressures would be greater to reach a comprehensive settlement and to return to 1967 borders. In essence, Kissinger structured the negotiation process to make his role indispensable to diplomatic progress. His threat to withdraw his services and to build increased reliance on mediation was designed to steer the parties away from deadlock.

Kissinger's success with Syria is explained by a similar combination of incentives and pressures. Kissinger sided with Syria on the return of the town of Quneitra, captured by Israel in the October War, and then used this support to exert pressure on President Assad. Pressing Syria, however, proved somewhat more difficult than pressing Israel. Given Soviet ties to Syria, the United States could neither threaten to withhold aid nor, indeed, promise significant compensation in the form of military assistance should an agreement be reached. By securing Syrian acquiescence to U.S. mediation, however, Kissinger was able to raise Assad's stake in a successful outcome. Not only did Washington hold the key to Quneitra but Kissinger convinced Assad (as he had convinced Israeli leaders) that nonagreement alternatives were perilous: a breakdown of the negotiations would leave Syria alone in its high-risk policy of confrontation with Israel.

To facilitate further concession making, Kissinger offered both sides a number of assurances and afforded each the obvious political advantage of responding to a U.S. proposal rather than to the demands of the other. The United States pledged to Syria a continued effort to secure the implementation of Resolution 338 and eventual Palestinian participation in subsequent negotiations. A package of assurances was also offered to Israel: a pledge that UN peacekeeping forces would not be withdrawn without Israel's assent; U.S. monitoring of the agreement; a promise of long-term U.S. military aid; and a delicately managed indirect pledge to support Israeli counterterrorist activity against political threats emanating from Syrian territory. With these third-party guarantees against non-performance in place, the parties were then able to proceed toward their first agreement.

Integrative Strategies: The Mediator as Formulator

Syria and Israel needed to overcome their resistance to the principle of undertaking mutual concessions. Kissinger was therefore compelled to formulate a number of proposals that identified (and provided) joint benefits for the parties, expanding the area of common ground between them. He accomplished the latter with great finesse around two key issues. First, he circumvented Israel's refusal to engage in negotiations until Damascus submitted a list of Israeli POWs and permitted Red Cross visits. He skirted this problem by persuading the parties to accept a proposal that would distinguish between prenegotiation gestures and concessions made in the context of a formal negotiation process. In essence, he proposed that Washington serve as a trustee for both sides: Syria would submit the names of the Israeli POWs to Washington; Israel would offer a concrete proposal for disengagement in exchange for the list; after the Red Cross visited the POWs in Syria, Kissinger would then transmit Israel's ideas to Damascus (Kissinger, 1982). With the success of this prenegotiation minuet, the parties were then able to engage in a concession-making process that led to an agreement.

The extent of Israel's withdrawal from the Golan was the second issue requiring a U.S. proposal. Essentially, Kissinger reframed the issue into its strategic and symbolic dimensions, suggesting that Israel could withdraw from Quneitra because the town was of no strategic value. Israel could retain the hills west of the town as strategic vantage points without undertaking any withdrawal that undermined Israeli security interests. Once Jerusalem agreed to relinquish Quneitra, the issue of withdrawal was then susceptible to greater subdivision and trade-offs.

IMPACT OF U.S. MEDIATION ON THE SYRIA-ISRAEL NORMATIVE ORDER

It is useful to approach the question of whether Kissinger's efforts fostered the creation of new norms for conflict management from both a short-term and longer-term perspective. In the short term (1974–1975), the mediator's impact on the conflict was significant. Kissinger persuaded the parties to accept the idea of U.S.-mediated negotiations, having created a sense of urgency about the absence of credible alternatives to mutual concession making. By facilitating a zone of agreement and redefining issues in a way that did not threaten core values, Kissinger was able to encourage limited learning among the disputants; Syrian and Israeli officials now believed limited functional cooperation could coexist with competition in an adversarial relationship. More precisely, with U.S. and UN assistance the parties managed to establish a set of rudimentary rules for regulating their competition as well as limited institutionalized peacekeeping procedures for monitoring compliance with these rules. Mediation reduced the intensity of the conflict in the short term by creating a credible tripwire mechanism to safeguard against surprise attack or war by miscalculation; it also fostered new practices and instrumental ends. It failed, however, to generate new principled ends or goals. Unfortunately, since mediation produced a reduction in conflict intensity without a concomitant reinforcement and extension of new behaviors, it precluded the creation and internalization of new norms.

Mediation is most likely to influence the creation and internalization of new norms for conflict management when: (1) the preference structures of the parties regarding conflict management are altered by new learning; (2) repeated behavior, reflecting new learning, generates new expectations and additional incentives to manage greater risks of accommodation with third-party assistance; (3) new learning, risk taking, and compliance are consistently rewarded with financial, military, and diplomatic guarantees; and (4) new behaviors and intentions are made congruent with other transnational conflict-management norms (Mandell and Tomlin, 1991).

Using these criteria as a reliable guide for testing for the presence of a normative transformation, it may be argued that in the Syria-Israel case mediation has neither generated new expectations nor fostered new norms. To begin with, although Kissinger did make effective use of pressing, compensation, and integration strategies to stabilize Syria-Israel relations in the aftermath of the October 1973 War, he did not significantly alter the preference structures of the parties (Carnevale, 1986). Neither Syrian nor Israeli leaders had any incentive to envision the longer-term benefits of self-binding commitments, sustained reciprocity, and increased reliance on mediated negotiations. Indeed, such short-term calculations were congruent with the disputants' assumption that the May 1974 disengagement agreement was neither a peace agreement nor a first step in a continuing peace process. Thus neither side expected or encouraged subsequent U.S. mediation efforts similar to those sought by Egypt and Israel after their first disengagement agreement.

Second, though Kissinger fostered limited change in the conflict management behavior of the parties, the mediation process failed to produce the momentum necessary for reinforcing and transforming new learning. In the absence of new expectations about expansion of the domain of functional cooperation, the parties had little incentive to engage in more risk-taking in order to establish new agreements.

Third, in the aftermath of the 1974 agreement the mediator did not reward Syria and Israel sufficiently for engaging in behavior that complied with three developing norms of reciprocity, functional cooperation, and reliance on mediated negotiations. Beyond sustaining a historical commitment to Israel, Kissinger showed little incentive to offer additional compensation that would encourage further peacebuilding momentum. The prospect of conferring rewards was complicated by the lack of U.S. diplomatic and military leverage with Syria in the mid-1970s. Constrained in its capacity to offer rewards, the United States was then prevented from sanctioning the parties for not pursuing subsequent peacebuilding initiatives.

Finally, the mediation process undertaken in 1974 did not compel the parties to make any commitments to the international community about permissible and impermissible behavior. Because of their quest for unilateral advantage and their need to avoid any additional self-binding commitments, the parties insisted on retaining war as a tool to right international wrongs (Kegley, 1975). Under such conditions, U.S. mediation was unable (despite the availability of skilled mediators) to build on new Syrian-Israeli limited functional cooperation to transform longer-term expectations about conflict management.

The foregoing analysis of the limits of U.S. mediation in transforming the normative order of the Syria-Israel conflict should not be understood as a condemnation of Kissinger's efforts. Rather, the analysis demonstrates that when new conflict-management behavior is not sufficiently reinforced and internalized, disputants fail to adjust their mutual expectations of appropriate behavior over time, a situation that precludes the development of new norms of conflict management.

The costs of a stalled normative transformation in the period between the 1974 agreement and the initiation of the Madrid Peace Conference in 1991 have, unfortunately, been enormous. Lacking embedded incentives and expectations for extending the domain of cooperation beyond the terms of their 1974 disengagement agreement, Syria and Israel developed new sources of intractability with the engagement in Lebanon's civil war of 1975–1976 and Israel's invasions of Lebanon in 1978 and in 1982. This spatial shift in the conflict fueled the quest for unilateral advantage as well as the avoidance of any new military confidence-building measures (CBMs) or additional self-binding political commitments. Such compound intractability led only to the creation of tacit "red lines" for regulating Syrian and Israeli intervention in Lebanon, with no concomitant development of collective expectations about permissible behavior. Indeed, the absence of a hurting stalemate created a stable status quo, successfully reinforced by extended reliance on institutionalized peacekeeping arrangements (UNDOF), which ultimately worked against any consideration of alternative peacebuilding initiatives. Moscow and Washington—engaged in intense superpower regional competition until the mid-1980s—found the diplomatic positions of their respective clients to be congruent with their own strategic interests. So the superpowers also lacked incentive to press the parties for new concessions that might extend the cooperative dimension of their own adversarial relationship. A tacit agreement prevailed on all sides to safeguard the politicomilitary status quo and avoid mediation of this intractable conflict.

Equally important in blocking normative transformation in the years following the 1974 disengagement agreement was the imperviousness of Syrian and Israeli leaders to successful peacebuilding efforts in other components of the Arab-Israeli conflict system. For example, the Egyptian-Israeli disengagement agreements of 1974 and 1975 and the formal peace treaty that followed in 1979 produced no positive spillover of additional learning and negotiating momentum for Damascus and Jerusalem.

In direct contrast to the Syria-Israel experience, U.S. mediation efforts in the Egypt-Israel case successfully reduced conflict intensity, induced behavioral change, and fostered the creation of new norms for conflict management. Spanning a period of six years, the mediation process initiated by Kissinger and completed by U.S. president Jimmy Carter guided Egypt and Israel through a series of steps that facilitated the delegitimation and decay of old norms; encouraged a mutual adjustment of expectations through repeated reciprocal acts of concession-making and expansion of functional cooperation; and reinforced, rewarded, and guaranteed compliance behavior with sustained financial and military support. Most important, continuous U.S. mediation fostered a number of discrete elements of a new normative order, which over time became linked and integrated in a way that generated further transparency and information sharing. Briefly, the components of this new order included: (1) rules to govern behavior and manage transactions in a routinized manner; (2) a collective expectation of what constitutes permissible and impermissible behavior; (3) clearly delineated boundaries around specific functional domains; and (4) a "tripwire" to signal a violation of an accepted rule and to allow for mobilizing a timely response (Mandell and Tomlin, 1991).

IDENTIFYING BARRIERS TO NORMATIVE TRANSFORMATION

Syrian and Israeli leaders demonstrated a growing interest in conflict de-escalation during the course of their bilateral talks in Washington from October 1991 to August 1994. On different occasions, both sides exercised self-restraint, floated trial diplomatic balloons, engaged in conciliatory gestures and, in the public domain, discussed the requirements for peace.[1] Despite this process of tacit signaling, however, the parties have yet to undertake the normative shift from a conflict-management order whose legitimacy is rooted in the use of armed force and the maximum pursuit of national interest to a newer order grounded in restraints on the use of force, moderation of competition, and the conscious coordination of behavior among adversaries.

To better understand this "stalled" or sporadic transition in Syria-Israel relations and, by extension, potential strategies for addressing such challenges, it is vital to identify clearly the barriers to normative transformation. In successful transformations, as evidenced by the Egypt-Israel case, disputants are motivated to move through a number of stages in which they gradually discard the norms of the old order. Third-party-assisted negotiations make the transition to a new order possible. Parties build a commitment and reliance on mediation and in the process learn the benefits of triadic negotiations. By engaging repeatedly in reciprocal acts for which they are consistently rewarded, adversaries become willing to take additional risks to expand their domain of functional cooperation. Most important, when deadlock occurs parties can rely on prior compliance behavior as a source of encouragement to persevere, avoid backsliding, and move toward an interdependent future more enticing than the prevailing status quo. Finally, their transition to the new order is completed when they internalize new conflict-management behavior and develop partner-specific norms that shield their emerging relationship from regional turbulence.

Given the definition from Kegley and Raymond (1990:16) that "norms are quasi-authoritative guides to behavior which contribute to social order by building a consensus on procedure as well as substantive matters," why have Syria and Israel proved unable to generate such a consensus in the realm of peacebuilding? Explanations of their resistance to subsequent interim disengagement agreements and to normative transformation are suggested by a number of barriers, generated by the disputants and the mediator alike.

The Disputants' Calculus

An examination of the disputants' calculus in the Syria-Israel conflict system since 1974 reveals several barriers to conflict management. The first barrier has to do with inertia exhibited by both Syria and Israel. Their extended reliance on institutionalized peacekeeping, which initially stabilized their interactions and expectations, later worked against consideration of additional risk-taking measures and concession making. As Stein (1987:65) notes, "leaders attend to the sunk costs of institutions and practices already in place and give considerable weight to these costs in considering alternative arrangements. Lags produced by custom and usage work against change in favor of established procedures of conflict management." Satisfied with the status quo and lacking either military, financial, or diplomatic incentives to continue the peacebuilding process begun in 1974, both sides have sought carefully to encapsulate military-strategic interaction on the Golan Heights while simultaneously pursuing unilateral strategic advantage in Lebanon.

A second barrier to normative transformation is explained by the parties' failure to make explicit their longer-term peacebuilding goals. Such hesitancy stems jointly from a refusal by Damascus and Jerusalem to agree to end the state of belligerency between them and their refusal to adhere to the principle of nonuse of force to resolve disputes. By retaining the "resort-to-force" option, the parties inevitably reinforce high levels of mistrust and suspicion that in turn preclude consideration of those longer-term goals that might discourage unilateral action.

This vicious cycle of short-term calculations provides the basis for a third explanation of Syrian and Israeli resistance to normative transformation. That is, even with the 1974 Golan agreement conflict-management norms have been insufficiently developed and grounded, a situation that leads to a persistent conflict with self-interest. For states preoccupied with managing an acute security dilemma, deep-seated vulnerabilities may be only partially resolved by evolving norms of conflict management that emphasize regularity and consistency of behavior (Goertz and Diehl, 1992). Under such conditions, Syria and Israel have been more concerned about reducing the risks of war than about distributing the future benefits of cooperation (Stein, 1987). This suggests that a strong aversion to war may be a necessary but insufficient condition for fostering and internalizing new norms of conflict management.

Finally, given that Syria and Israel have been hesitant to move in the direction of building a regime of common interest, a fourth explanation of resistance to normative transformation suggests that conflict-management norms are likely to vary in strength and acceptance over time. Where evolving norms such as reciprocity and functional cooperation are valued differently by disputants over time, we can expect a differentiated impact on behavior (Goertz and Diehl, 1992). Israeli and Syrian leaders have accepted new conflict-management practices (as distinct from fully internalized norms and principles) during the past two decades to the extent that these practices have been deemed congruent with national self-interest. As a consequence of competing understandings and asymmetrical rates of learning, however, Israel and Syria have each tested the limits of these new practices, especially in Lebanon. Israel has tended to view compliance with new conflict-management practices as an opportunity to strengthen deterrence and arms race stability and to sustain the possibility of longer-term political accommodation. For Syria, deterrence and arms race stability have been equally important priorities but the acceptance of new conflict-management practices has (until very recently) not extended to longer-term consideration of the benefits of greater accommodation with Israel. Israel has expected evolving norms of conflict management to lead ultimately to a full normalization of relations with Syria; Syria has understood such embryonic norms more as tactical "holding actions" that will create the conditions in which Israel will ultimately acquiesce to Syrian demands. With each side highly cognizant of the particular value that its counterpart attaches to the "rules of the game," Syria and Israel have assiduously ignored ripe moments for conflict de-escalation, preferring at each juncture to avoid undertaking the domestic groundwork necessary for concession making and significant peacebuilding policy shifts.

The Mediator's Calculus

Although Kissinger sensed the possibility of leading Egypt and Israel through a series of interim steps that would culminate in a formal peace treaty, no comparable long-term goals were articulated by successive U.S. administrations for the Syria-Israel relationship. On the contrary, the difficulties encountered in producing the 1974 Golan disengagement agreement were such that no American mediator wished to tackle the conflict again until October 1991, when the Madrid Peace Conference was initiated in the aftermath of the Gulf War. The longer-term benefits to the United States of engagement in mediation of the Syria-Israel conflict throughout the late 1970s and 1980s were perceived to be minimal, and the reputational costs of failure high. Even after the Egypt-Israel peace treaty of 1979 and Israel's invasion of southern Lebanon in 1982, where Syria and Israel clashed in air battles, Washington failed to articulate ambitious peacebuilding goals beyond its initial goal of stabilizing the Syria-Israel front after the October War of 1973. With no compelling ripe moments for diplomatic intervention and in the wake of the killing of 250 U.S. Marines in Beirut in October 1983, American leaders had little incentive to exercise any form of mediation with muscle. This U.S. attitude of benign neglect and sporadic engagement with the Syria-Israel conflict throughout the 1980s was, unfortunately, reinforced by the disputants themselves. Neither side signaled a willingness to rely on U.S. mediation to negotiate additional interim agreements, which were a proven way to foster confidence-building momentum in the Arab-Israeli conflict.

Other barriers to normative transformation—beyond the limited success of prior mediation efforts and the reluctance of the parties to expand the cooperative component of their adversarial relationship—have presented equally formidable challenges to potential U.S. mediators. For example, U.S. political and military leverage with Israel and Syria has traditionally been highly asymmetrical over the past twenty years. Although U.S. policymakers have maintained consistently high levels of influence with and access to Israel's decisionmakers, access to Syria's leadership has until recently been circumscribed by Damascus's close relationship with its Soviet patron. Supported by a regular flow of arms and aid from Moscow until the mid-1980s, President Assad had little need to acquiesce in the face of U.S. threats and promises. Washington could offer Syria few rewards for compliance with new forms of conflict-management behavior. The United States possessed neither sufficient sanctioning power to enforce a developing norm (especially reliance on mediation) nor credible means for punishing the parties for failing to expand their domain of functional cooperation.

A long history of failed Middle East peace initiatives reminded U.S. policymakers that it was counterproductive to force concessions from Israel when its Arab neighbors refused to make concessions in kind. In this connection, then, where the mediator's relationship and influence with each of the parties is vastly different, conventional strategies of manipulation, pressing, integration, and compensation are likely to be collectively insufficient for overcoming inertia. Indeed, this condition of deadlock is likely to be exacerbated to the extent that the mediator fails to identify a new formula for agreement and is unable to persuade the parties to articulate explicit public commitments—congruent with transnational norms of conflict management—about the nonuse of force. When mediation cannot produce these key anchors of a new normative order, it fails to serve as a transitional link between a prevailing dysfunctional conflict system and a newer one grounded in norms of constructive conflict management. This is especially problematic in the Syria-Israel case, where the parties have developed a series of tacit signals that over time have amounted to an informal normative order of conflict management that always leaves both sides with a convenient exit strategy.

REFRAMING U.S. MEDIATION STRATEGIES TO SUSTAIN CONFLICT-TRANSFORMATION MOMENTUM

The preceding lengthy list of barriers to normative transformation raises the question of how the United States can better use its mediation resources to generate and sustain transformation momentum and overcome the current deadlock in Syria-Israel relations. To be sure, mediators face daunting challenges in de-escalating and transforming protracted conflicts, which are best understood as ongoing conflict processes rather than as specific events with distinct end points. Exhibiting high levels of inertia and stability in their capacity to resist change, protracted conflicts like that between Syria and Israel tend to reduce the effectiveness of traditional intervention strategies and therefore undermine motivation for third-party intervention. If the United States is to strengthen its capacity to undertake mediation for the long haul in the Syria-Israel conflict, Washington will need to reconceptualize motivational and outcome rewards and to rethink mediator influence strategies such that new learning by the disputants is quickly embedded, reinforced, and ultimately internalized as new norms of conflict management.

During the past four decades, while intermediaries have been motivated to intervene in the Arab-Israeli conflict to facilitate a process through which adversaries can better manage their conflict, they have also been motivated by the potential for an actual settlement or "outcome reward" that advances the interests of both the parties and the mediator (Mitchell and Webb, 1988). Thus, in working toward a more durable settlement of the Syria-Israel conflict, Washington will likely be rewarded by enhanced influence with the parties, strengthened regional security arrangements that forestall conflict escalation, and greater status as an international mediator capable of fashioning a key component of the new post–Cold War world order.

As of December 1994, the Clinton administration is well placed to reap the benefits of mediating the Syria-Israel conflict. Syria's leaders, who no longer have generous access to Russian financial and military aid and who, since the Gulf War, wish to be more fully integrated into the international community, now see cooperation with U.S. mediation efforts as the best strategy to constrain Israeli military power and win greater financial assistance and diplomatic acceptance among Western nations in particular. For Israel, the May 4, 1994, Cairo Agreement with the Palestine Liberation Organization and the October 26, 1994, peace treaty with Jordan, along with persistent fears of another quantum leap in the Middle East arms race, have all made Israeli leaders more amenable to serious peacebuilding negotiations with Damascus. Furthermore, both sides are now publicly exchanging views on the general formula *full peace* (to be offered by Syria) *in exchange for full Israeli withdrawal from the Golan Heights.* An active U.S. mediator clearly has an opportunity under these conditions to flesh out the meaning of this formula and to offer the bridging proposals, compensations, and guarantees necessary for an agreement.

Unfortunately, as evidenced by President Clinton's October 27, 1994, trip to Damascus, although strong mediator motivation and the presence of a ripening moment are necessary they are not sufficient conditions for success. The U.S. president took the unusual step of traveling to the Middle East only two weeks before the November 8, 1994, congressional midterm elections to witness the signing of the Israel-Jordan peace treaty on October 26, 1994. Clinton hoped a direct, personal venture into Arab-Israeli peacemaking would remove Syria as the last obstacle to a comprehensive peace and, in so doing, strengthen support for Democrats at the polls as well as boost his own leadership and foreign policy credentials. This was a risky step not only domestically but also internationally: this was to be the first time that a U.S. president visited a country that the State Department officially continues to accuse of sponsoring terrorism.

None of this boded well for a breakthrough in the deadlocked Syria-Israel peace talks.

After four hours of private meetings with President Assad on October 27, Clinton failed to win any substantive concessions from the Syrian leader. At best, Assad agreed only to extend the timing for an Israeli withdrawal from the Golan from one year to eighteen months and to consider opening some form of diplomatic relations with Israel after the first phase of Israel's withdrawal (*New York Times*, December 31, 1994). Not only did Assad fail to condemn terrorism publicly at a joint news conference with President Clinton, he also displayed little eagerness for peace with Israel. He was clearly uninterested in using the unique opportunity of a presidential visit to provide reassuring signals to a suspicious Israeli public (*Newsweek*, November 7, 1994). Although Clinton and his aides tried to demonstrate new signs of flexibility in Assad's utterances, Israel's leaders remained unimpressed and concerned that a high-level presidential intervention had not added any new momentum to the peace process. Upon his return to Washington, Clinton maintained that he had made an investment in peace, whereas critics noted that the president had received nothing for this significant investment of American prestige; only Assad gained additional international legitimacy and respectability (*Time*, November 7, 1994).

Despite the lack of serious diplomatic progress at the level of presidential summitry, Clinton's intercession did breathe new life into the quiet, private, face-to-face meetings of Syrian and Israeli officials in Washington during the last six months of 1994. While not to be equated with the Oslo-style secrecy and urgency of the Israeli-Palestinian talks of 1993, these discussions were the first to include the Syrian and (then-) Israeli military chiefs of staff, Major General Hikmat Shihabi and Lieutenant Ehud Barak. Held on December 21 and 22 respectively, these latest discussions provided military experts an opportunity to better understand each other's security concerns. The talks did not succeed in narrowing the gap on future security arrangements but did leave open the door to further indirect exchanges to be managed through U.S. mediation efforts.

NEXT STEPS

For Washington to capitalize fully upon these latest developments, the United States must define new goals and employ different strategies to facilitate both a formal peace and the internalization of new norms of conflict management by Damascus and Jerusalem. Beginning with the end in mind, U.S. mediation efforts must become increasingly anticipatory and self-starting. Informed observers already expect that Syria and

Israel will sign a formal peace treaty in exchange for a phased Israeli withdrawal from the Golan Heights. Using the Egypt-Israel peace treaty as a ready benchmark, Israel will relinquish political sovereignty over the Golan Heights while surrendering military control incrementally in three phases of geographic disengagement and demilitarization. The final handing over of territory will coincide with the commencement of full normalization of Syria-Israel relations. The process will take several years to complete, depending on the duration and accomplishments of each phase.

At this juncture, Israel is willing to withdraw on the Golan Heights but refuses to commit itself on just how far until Syria agrees to establish normal ties. Israel is also insisting that demilitarization be asymmetrical, with the demilitarized buffer zone extending further on Syrian territory. As part of the broader package of security arrangements, Israel's leaders also want to maintain permanent observation posts on the Golan, have U.S. troops serve as peace observers and a tripwire between the two sides, and witness a reduction, over time, in the size of Syria's standing army. To date, Damascus has rejected all of these Israeli demands, arguing that they are neither consistent with the meaning of Security Council Resolutions 242 and 338 nor integral to the spirit of the October 1991 Madrid Peace Conference. Anxious to forestall full normalization with Israel, Syria has, with minor periodic modifications, insisted on the full return of the Golan Heights before opening diplomatic and trade relations with Jerusalem (*New York Times*, December 31, 1994).

In order to break the impasse, U.S. mediation must focus on the discrete phases of peacebuilding, with demands and obligations on the disputants and the mediator weighted and sequenced differently in each phase. For example, Secretary of State Christopher needs to anticipate: (1) the package of security arrangements and compliance measures to be integrated into each phase; (2) the scope and timing of the withdrawal of Syrian and Israeli forces from Lebanon; (3) the management and control of water resources; (4) the removal of Israeli settlements on the Golan Heights; (5) the adjustment of international borders; (6) post-treaty compliance measures (Schiff, 1993); and (7) potential cultural barriers to mediated agreement (Kimmel, 1994).

Bridging cultural differences may prove the greatest mediation challenge of all, as Syria and Israel have widely different expectations regarding the purpose, process, substantive issues, and outcomes of mediated negotiations. For Israel, such negotiations are expected to accomplish a number of confidence-building tasks leading to new security arrangements (in the context of phased withdrawal from the Golan Heights) and full normalization of relations with Syria underwritten by U.S. military and financial guarantees. For Syria, by contrast, mediated negotiations are expected to, among other things: validate Syria's pivotal strategic and Arab leadership role in the peace process; ensure equality of status in negotiations with Israel; integrate Syria more fully into the international community and thus attract foreign aid; remove the stigma of Syria's support for international terrorism; and produce a more stable military relationship with Israel along with limited forms of political cooperation.

The foregoing suggests that Syria and Israel have conceptions of peace that are not easily understood by each other. Although these two disputants have been holding sporadic bilateral talks over the past two years, they have not to date produced a level of intercultural communication sufficient for interlocutors to develop greater empathy and mutually shared perceptions of the external environment they confront (Kimmel, 1994). From this perspective, then, U.S. intervenors will need to ensure that Damascus and Jerusalem send and receive signals that strengthen collaborative problem solving and extend room for diplomatic maneuvering, rather than to encourage the more rigid bargaining behavior undertaken to prevent a loss of face. Additionally, it would be counterproductive for U.S. intervenors to be guided by their own urgent sense of time as Syrian and Israeli leaders carefully weigh the profound risks and consequences of expanding their domain of politicomilitary cooperation.

With clear goals and a strong awareness of cultural imperatives in mind, mediators are better able to control the interaction of demands and obligations that ultimately produce the confidence-building momentum and incentives needed for additional self-binding commitments. To ensure the kind of third-party engagement necessary to reinforce new learning, the United States must tie its intervention strategies more explicitly to requirements for effective arms control arrangements and regime building. Only by helping the disputants manage different kinds of performance risks over time can the United States avoid facilitating another short-term, plateaulike agreement beyond which the parties have no incentive to continue peacebuilding efforts.

When third-party intervention is conceived of exclusively as a power-based activity in which carrots and sticks are applied to alter the preference structures of disputants, mediation tends to become a technical fix for stabilizing and managing short-term strategic interactions. To succeed in protracted regional conflicts, however, mediation is best conceived of as a norm-generating mechanism for influencing the longer-term behavior and capacity of states to develop and internalize self-enforcing and cooperative norms. Incentives, rewards, and punishments, seen from this perspective, become integral contributions in building new relationships among adversaries rather than simply instruments for constructing new agreements based on narrow self-interest. Furthermore, by adopting a norm-based approach to pacific intervention, mediators become more sensitized to the ways in which disputants signal their intentions to each other and develop rules to manage transactions (Kegley and Raymond, 1990). A norm-based approach will also better direct the mediator to those intervention strategies and reward structures most likely to be helpful in facilitating among adversaries new patterns of repeated behavior that ultimately embed a habit of cooperation.

In the context of the Syria-Israel case, if the United States adopts a more deliberate normative focus it will have to realign its strategies of pressing, integration, and compensation accordingly. It will have to continuously expand opportunities and incentives that reinforce new learning and internalize new norms of conflict management. Operationally, this means that when the United States decides to press the parties, the mediator should motivate concession making by applying positive inducements before invoking threats and negative sanctions (Pruitt and Carnevale, 1993). The U.S. mediator need not press the parties simultaneously nor compensate them in identical measure: Damascus and Jerusalem are likely to have different security and compensation needs across the various phases of the withdrawal and normalization process.

Washington will be well positioned to sustain its involvement in the arduous process of conflict transformation to the extent that it reconceptualizes compensation commitments and compliance guarantees as dynamic resource variables that can be adjusted and distributed in relation to developments within the process itself. Essentially, the parties will have to stretch to win their compensation and the United States will not be compelled to offer open-ended commitments and unlimited blanket guarantees. More precisely, Washington might consider "reverse obligations" that would gradually reduce its military and financial commitments to Syria and Israel as they move toward a more stable and secure footing. In this way, the obligations of conflict management, including the internalization of new norms, would ultimately be shifted back to the parties. The United States would bear the heaviest burden at the outset but its contribution would gradually decrease, an approach feasible only to the extent that other third parties increase their levels of material support. Since it precludes long-term reliance and dependence on U.S. mediation assistance and compensation, such an approach would appear at first glance to run counter to effective norm creation. But given the growing requirement for the United States to be involved in several new regional and ethnic conflicts simultaneously, this intervention approach is congruent with emerging U.S. foreign policy commitments. It allows for sustained U.S. involvement in the Syria-Israel conflict-transformation process through varying degrees of resource commitments over time. Washington's capacity for continuous third-party engagement, as distinct from intensive short-term assistance, is the key to the normative transformation of the protracted Syria-Israel conflict.

CONCLUSION

With several longstanding bilateral conflicts in the Arab-Israel conflict system now approaching resolution, the United States has a unique opportunity to facilitate a formal peace between Syria and Israel. Valuable in its own right, such an agreement would do much to anchor peaceful relations more permanently throughout the Middle East. Although the parties accomplished an initial de-escalatory step more than twenty years ago, they have yet to develop sufficient political will to transcend their quest for expanded politicomilitary accommodation. Damascus and Jerusalem have expressed their desire for another U.S.-brokered accord. The challenge facing the Clinton administration at this juncture is twofold. The administration must first engage the parties in a way that creates incentives for them to take risks, discard old norms, and establish a new normative order that precludes the use of force to resolve future problems. Second, it must convince Congress that in spite of U.S. experience and commitments in Somalia, Bosnia, Haiti, Rwanda, and elsewhere, facilitating and guaranteeing a Syria-Israel peace treaty in conjunction with other third-party support is fully congruent with U.S. interests. By addressing these challenges creatively, the current administration can do much to resolve a conflict that is otherwise headed for another cycle of armed conflict.

NOTE

1. In the first six months of 1994, for example, both sides demonstrated empathy for each other's constraints, developed a commitment to the peace process amid sporadic conflict in Lebanon, and described the achievement of peace to domestic audiences as a strategic objective.

REFERENCES

Carnevale, P. (1986). "Strategic Choice in Mediation." *Negotiation Journal* 2, 1: 41–56.

Goertz, G., and Diehl, P. F. (1992). "Toward a Theory of International Norms: Some Conceptual and Measurement Issues." *Journal of Conflict Resolution* 36, 4: 634–664.

Kegley, C. W., Jr. (1975). "Measuring the Growth and Decay of Transnational Norms Relevant to the Control of Violence: A Prospectus for Research." *Denver Journal of International Law and Policy* 5, 2: 425–439.

Kegley, C. W., Jr., and Raymond, G. A. (1990). *When Trust Breaks Down: Alliance Norms and World Politics*. Columbia: University of South Carolina Press.

Kimmel, P. R. (1994). "Cultural Perspectives on International Negotiations." *Journal of Social Issues* 50, 1: 179–196.

Kissinger, H. (1982). *Years of Upheaval*. Boston: Little, Brown.

Mandell, B. S., and Tomlin, B. W. (1991). "Mediation in the Development of Norms to Manage Conflict: Kissinger in the Middle East." *Journal of Peace Research* 28, 1: 43–55.

Mitchell, C. R., and Webb, K., eds. (1988). *New Approaches to International Mediation.* Westport, Conn.: Greenwood.

Pruitt, D. G., and Carnevale, P. J. (1993). *Negotiation in Social Conflict.* Pacific Grove, Calif.: Brooks/Cole.

Schiff, Z. (1993). *Peace With Security: Israel's Minimal Security Requirements in Negotiations With Syria.* Washington, D.C.: Washington Institute for Near East Policy.

Stein, J. G. (1987). "A Common Aversion as a Strategy of Conflict Management." In G. Ben-Dor and D. Dewitt, eds., *Conflict Management in the Middle East.* Lexington, Mass.: Lexington Books, 59–77.

PART THREE

INTERNATIONAL MEDIATION: THE RANGE OF PRACTICE

Chapter Seven

Mediation in Internal Conflicts: Lessons from Sri Lanka

Kumar Rupesinghe

Social science approaches to mediation of internal conflicts have evolved dramatically in recent years, from obscure and somewhat arcane academic and diplomatic exercises rooted in Western attempts at understanding and managing the superpower confrontation, to an increasingly popular tool for peacemaking and peacebuilding at the disposal of people at every level in the global community. With the collapse of the Soviet Union and the emergence from the overbearing shadow of the Cold War of dozens of violent internal conflicts—now the predominant manifestation of conflict in the world—the challenges of disseminating and applying conflict resolution techniques and methodologies in what is perceived as a "new world of disorder" have grown in scope and urgency (Rupesinghe, 1992).

This chapter examines some of the salient characteristics of violent internal conflict and the applicability of current theoretical approaches to conflict resolution in violent or potentially violent internal conflicts. Using Sri Lanka as a case study, it discusses the two most promising attempts to negotiate a peaceful settlement of the conflict between the Sinhalese majority and the Tamil minority and suggests some of the reasons these efforts failed. Finally, the chapter looks at some of the lessons learned and presents the case for a comprehensive approach to peacebuilding in the Sri Lankan and other contexts. It is argued that in a multidimensional, protracted social conflict such as Sri Lanka's, where traditional approaches have consistently failed to bring peace, an alternative to deadlock is a multisectoral approach to conflict transformation that emphasizes creating sustainable frameworks for citizen-based peacebuilding initiatives.

CONFLICT THEORY AND PRACTICE

The theory and practice of conflict resolution largely evolved in the context of the Cold War. Predominantly Western and rationalistic in its discourse and focused on the interplay of states and state actors in relation to the superpower competition, little emphasis was placed on the resolution of internal conflicts, let alone their long-term transformation. And although much of the theorizing, methods, and techniques explored may have applicability to violent internal conflicts, overall their relevance remains problematic.

Within conventional Western paradigms, there are certain assumptions that are largely unstated but that need to be deconstructed if we are to understand why conflict theory has not been more useful in resolving the violent internal conflicts occurring today. Much of the large and growing literature on conflicts and conflict resolution originated in the United States and Europe and generally presupposes a domain of "rationality" where all the parties, more or less, share certain central values such as equality and recognition of the rule of law. The modern division of labor in Western societies assumes that members are involved in multiple roles and attached to a variety of interests. Recognizing that this complexity gives rise to conflict, societies develop institutions and mechanisms to resolve conflicts in specified ways. Gradually a culture of negotiations emerges and a complex network of arbitration and dispute resolution becomes increasingly professionalized, often with the stable, modern state assuming the role of mediator.

In recent years, nontraditional approaches to third-party mediation and resolution of conflict have become more prominent for a variety of reasons, both positive and negative. These reasons include the development of more effective negotiation or facilitation skills and methods, a growing awareness of the complexity and intractability of many deep-seated internal conflicts, and the success of nongovernmental initiatives in exercises such as the recent Norwegian facilitation of discussions on an Israeli-Palestinian peace accord. At the same time, there has been a growing awareness at all levels of the international community of the failures and limitations of traditional forms of bilateral or multilateral diplomacy when applied to conflict resolution, and in particular of the inherent limitations of an international system in which the concepts of state sovereignty and noninterference retain great potency.

Based on the outcome sought, both traditional and nontraditional third-party approaches can be divided into two major streams—partial settlement of specific issues, or integrative conflict resolution and transformation. This transformative process is concerned with "broader social structures, change and moving toward a social space open for co-operation, for more just relationships and for non-violent mechanisms for handling conflict" (Hoffman, 1992:278). When applied in a transformative process, nonprescriptive methods of analyzing root causes and exploring mutually acceptable compromises involve empowerment of local people. One of the principal aims of that empowerment in situations of violent conflict must be to recapture or secure the democratic space necessary to transform the conflict and sustain peace.

In this description of conflict transformation, one can see the utility of incorporating many of the concepts, frameworks, skills, and tools derived from Western approaches to conflict resolution. However, it is also crucial to recognize the limits of those approaches in relation to protracted social conflicts in non-Western societies. Take, for example, the approach of John Burton and others, who have focused on the meeting of basic human needs or ontological and biological drives for survival. Human needs theory posits that basic needs for security, identity, and recognition are nonnegotiable and cannot be compromised. Frustration or suppression of basic needs is seen as a primary source of conflict. Thus, in third-party conflict resolution based on human needs theory—usually carried out in a problem-solving workshop setting—an analytical approach is used to determine the overall nature of the conflict or intertwined conflicts and to identify the potential actors, and then to facilitate movement of the parties beyond stated positions or interests to the common ground of basic human needs. This type of approach can encompass attitudes, interpersonal relationships, and social, political, and economic structures. Ultimately, the goal of the process is to "rationally" transform conflictual attitudes and situations (Hill, 1982).

One example of the problem-solving approach aimed specifically at ethnic and national conflicts is the concept of the "public peace process," developed by Harold Saunders and others. Because the basic issues in ethnic and national conflicts are rooted in national and cultural identity, historical grievances, fear, hostility, and dehumanization, it is assumed that they are nonnegotiable and can only be addressed by working at fundamental human levels. This work involves engaging people in a nongovernmental political process of sustained dialogue to change perceptions, build new relationships, and create an environment conducive to peace, as opposed to the search for technical solutions between negotiators at the bargaining table (Kramer, 1993).

Although the notion of basic needs and the problem-solving workshop approach have been major conceptual contributions to conflict resolution theory and practice, various scholars have noted some limitations. These include distortions caused by faulty communications, coping with the asymmetrical power balance in some conflicts, a lack of common cultural ground between actors in others, and so on. Perhaps more fundamentally, in practice problem-solving workshops generally are not conducted with the active parties to a conflict, but rather with those who may be able to exert some influence on political, social, and economic processes. This disjunction and problems of reentry into the conflict system make successes at the workshop level difficult to transfer in meaningful ways to a political negotiation process.

The limitations of the workshop, problem-solving approach are most apparent in violent internal conflicts such as Sri Lanka's, where there is a high degree of polarization between the parties and where stereotyping and demonization have taken root. A more promising approach is the transformative one, in which reaching agreement on outstanding issues as quickly as possible can be seen as secondary to addressing the overall conflict process and coming to terms with the historical background and pace of conflict processes. If the goal being pursued is the building and/or revival of indigenous political, social, and economic mechanisms and attitudes that militate against the use of violence to resolve conflicts in a given society, what is needed is a broad, open-ended, and dynamic process.

Because of the complexities of internal conflicts, one of the great challenges for general conflict theory is how to develop a comprehensive framework for peacebuilding strategies that combines traditional linear approaches with transformative ones. Lederach has propounded strong arguments for combining an "elicitive" approach in conflict resolution with the "prescriptive" approaches rooted in Western cultural and ideological assumptions (Lederach, 1994a).

CHARACTERISTICS OF VIOLENT INTERNAL CONFLICT

In general, internal conflict can be defined as conflict taking place primarily within the borders of a given state. Internal conflicts often occur between the state and the civilian population. While the civilian population may or may not belong to an ethnic or minority group different from that of the dominant elite, these conflicts often involve a notion of identity, a concept of security, and a feeling of well-being. Burton (1986) emphasizes the importance of the core sense of identity. Azar has made many important contributions in this area, particularly in his definition and description of protracted social conflicts as not merely interest-based but also involving many social, political, and economic dimensions. He suggests that the most useful unit of analysis in protracted social conflict situations is the identity group—racial, religious, ethnic, cultural, and others; and maintains that an identity group is a more powerful unit of analysis than the nation-state (Azar and Burton, 1986). Northrup (1989) defines identity as "an abiding sense of the self and of the relationship of the self to the world, a system of beliefs or a way of construing the world that makes life predictable rather than random." Defined in this way, identity is more than a psychological sense of self; it encompasses a sense of self in relation to the world and may be experienced socially or psychologically. Conflicts that involve a core sense of identity tend to be intractable largely because of the dynamics of the conflict rather than because of any rational assessment of benefits in perpetuating the conflict. Azar (1986) has pointed out that intractable conflicts, while sometimes stemming from a single grievance, escalate "to dominate and absorb most of the energies and resources of all sides, ultimately involving every aspect of inter-communal relations." In these instances, conflict resolution can be seen as a means of changing the conditions of intractability.

Some of the characteristics of internal war include the fragmentation of societies, communication breakdowns between segments of society, the militarization of the conflict, increased flows of refugees and the internally displaced, the stereotyping and/or demonization of others, internationalization of the conflict (but rarely of attempts at mitigation or resolution), and massive violations of human rights and severe breaches of humanitarian law, particularly against civilians. In addition, partly because of the multifaceted and complex nature of most protracted social or communal conflicts and the societal fragmentation they engender, attempts at peacemaking are often sporadic and uncoordinated.

In conflict situations marked by fragmentation and miscommunication and/or disinformation, linear, elite-level approaches to conflict resolution rarely bring lasting results and apparently must be supplemented by other approaches. At one level, this necessitates looking at conflicts within political frameworks that take into account social, economic, and historical factors. It also implies a recognition that in specific conflict situations many actors and institutions need to be involved in the transformation process, and that each phase in a conflict may necessitate a different type of intervention by different actors or combinations of actors.

In terms of the fragmentation of society, perhaps the most critical aspect of internal conflicts is the disempowerment of local communities. In these internal situations, armed protagonists readily target civilians. Humanitarian assistance necessitated by economic and social disruption becomes increasingly important; humanitarian agencies working in difficult circumstances created by conflict begin to negotiate with the armed protagonists; and the civilian population becomes increasingly passive. Meanwhile, attempts are made at external mediation. Fact-finding missions come to the country (in Sri Lanka there have been over 180 such missions in the last ten years); yet, however well-meaning, fact-finding is often uncoordinated and the last mission is not acquainted with the previous one or its findings.

As external mediation becomes more dominant, local actors are further disempowered. Many of the most capable people in the country service the humanitarian agencies, dispensing billions of dollars for humanitarian relief, while not even 1 percent of those funds are invested in peacebuilding. Clearly, it is important to shift that balance so that international agencies will empower local institutions and organizations and invest more resources in peacebuilding.

THE SITUATION IN SRI LANKA

Against a backdrop of spiraling communal violence (Brogan, 1992), the period from 1957 to 1994 saw ten major internal peace initiatives involving the Sri Lankan government (Rupesinghe and Verstappen, 1989; Rupesinghe, Verstappen, and Philips, 1993). In 1957 and again in 1965, attempts were made at a negotiated accommodation, with proposals to make Tamil a national minority language and allow the use of Tamil in the administration of the northern and eastern provinces. The 1965 initiative also proposed limited economic development powers for District Councils. However, because of pressure from the Buddhist clergy and other Sinhalese chauvinist groups, neither the Bandaranaike-Chelvanayagam pact of 1957 nor the Senanayake-Chelvanayagam pact of 1965 was enacted. It was not until 1983, in the wake of the July pogroms against Tamils and under pressure from India, that negotiations between the government and Tamil political leaders resumed, leading to the Round Table Conference of that year. The following year, an All Party Conference was convened. In 1985, India sponsored two rounds of talks in Thimpu, Bhutan. In 1986, the Sri Lanka government resuscitated the political-party approach in the Political Parties Conference. In the wake of direct Indian intervention in 1987, the Indo-Lanka Accord was formulated, followed by another All Party Conference in 1989, dialogue with the Liberation Tigers of Tamil Eelam (LTTE) in 1990, and most recently, in 1992, the establishment of a Select Committee of Parliament (see Table 7.1).

Table 7.1 Peace Initiatives

Initiative	Year
Bandaranaike-Chelvanayagam Pact	1957
Senanayake-Chelvanayagam Pact	1965
Round Table Conference	1983
All Party Conference	1984
Thimpu, Bhutan Talks	1985
Political Parties Conference	1986
Indo-Lanka Accord	1987
All Party Conference	1989
Dialogue with the LTTE	1990
Select Committee of Parliament	1992

Here we shall consider the strengths and weaknesses of the two most significant of these peacemaking attempts.

India's Role as Peacekeeper

The most significant external intervention in the Sri Lankan conflict has been that of India. Given its geographical proximity, its geopolitical interests, and its own large Tamil population concentrated in Tamil Nadu, India has been by no means disinterested in Sri Lanka's internal strife and the impact of Sri Lankan Tamil separatism on its own restive Tamil population. As Crossette has noted:

> Politically, every one of India's smaller neighbours has been the victim of Kautilyan [similar in connotation to Machiavellian] intrigue since the death of Nehru in 1964 and the subsequent consolidation of power by his daughter, Indira Gandhi, a few years later. Except for two brief historical moments in 1977–79 under a Janata Party government and in 1989–90 when Prime Minister Vishwanath Pratap Singh and his foreign minister, Inder Kumar Gujral, pledged to stop playing dirty tricks on the neighbours, Indian policymaking on Sri Lanka, Bangladesh, Nepal, Bhutan, and to some extent Maldives and Pakistan (a special case) was a game for intelligence agents, schemers in the Ministry of External Affairs, and viceregal diplomats in imperial cloaks. (1993:110–111)

Muni, in his detailed and perceptive account of India's involvement in the Sri Lankan conflict, presents a more nuanced view of Delhi's motivation:

> India's objectives and interests underlying its mediatory role in Sri Lanka were several and varied. They ranged from the sublime to the obtuse, involving the narrow objectives of the ruling Congress Party to consolidate its alliance with the regional All India Anna DMK Party of M. G. Ramachandran to perpetuate its influence in Tamil Nadu; the stalling of Tamil separatism in Sri Lanka and its undesirable consequences in India; as well as keeping Western and other inimical external influences away from Sri Lanka and the Indian subcontinent as a whole. No less important for India was the objective of ensuring and strengthening peace and stability in its neighbourhood because the conflicts like the one in Sri Lanka had serious spillover implications for India itself. The order of priorities and the nature of these objectives were continually reformulated as the dimensions of the conflict and India's mediatory role evolved through various stages. (1993:166)

The first phase of the Indian approach to the Sri Lankan conflict, which lasted up to 1987, was characterized by active diplomatic engagement through high-level political meetings, shuttle diplomacy, consultations with the main protagonists, and the establishment of formal frameworks for negotiation. Covertly, India was also engaged in arming and training Tamil militants in Tamil Nadu. In mid-1987, Indian involvement shifted and deepened dramatically with the dispatching of peacekeeping forces to monitor the ill-fated cease-fire between the Tigers and the Sri Lankan army and the signing of the Indo-Lanka Accord. At the height of India's Sri Lankan operation, more than 120,000 of its troops were in the country; 7,000 were killed and many more wounded (De Silva and Cowper,

1993), and since 1990, when the last contingent of the force departed, India's involvement has been reluctant and low profile.

India's military and political debacle undermined the leverage that Delhi had developed with the Tamil militants by arming and training them in camps in Tamil Nadu, dispelled whatever perception existed among the Sri Lankan government and public of Indian impartiality and utility in the peace process, and eroded the Indian public's support for further military intervention in Sri Lanka. In May 1991, ten months after the Indians withdrew from Sri Lanka, Rajiv Gandhi was killed in a suicide bombing at an election rally in Madras; it was believed that this action was carried out by the LTTE in retaliation for the Indian peacekeeping force's turning on the LTTE when they breached the cease-fire accompanying the Indo-Lanka Accord.

Throughout the Indian mediation effort, Indian diplomats and leaders had difficulty in getting Colombo to accept proposals because of personality clashes (primarily between Mrs. Gandhi and President Jayewardene and later between President Premadasa and Rajiv Gandhi) and also because the Sri Lanka government saw Indian involvement as unwanted interference. Even when top levels of government came to understandings, bureaucrats and other Sinhalese interest groups who bitterly opposed progress toward a settlement often undermined them and, by extension, the credibility of both the government and the mediator. At the same time, India demonstrated arbitrariness in its relations with Tamil militants and rarely made any effort to coordinate the positions of the various militant groups. Furthermore, India made no attempt to bring leaders of the two sides into face-to-face meetings, largely because of the antipathy between the sides and because of the Sri Lankan government's objections to legitimizing "the enemy." India failed to foresee the Sri Lankan leadership's shift to a stance of open and public antagonism when Premadasa took over as president from Jayewardene. It also underestimated the tenacity, capability, and external backing of the LTTE.

In more specific terms, the Indian peacekeeping effort was fatally flawed first because Delhi misjudged its ability to deliver compliance from the LTTE and other Tamil militant groups and failed to involve the LTTE as a signatory. Second, the terms of reference for Indian troops on the ground were dangerously unclear, and despite the forces' multicultural makeup, cultural differences and misperceptions led to mistakes in dealing with Sri Lankan civilians and converted a largely welcoming, war-weary population to open hostility.

Assessing the Accord

Although the Indian intervention can be viewed as disastrous in many respects, the Indo-Lanka Accord also can be seen as focusing many of the outstanding issues and as offering a framework for the ultimate resolution of the conflict. In this regard, the major points of the accord were:

- Affirmation of the unity, sovereignty, and territorial integrity of Sri Lanka
- Acknowledgment of Sri Lanka as a multiethnic and multilingual society consisting of Sinhalese, Tamils, Muslims, and Burghers
- Recognition of the northern and eastern provinces as areas of historical habitation of the Tamil-speaking Sri Lankan people
- The proposed formation of an administrative unit comprised of the northern and eastern provinces

Despite the accord's imprecision concerning processes and time frames, dilution of the concept of a Tamil "homeland" (*eelam*), inattention to the protection of Sinhalese settlers in predominantly non-Sinhalese areas, vagueness regarding the scope of devolution of powers, and lack of constitutional guarantees, it still constituted a framework for addressing many of the major issues of the conflict. In the medium term, it also created the space for a period of respite and negotiation in the conflict that came to be known as the Premadasa-LTTE "honeymoon."

Yet beyond the specific elements of the accord itself, its faulty imposition radically altered power relationships within Sri Lanka by demonstrating the country's geopolitical vulnerability to the regional superpower, shifting the government away from its Sinhalese-chauvinist position, and destroying the patron-client relationship between the LTTE and the Indian government. It also dispelled a myth cherished by many Sinhalese—that of India's desire to exercise hegemony over the island. Nevertheless, despite setbacks it has encountered, seven years later the accord remains a valid framework for a long-term political solution to the Sri Lankan conflict.

The Premadasa-LTTE "Honeymoon": Lessons for the Future

Under pressure from newly elected President Premadasa, India agreed to begin withdrawing its peacekeeping troops during 1989. Indian military operations were cut back, leaving the field in the north and east to the LTTE and its rivals, a situation that led to internecine fighting between the Tamil militant groups. At the same time, Premadasa began negotiations with the LTTE.

Judging by their public statements, the LTTE trusted President Premadasa. They had demonstrated their goodwill by officially registering themselves as a political party and publicly reiterating that they would welcome elections and enter the democratic process. Premadasa, meanwhile, was emphatic that he would do his utmost to bring the Tamil militants into the democratic process, making it clear that even the handing over of weapons would be secondary to that goal. Given the goodwill on both sides, what is surprising is that the situation changed so dramatically and that the two sides redeclared war on each other. Nevertheless, lessons can be learned by examining some of the shortcomings of the negotiation process.

For one, the period of negotiation was too protracted. There is good reason to believe that an agreed timetable and a well-planned implementation program would have helped both sides to focus on the difficult issues. A complementary problem was caused by the limited machinery of the negotiations, which consisted of periodic visits by the LTTE representatives to Colombo and subsequent shuttle diplomacy by the negotiator Saul Hameed. At no time did the LTTE leader Prabharakan and President Premadasa meet and attempt to consolidate any developing mutual trust. Misunderstandings could have been avoided if there had been adequate machinery to accelerate the peace process and a group of officials in charge of sustaining its implementation. The absence of such a body was felt when hostilities suddenly erupted and there was no way to monitor and act on cease-fire violations. There was obviously a need for secrecy so that certain details of the proceedings could not be made public, but the way in which the process was communicated could have been improved; after all, the negotiations between the two sides were historic and crucial and a significant departure from past practice. The opposition parties did their best to undermine perceptions of progress and hector the government; and against this background government spokesmen made contradictory and sometimes provocative statements that hindered the confidence-building necessary to sustain the peace process.

By May 1990, suspicions had become more manifest and statements by both sides more acrimonious. Some of the issues generating misunderstanding and tension were the ambiguity of the policy for disarming guerrilla forces; the opening of discussions with one of the LTTE's rivals, the Eelam People's Revolutionary Liberation Front; delays in the holding of a referendum on merger of the northern and eastern provinces and the legal difficulties in dissolving the existing government in the eastern province; the manning of police stations and the redeployment of security forces without warning and consultation; the mixed messages being propagated by government spokesmen; and the collection of taxes in Tamil areas. With hindsight, it is possible to see how these shortcomings in the dialogue process could have been rectified and some of the harmful political gestures avoided.

Convergence and Cleavages

Despite the widespread violence since 1983 and the increasing militarization of the conflict, by 1994 the various attempts at resolution had clarified the major issues—particularly Sinhalese willingness to devolve a substantial amount of autonomy to the Tamil minority and Tamil acceptance of a federal solution—thus providing what could form a general framework for an ultimate settlement. The principal areas where there have been indications of varying degrees of greater convergence are:

1. Institutional linkages between the northern and eastern provinces, such as the establishment of common institutions—for example, a sole governor, high court, and educational system
2. Constitutional guarantees of provincial powers
3. Devolution of powers to the Tamil-dominated provinces for the maintenance of law and order
4. Establishment of a national policy on land settlement
5. Equitable economic development
6. The need for confidence-building measures to dissipate mutual hatreds and suspicions on both sides

At the same time, the negotiation process has repeatedly been found wanting in the following crucial areas:

1. Inadequate will on both sides to overcome the resistance of political, religious, and other extremist elements and resolve the conflict
2. The propagation of intransigent or incendiary political positions for the consumption of particular constituencies
3. Reliance on military solutions
4. Hardening of public attitudes toward other groups
5. Inability of political leaders on both sides to overcome personal animosities toward their counterparts
6. A lack of consensus within both the Sinhalese and Tamil communities
7. A disparate and relatively weak peace constituency

The Failure of Traditional Mediation

The history of Sri Lanka's conflict and attempts at conflict resolution has been one of too-little, too-late reactions to the escalating spiral of violence. Far too often, the visceral and ad hoc responses have been to manipulate peace processes for short-term partisan gain and to counter violence with greater violence. Hence the killing, displacement, trauma, and material destruction have continued virtually unabated.

One of the major obstacles to a settlement has been the way the conflict has been conceptualized by the actors themselves and by third parties. Resolution of the conflict would therefore depend on reconceptualization—on identification and recognition of all the actors involved, as well as transformation of the political, social, and attitudinal constructs that have perpetuated the conflict. Unfortunately, in a society such as Sri Lanka that is polarized by rigid and antagonistic ethnic stratification and memories of recent carnage, such transformation will require great investment.

In a multidimensional, protracted social conflict such as Sri Lanka's, where traditional linear approaches to peacemaking and peacekeeping have consistently failed, there is, I would suggest, an alternative to deadlock. That alternative is a multisectoral and multilevel approach to conflict transformation that emphasizes the creation of frameworks for developing sustainable, citizen-based peacebuilding initiatives, the effective linking of those initiatives to the parties to the conflict, and the development of an overall environment conducive to making peace and sustaining it. Furthermore, in virtually all situations of protracted conflict like Sri Lanka's there exists an abundance of indigenous expertise, goodwill, and potential resources for the development of new approaches. Central to this approach is the concept of strategic planning of sustainable peacebuilding processes and, ultimately, sustainable peace, as well as the development of engaged, visible, and varied constituencies for peace that are linked to the political elites on all sides and also to external supporters of peacemaking.

DESIGNING PEACE PROCESSES

Peacebuilding requires a strategic design, the articulation of a framework, the identification of gaps in the mediation process, and the development of an overarching plan that provides for sustainable peacemaking at different levels. It also demands the development of peace constituencies concerned with particular conflicts at both the national and international levels. One possible design model is shown in Table 7.2.

As illustrated in Table 7.2, the long-term success of peace processes involves bringing together a variety of conceptual and organizational elements. Although there can be significant similarities in the techniques used in the prenegotiation and actual negotiation phases, the two need to be clearly distinguished by distinctive designs and strategies. The "strategic intent" of the prenegotiation phase is to reduce the sources of intractability as well as to create an environment in which parties to a conflict are able and willing to move from violent confrontation to the negotiating table. The prenegotiation phase is, therefore, a process for moving toward resolution rather than conflict resolution itself. It is during the prenegotiation phase that problem-solving techniques can be useful in defining and developing a citizen-based peace process. Problem-solving has also helped induce influential leaders on either side of a conflict to seek and agree on common objectives. Success in problem-solving is fragile,

Table 7.2 Designing Peacebuilding

Level 1 The International Framework
- Monitoring
- Lobbying (UN, donors, business, others)
- Support coalitions (humanitarian agencies, other interested parties)
- Establishing an international forum
- Providing resources for citizen-based peacebuilding

Level 2 Regional Frameworks
- Providing regional frameworks
- Lobbying (regional governments)
- Linking (regional organizations)

Level 3 National Frameworks
1. Prenegotiation phase
   - Creating political will for negotiations
   - Developing strategic alliances among:
     - business community, mass media, politicians, religious leaders, community leaders, eminent persons, diaspora
   - Designing public peace process
   - Designing community development as peacemaking
   - Creating economic plan
2. Negotiations
   - Building infrastructure for negotiations
   - Preparing technical papers and agendas
   - Free text
   - Timetables
   - Defining issues

however, because the middle-class intellectuals who are often involved in such exercises may have little influence with the parties to a conflict.

Developing a citizen-based peace process means creating a peace constituency and getting parties to be accountable to it, expanding the space for democratic action, developing political will, creating social networks that can persuade parties to negotiate, and establishing linkages between communities in conflict as well as within the political process. Models of community development aimed at linking communities and, ultimately, at peacemaking, and the concept of public peace processes pioneered by Harold Saunders (Kramer, 1993), can be useful in developing environments within which formal negotiations can succeed.

It is clear that peacemaking in complex and protracted social conflicts requires that efforts be pursued at different levels simultaneously. Even when formal negotiations do become possible, they alone are unlikely to provide a basis for long-term conflict transformation. Indeed, formal negotiations often disintegrate because of a failure to involve some of the crucial actors. The tendency of parties to use the negotiating process as a forum for publicity and point-scoring against each other also undermines negotiations, and in the worst cases the glare of publicity can heighten and perpetuate a conflict. On the other hand, the development of an active, multilayered, and effective peace constituency can create an environment conducive to counterbalancing negotiating setbacks and keeping the formal process on track.

Skilled facilitators can also introduce into seemingly intractable situations "icebreaking" or other innovative approaches, for example, by acting as messengers or enabling the use of a "free text" in which parties note their evolving agreements and disagreements. Another possible negotiating element is the provision of a larger canvas for discussion of issues not directly related to the conflict, such as economic or social development that involves external funding. Meanwhile, the development of strategic constituencies can provide a basis for other broad, peace-related initiatives.

Recent history has shown that a wider political framework and power relationship can be instrumental in persuading parties to enter into ceasefires or negotiations. The U.S. umbrella in the Middle East is one example of this; NATO's involvement in Bosnia is another. Involving outside actors and placing a local conflict in a wider context, whether global, regional, or both, can decrease the salience of that conflict. In the case of Sri Lanka, it is evident that India cannot be ignored in any effort to achieve lasting accommodation.

Although some of the approaches mentioned may have their own inherent design, logic, and momentum, it is important that they be complementary to each other, consistent, and sustained, and that the linkages between them be understood.

Frameworks for Sustainable Peace

Contemporaneous successes and failures suggest that there are a number of prerequisites for initiating the prenegotiation stage, attaining viable comprehensive peace settlements, and embedding mechanisms and attitudes so as to sustain and develop such settlements over an indefinite period.

Understanding root causes. It is abundantly apparent from recent experiences in Somalia, the former Yugoslavia, Sri Lanka, and elsewhere that there is a need for a clear conceptual and theoretical understanding of the root causes and the sources of intractability of a given conflict.

Ownership of the peace process. The second principle for ensuring sustainability must be the empowerment of local actors as the primary architects, owners, and long-term stakeholders in the peace process. Imposed settlements that do not involve representatives of the majority who favor a peaceful solution and that gloss over the root causes of conflict are likely to simply postpone further confrontations.

Identifying all the actors. Accurate identification must be made of all significant actors—the visible and articulate elites as well as the less visible, less articulate, but still influential opinion shapers and leaders. In situations of violent conflict, it is imperative that nonmilitary actors be fully involved in the process. Exclusive reliance on highly visible political or military elites has proved disastrous in the former Yugoslavia, Somalia, and Sri Lanka, to give only three examples.

Identifying facilitators. Accurate identification must also be made of who has the background knowledge, as well as analytic and mediation skills, to make a positive contribution in the design of a particular peace process.

Setting a realistic timetable. Another crucial element of a peacebuilding design should be an understanding of the stages of conflict resolution and of the need for realistic timetables for accomplishing such phases as the identification of root causes and significant actors, through cease-fires, to the elaboration of mechanisms of political and social accommodation. Those involved in designing the peace process must also devote an adequate amount of their time to the process.

Sustaining the effort. A comprehensive approach also requires from sponsors a sustained commitment to adequate investment of financial resources and patience, and a complementarity of efforts and resources.

Evaluating success and failure. Another key element of any peacebuilding design should be a process for evaluating whether the main interests of the parties are being addressed, the precedents and principles used in searching for a solution and their usefulness, the obstacles encountered, factors that led to progress, alternatives and missed opportunities, coordination with other peacemaking activities, and lessons to be learned from the process. Failures must be reported on and "institutional memories" developed so that practitioners can learn from experience.

Strategic constituencies. Strategic constituencies must be identified if peace processes are to be sustained over time. Such discrete and interlinked networks could include the media, human rights and humanitarian institutions, religious institutions, independent scholars, former members of the military, members of the business community, intergovernmental and governmental officials, and donors. To maximize their impact, various constituencies can form strategic alliances focused on a particular conflict, aspects of violent conflict, or the overall goal of prevention. One of the principal aims of these strategic groups should be to help cultivate the political will necessary for peacebuilding. But also of crucial importance is their role in directly influencing the prenegotiation and negotiation stages and helping to form and sustain the linkages between parties to conflict, NGOs, and the intergovernmental community, and between strata within the conflicting societies.

CONCLUSION

In dealing with multifaceted, protracted internal conflicts such as Sri Lanka's, there is a need to draw on all the relevant resources available, particularly those found within the region of conflict, and to establish positive and purposeful linkages between them. This implies the development of forums, systems, and networks; an analysis of the root causes of conflicts; identification of all the principal actors and of which ones are best suited to intervene effectively; an understanding of conflict dynamics; a recognition of windows of opportunity for intervention; and a division of labor so that duplication of effort is avoided. In the latter case, it is essential to have a precise understanding of the comparative advantages of the relevant bodies, organizations, or individuals, and of the areas of specialization of those who are best suited to enter into mediation, negotiation, and long-term transformation of the conflict.

External and internal input into peacebuilding designs should be combined with particular strategies for particular conflicts, as each conflict situation should dictate how the process is designed. However flexible the responses, the goal remains the same—not just to get to "yes" but also to invent in each specific case a strategy that fosters "sustainable reconciliation" (Lederach, 1994b) through the development of multifaceted and multisectoral approaches, mechanisms, institutions, and attitudes that are rooted in accountability to citizens and that maintain indefinitely the momentum of peace.

REFERENCES

Azar, E. (1986). "Management of Protracted Social Conflict in the Third World." Paper presented at the Fourth ICES Annual Lecture, Columbia University. Mimeograph, Center for International Development and Conflict Management, University of Maryland.

Azar, E., and Burton, J., eds. (1986). *International Conflict Resolution: Theory and Practice*. Brighton, Sussex: Wheatsheaf Books.

Brogan, P. (1992). *World Conflicts: Why and Where They Are Happening*. London: Bloomsbury.

Burton, J. W. (1986). "The History of International Conflict Resolution." In Azar and Burton, *International Conflict Resolution*.

Crossette, B. (1993). *India: Facing the Twenty-First Century*. Bloomington: Indiana University Press.

De Silva, M., and Cowper, R. (1993). "New Delhi Has Score to Settle." *Financial Times*, October 27.

Hill, B. J. (1982). "An Analysis of Conflict Resolution Techniques: From Problem-Solving Workshop to Theory." *Journal of Conflict Resolution* 26, 1: 109–138.

Hoffman, M. (1992). "Third-Party Mediation and Conflict Resolution in the Post–Cold War World." In J. Baylis and N. J. Rengger, eds., *Dilemmas of World Politics*. Oxford: Oxford University Press.

Kramer, J. (1993). "A Public Peace Process." *Timeline,* September/October, 8–11.

Lederach, J. P. (1994a). "Conflict Transformation in Protracted Internal Conflicts: The Case for a Comprehensive Framework." In K. Rupesinghe, ed., *Conflict Transformation*. London: Macmillan.

Lederach, J. P. (1994b). *Building Peace: Sustainable Reconciliation in Divided Societies.* Tokyo: United Nations University.

Muni, S. D. (1993). *Pangs of Proximity: India and Sri Lanka's Ethnic Crisis*. London: Oslo/Sage.

Northrup, T. A. (1989). "The Dynamic of Identity in Personal and Social Conflict." In L. Kriesberg, T. A. Northrup, and S. J. Thorson, eds., *Intractable Conflicts and Their Transformation*. Syracuse: Syracuse University Press.

Rupesinghe, K. (1992). "The Disappearing Boundaries Between Internal and External Conflicts." In K. Rupesinghe, ed., *Internal Conflict and Governance*. London: Macmillan, 1–26.

Rupesinghe, K., and Verstappen, B. (1989). *Ethnic Conflict and Human Rights in Sri Lanka: An Annotated Bibliography*. London: Hans Zell.

Rupesinghe, K., Verstappen, B., and Philips, A. S. *Ethnic Conflict and Human Rights in Sri Lanka: An Annotated Bibliography. Vol. 2. 1989–1992*. London: Hans Zell.

CHAPTER EIGHT

The Yugoslavian Conflict, European Mediation, and the Contingency Model: A Critical Perspective

Keith Webb with Vassiliki Koutrakou and Mike Walters

It is the aim of this chapter to engage in a friendly debate with Fisher and Keashly. Their stimulating article (Fisher and Keashly, 1991) restates the contingency model of mediation in a precise, accessible, and plausible manner. The argument here, however, is not that they are wrong, but that the model they present oversimplifies real-world situations in such a way as to require considerable modification of their conclusions. This oversimplification may be attributable in part to the origins of much early work on the contingency approach, which came from a psychological or social-psychological perspective, with the substantive roots in industrial and organizational conflict resolution. The argument will be made, and demonstrated by reference to the conflicts in the former Yugoslavia, that international and sometimes interethnic strife is very different, and that what may be true in one context may require considerable modification in another.

This argument does not mean, however, that there are no generic features in conflict and that insights generated in one context, situation, or case cannot be meaningful in another. If this were not so, social science as a basis for social action would be a dubious activity.[1] In order to act successfully in the world, it is necessary to predict outcomes; there are few social actions of any consequence at any level that do not have as an important component an element of expectation about the future. Such an expectation may be based on a number of sources—such as other actors' motives, beliefs in rationality, or a knowledge of how others perceive the world—but in social science it will often derive from a comparison with examples of what has happened before. The adequacy of an expectation thus derived will depend on a number of factors. First, it will involve an interpretation of past events; that is, a theoretical construal of the past. Such construals may be erroneous as a consequence of measurement problems or may be rooted in radically different theoretical outlooks; in either case, error may become magnified with the passage of time (Nicholson, 1992; Webb, 1992). Here I will maintain that Fisher and Keashly, while drawing attention to important elements of the intervention process, simplify in regard to the implications of those elements.

Second, the capacity to generalize from past events as a guide to action—that is, to predict—requires that the future event be classified or categorized as in some sense "the same" as past events. In a nontrivial sense, however, few macropolitical events are "the same" to the extent that we can overlook the strong likelihood of variance. Although we may identify something as a revolution, a war, or capitalism, it will not conform to any similarly identified phenomena sufficiently to permit prediction. Hence it is not possible to approach any form of social engineering—which third-party intervention essentially constitutes—in a formulaic manner. The intervenor, whether a private individual, the Secretary-General of the United Nations, or a state, though perhaps guided by principles must always struggle to remain attuned to the situation. Particularly in an intense and complex conflict such as that in the former Yugoslavia, the situation is in constant flux and intervention strategies must be maximally flexible. To argue that there is a "right" kind of strategy for particular conditions of conflict assumes a degree of stasis that is rarely found. For example, in much international and interethnic conflict parties are not wholly unified and homogeneous—a condition that can vary greatly in response to battlefield success or failure—so that to typify a conflict as being at a particular stage or level is frequently to overlook the range of variation within groups.

THE CONTINGENCY APPROACH TO MEDIATION

Fisher and Keashly (1991), developing the ideas of previous contributions (Fisher, 1972, 1986; Glasl, 1982; Prein, 1984; Sheppard, 1984), argue that the type of third-party intervention should match the characteristics of the conflict. They make a strong distinction between types of intervention, and particularly between mediation and consultation in terms of the functions performed by the intermediary. They suggest that the distinction there is "clear-cut" and that there has been an "unfortunate blurring of the boundaries." Although the distinction between mediation and consultation is primarily functional, it is also clear that these functions are performed by different kinds of bodies. Following Wright (1965), they maintain that conflict, a dynamic process, can be broken down into stages—discussion, polarization, segregation, and destruction—and that between these stages there is variation in communication, perception, trust, issues, and conflict-management techniques. Congruent with the different stages are different mixes of subjective and objective elements of the conflict, with subjective factors such as misperception and miscommunication becoming more salient as the conflict develops. Fisher and Keashly note that all approaches to conflict are limited and that particular approaches are relevant to particular stages, concluding that "it is not surprising that frustration and failure are often the result." There is a need, therefore, to sequence and coordinate the intervention strategies. They suggest that the failure of much mediation is a consequence of inappropriate interventions.

My contention here is that at important points this optimistic thesis does not match the reality of international and interethnic conflict. For example, is the functional differentiation of intervention strategies as clear-cut as is suggested? And can complex conflict situations be adequately characterized by the four stages that Fisher and Keashly propose? Moreover, the distinction between subjective and objective factors of a conflict seems questionable; from whose point of view are these factors objective or subjective? Finally, the political feasibility of sequencing and coordinating intervention is doubtful; this entails assumptions about the nature of the international system that are difficult to justify.

BACKGROUND TO THE CONFLICT IN THE FORMER YUGOSLAVIA

Yugoslavia became a state only in 1918, and was "a new country of old peoples" (Ramet, 1992:xv). The origins of the Yugoslavian conflict lie deep in a turbulent, often violent past. As a result of the Versailles settlement, the different territories were merged into a single state and became a unified kingdom. Nevertheless, interwar relations, particularly between the Serbs and Croats, were often marked by violence. During the Second World War the kingdom was conquered by Germany and partitioned, with Croatia being given the status of an independent state. It was a brutal state, in which hundreds of thousands of Serbs were killed by the Ustache as mass conversion to Catholicism was attempted. At the end of the war, Tito's Partisans wreaked vengeance by killing hundreds of thousands of Croats. Tito became a liberator and hero in the eyes of many Yugoslavs, and with some help from the Red Army he established a communist state. Here communism was not simply imposed by the USSR, as in many East European states, but a home-grown product, domestically legitimated and not dependent for its survival on the Red Army. Indeed, though he initially held many Stalinist ideas, soon after coming to power Tito broke with Stalin.

Tito ruled until May 1980, and it was with his death that the Yugoslavian state gradually began to unravel. Although Tito suppressed dissidence, sometimes with considerable force, he also accorded a degree of local and regional autonomy (Sword, 1991:159–160). Six "ethnic" republics were established that had considerable autonomy, though in other cases peoples were so ethnically intermingled that such divisions were not possible. But even in the ethnic republics there was heterogeneity; for example, 14 percent of the population of Croatia was ethnically Serbian, and 17 percent of the population of Macedonia ethnically Albanian. In the postwar years, however, ethnic and religious tensions were managed by the overarching rule of the Party, through decentralization, and by Tito in his capacity as arbiter. Nevertheless, Tito bequeathed his successors a complex and unworkable constitution that was designed for federalism in a one-party state, so that elites in different states began to make demands that could only be satisfied by seriously weakening the center.

With Tito's death the demands for greater autonomy—fueled by serious economic decline and competition between the republics—increased. Tito left Yugoslavia with a foreign debt of $19 billion that continued to grow after his death. By 1986, the standard of living had fallen by a third and inflation was approaching 100 percent. Throughout that decade competition spurred by intense economic frictions mounted between the republics, and by 1991 an internal trade war broke out when Serbia banned imports from Slovenia and nationalized stores, factories, and gas stations belonging to Croatian firms. Slovenia and Croatia countered by imposing taxes on Serb properties and blocking deliveries to Serbian oil refineries. The decade also saw the erosion of the authority of the ruling party, the League of Communists in Yugoslavia (LCY), as the political agenda became framed in terms of centralization versus federalism, liberalism versus conservatism, and was increasingly dominated by economic concerns that often found nationalist expression. In 1987, the Serbian nationalist Slobodan Milosevic came to power and pursued a vigorous centralist program that stimulated resistance from other republics in the form of increased pressure for a confederal arrangement. In 1990, Franjo Tudjman was elected in Croatia, and in reviving Ustache symbols he reawakened memories of past atrocities. In response, Serbia threatened to occupy Serb areas of other republics and to defend its ethnic brethren if confederation went forward.

By 1989, Slovenia was threatening to declare independence and there were rumblings of discontent from the Serbs in Croatia; meanwhile the influence of the LCY waned even further with the election of noncommunist parliaments in Slovenia and Croatia and the general delegitimization of communism throughout Eastern Europe. An arms buildup had begun in several of the republics and ethnic killings had taken place, particularly in the border areas between Serbia and Croatia, while in Slovenia federal positions had been attacked. In 1991, Slovenia and Croatia declared independence. In an attempt to draw into the conflict the Serbian-dominated federal army, Croatian Serbs began a guerrilla campaign, and the federal army indeed attacked Croatia. Thus the civil war finally broke out and was waged with a ferocity that had not been seen in Europe since the Second World War. Massacres of civilian populations, ethnic cleansing, rape as a political weapon, concentration camps, and other war crimes became the stuff of daily news; the Geneva Convention might never have been written. In 1992, the war spread to other republics; particularly to Bosnia-Herzegovina, where Serbs rebelled against a vote by Muslims and Croats to secede from a Serbian-dominated rump Yugoslavia, thus adding a Muslim element to the Serb-Croat conflict.

The civil war in the former Yugoslavia is marked by three elements that are relevant to the contingency model of intervention. First, because of the extreme intermingling of populations it is an irredentist conflict of a kind that is peculiarly complex. Irredentist conflicts always involve such intermingling, but in this case the dispersion of populations—particularly the Serbs, Croats, and now Muslims—has led to a localized war that is disaggregated into many fronts. There is no general, overarching situation for the parties; what is true of one locality may not be true of another. Hence, leaders at the communal level have trouble imposing their authority on local leaderships, and their efficacy as negotiating partners is limited at best.

Second, the war is marked by a kaleidoscopic shifting of alliances at both the national and local levels; the enemy of my enemy is my friend, but probably not for long. All parties are reacting to the practical exigencies of each moment in a situation of extreme violence and great uncertainty. This means that questions vital for the intervenor—"Who are the parties?" and "What are the relations between the parties?"—are constantly renewed on the agenda. For example, although the leaders of both the Croatian and the Bosnian Serbs were key actors, it is reasonable to assume that the real power lay with Milosevic. Who are the third parties that should be approached to intervene? It is clear from the large number of truces and cease-fires arranged by both the EC and the UN that republican leaderships of ethnic groups did not always have control of their forces.

Third, it must be recognized that intervention is not a neutral act (Mitchell, 1988); intervenors may genuinely desire peace (though that is not always the case) but will usually seek or accept the role of consultant or mediator for motives of their own. In international conflict (and the Yugoslavian conflict may now be defined as such), even though there may be attempts to coordinate intervention the interests of different states will mar the coherence of the activity. This is splendidly illustrated in Jabri's work on the Western Contact Group in Namibia (Jabri, 1988; 1990). These competing interests point to an important difference between industrial and organizational conflict on the one hand and international conflict on the other, namely, that in the latter the normative structure of the conflict is much weaker and less defined. In an industrial conflict, there are usually the ultimate limitations of domestic law to constrain the more extreme expressions of conflict; in international conflicts, and particularly in cases of civil war, however, such normative constraints are often abandoned. Indeed, at least part of the reason for the extremity of violence is that the norms of governance are themselves under contention. The international environment is not wholly anarchic, but the application of norms is certainly weaker than in the domestic environment.

AN OVERVIEW OF MEDIATION IN THE FORMER YUGOSLAVIA[2]

Third-party intervention in the former Yugoslavia has been an exercise in frustration. Rather than improving, the situation has constantly deteriorated through a widening of the conflict. During the post-Tito era before violence became extensive, third-party intervention was used as part of the normal diplomatic and economic intercourse. For example, because of the grave economic situation, financial institutions became involved in the relations between the republics. Once serious conflicts began, mediation on the ground in operational situations was often conducted by aid agencies, peacekeepers or monitors, troops attempting to get medical and food supplies through, and people dealing with the enormous problem of refugees. Indeed, in this conflict the creation of refugees was often a primary aim of the combatants. In addition, many groups were involved in second-track diplomacy, such as the Quakers or the U.K. Green Party, though as always they received much less reportage than the first-track exponents.

As the situation worsened, Serbia—the largest single unit—sought to maintain the federation, whereas Croatia and Slovenia in particular but also Kosovo, where there was strong anti-Serb feeling, desired a much looser confederation; and on June 25, 1991, both Slovenia and Croatia declared independence. Serbian insurgents in Croatia, supported by the largely Serbian federal army, then took up arms, and in Slovenia federal army units attempted to reverse the decision. From a military point of view, Slovenia was in a better position than Croatia, which is located between Slovenia and Serbia. The Slovenes had been building up their arms and were able to expel the federal forces. Croatia, however, with its long common border with Serbia and large indigenous Serbian population, was not able, when the Serbs invaded the militarily vulnerable Dalmatia, to resist so effectively.

With about one-third of Croatian territory controlled by the Serbs and some 400 fighters having been killed in the conflict, in September 1991 an EC-sponsored conference was held in The Hague. The EC was an appropriate third party since Yugoslavia, and later some of the republics, had aspirations to join it. This conference was chaired by Lord Carrington and attended by the leaders of Yugoslavia's six republics as well as several European foreign ministers; subsequently Carrington went to Yugoslavia and held discussions with both Milosevic and Tudjman. A moratorium was worked out on further moves toward independence by Croatia and Slovenia. Two committees were then formed to engage in separate discussions with the Croatians and the Serbians.

The EC mission was, however, beset with disagreement among the sponsors. Belgian foreign minister Mark Eyskens blamed Serbia for the war and, drawing on Belgium's temporary membership in the UN Security Council, tried to get the General Assembly to withdraw recognition of Yugoslavia; whereas from the vantage point of the EC presidency, Dutch foreign minister Hans van den Broek blamed Croatia. At the same time, Stipe Mesic, a Croat and head of the collective Yugoslavian presidency, called for a UN peacekeeping force to stop what he referred to as Serbia's aggressive war. Belgrade decried his attempt as unconstitutional. Serbia denied that it had any territorial ambitions, but also argued that if Croatia became independent the borders would have to be redrawn to bring under Serbian control those Croatian areas with large Serbian minorities. A succession of truces was worked out but proved ineffective, as did the presence of some 200 unarmed European monitors. Van den Broek proposed a lightly armed peacekeeping force and was supported by France and Italy, but Britain was cool to the idea and Germany refused to send any troops to Yugoslavia. Overall, then, European attempts to mediate in Yugoslavia were hampered by disagreements among the mediators; moreover, the parties themselves were adept at using the various meetings and conferences as high-visibility forums at which to urge their own causes.

In late September, the EC, though continuing with its mediation efforts, called on the UN to intervene; the Security Council members met informally in New York to consider the situation. Meanwhile, Italy and the Yugoslavian federal government appealed for a renewed EC mediation effort. Lord Carrington held talks with the Secretary-General's special envoy to Yugoslavia, Cyrus Vance, who then met with the leaders of the six republics. The basic impasse, however, remained: Croatia wanted independence, but within this framework could not allay the fears of its Serbian minority. The situation was not eased by the disagreement among the EC partners regarding recognition of Croatia, which was particularly important to Croatia as it sought international legitimation for its declaration of independence. Germany, however, recognized Croatia on December 19, reinforcing a view of many international observers that the bulk of the blame for the civil war lay with Serbia and its territorial ambitions.

The Hague conference was also hampered by the collapse of the various cease-fires. In Bosnia, the Croats and Muslims expressed apprehension that as Yugoslavia disintegrated Serbia would attempt to annex part of their territory, and in early October agreed to allow EC monitors into their territory in an effort to avoid becoming embroiled in the Serb-Croat war. Elsewhere, van den Broek brokered an agreement with the Croats that they would cease blockading the federal garrisons in return for withdrawal of federal forces from Croatia. The army, however, totally rejected the agreement. Here, as on numerous other occasions in both the Croatian and Bosnian conflicts, various actors in the conflict were able to act autonomously, but the leadership did not have control over the followers.

With the EC mediation faltering and the UN becoming more involved, still another international actor entered the arena—Soviet President Mikhail Gorbachev. With his reputation as a peacemaker and supported by historical Slavic ties with Serbia, Gorbachev believed that he could exert influence, particularly on the Serbs, where others had failed. He held separate meetings in Moscow with Tudjman and Milosevic, in which both pledged to end the fighting.

Yet little changed on the ground; the fighting continued. The EC Hague conference came up with a formula to accord special status to the minority groups in Croatia. Branco Kostic, federal vice president, said this status would have to be guaranteed by the EC, the UN, and the Conference on Security and Cooperation in Europe (CSCE). But the Serbian president—alone among Yugoslavia's six regional leaders, and despite having successfully introduced clauses to the effect that Serbian areas in Croatia would be demilitarized—later rejected the plan.

Milosevic's rejection of the peace plan left the Serbs isolated, with international opinion moving toward the position that force was needed in the mediation. Lord Carrington said that he doubted the economic sanctions threatened by the EC would work, but warned that the EC might well intervene militarily. The Serbian parliament responded by rejecting the peace plan, but also proposed amendments that would accord international control over the Serbian regions in Croatia while a vote was organized to determine which state the Croatian Serbs wanted to live in. After further interventions by Vance on behalf of the UN and further rejections of the peace plan by Milosevic, the EC finally imposed economic sanctions against Yugoslavia and was joined by the United States. Meanwhile, the EC was reconsidering a peacekeeping force. Also at this time, the first UN-brokered cease-fire came into effect after thirteen previous EC-brokered cease-fires had failed.

The EC further said that from January 15, 1992, it would recognize as states any of the Yugoslavian republics; this move had been anticipated by Germany's recognition of Croatia. Serbia responded that it would recognize Serb territories in both Croatia and Bosnia-Herzegovina, which would constitute a virtual annexation of large tracts of land. Croatian leaders then said that Croatian authority would be reestablished in all areas held by Serbs. The new UN President, Boutros-Ghali, responded by shelving the idea of a peacekeeping force. The EC and the UN began attempting to coordinate their mediatory activities, as Boutros-Ghali met with EC leaders in Paris and London. It was not until October of that year that a UN-brokered agreement led to the withdrawal of Serbian forces from Croatia.

At the same time as the recognition of the republics came into effect, the Bosnian Serbs were declaring themselves autonomous. It now seemed that what had happened in Croatia was likely to occur in Bosnia, and to prevent this the ethnic leaders in Bosnia agreed to a conference. This led to a referendum in which the majority of Bosnians voted for independence. In a meeting in Brussels, agreement was reached on a confederal Bosnia, but the Serbs requested more time to consult their constituency. In late March 1992, the Bosnian Serbs threatened to declare their own independence if Bosnia were recognized before institutional reforms were completed; on April 5 the EC did recognize Bosnia-Herzegovina as an independent state, and the following week the UN sent 100 military observers to monitor the situation. The fighting, however, became a three-way affair involving the Serbs, Croats, and Muslims, and was accompanied by a food shortage and major refugee problems. Though acting out of the best humanitarian motives, the UN was accused by some of abetting the aggressive designs of the parties.

By July, there were several groupings of nations involved in the Bosnian situation. While the UN was involved in mediation and the succor of civilians—including sending troops to secure the Sarajevo airport to ensure that food and medical supplies could be distributed—it also imposed wide-ranging sanctions on Serbia and Montenegro. Also that month the CSCE suspended Yugoslavia's membership and by December sent its representative, Swedish foreign minister Margaretha af Ugglas, to Belgrade to warn the Serb and Yugoslav leadership, which it held responsible for the war, that tougher sanctions would be imposed if the ethnic cleansing continued. However, the CSCE consistently rejected Bosnian Muslim calls for military intervention and backed efforts for a political solution. The Western European Union agreed to dispatch ships to monitor the sanctions, an operation that the United States and its NATO allies agreed to support. Later the Chinese (twice), as well as Greek, Italian, and Portuguese diplomats would also become involved. And finally, the EC was still active, with Lord Carrington engaging in shuttle diplomacy to arrange a Bosnian peace conference. But the London conference held in late August was not attended by the presidents of either Serbia or Montenegro, and the Bosnian Muslim president Alija Izetbegovic followed suit by declaring that he would not meet with the leaders of the Bosnian Serbs or Croats. Thus the conference ended in failure, and Lord Carrington resigned, to be replaced by Lord Owen.

Between the gestation of the Bosnian war and its evolvement into full-blown horrors, a shift occurred in goals. In the early stages, it was the Serbs who spoke of autonomy, and for a time it looked as if a Croatia-type war would be avoided through creation of a very loose institutional structure. This possibility, however, was damaged by the early recognition of Bosnia. Increasingly the orientations of all the parties, and particularly of the Croats and Muslims, who had the most to accomplish, moved away from ideas of loose unity and toward separation, the logic being that when the settlement finally came, control of territory and ethnic homogeneity would be crucial. Hence what had been a two-sided struggle, pitting mainly the Croats and Muslims against the Serbs, became in September 1992 a three-way struggle as the Croat forces sought to eject their erstwhile allies from the area around Sarajevo. Splits also occurred within the Serbian camp, first with respect to the international control of heavy artillery, to which the leadership agreed but with which there was again no military compliance, and second with respect to the integrity of Bosnia's borders. Milan Panic, who had been elected prime minister of Yugoslavia in July of that year, agreed that existing borders would be respected although the Bosnian Serbs rejected the existing borders.

At this stage, with the Bosnian Serbs controlling most of the major airfields, the United States proposed and the EC agreed to a no-fly zone over Bosnia. This led Bosnian Serb leader Radovan Karadzic to threaten to pull out of the Geneva talks and later to transfer his airforce to Serbia. At this point, Panic went to Beijing for talks with two Chinese leaders on possibly ending the war in Bosnia. Meanwhile, amid arguments concerning international control of artillery, about whether Serbia, as the rump of the Yugoslav federation, should inherit the UN seat, and about the deepening of the sanctions, the London conference reconvened in Geneva. In addition to the steering committee headed by Owen and Vance, there were five working groups covering confidence-building measures, economic questions, humanitarian affairs, minorities, and the division of former Yugoslavian assets. Subsequently, Owen and Vance went to consult with the Greek prime minister and Bosnia's Muslim president went for talks in Pakistan. Although denying that he was seeking arms, Izetbegovic was attempting to mobilize international Muslim support for the Serbian Muslims. Support later materialized from the Organization of Islamic Conference (OIC), which sought to pressure the UN for military intervention beyond peacekeeping and to rescind the ban on arms purchases by the Muslims. This marked the second time the OIC had made such a request. The Muslims were at this time under severe pressure from the Serbs, especially in Sarajevo, and short of weapons with which to resist them.

By the end of October 1992, the UN and EC mediators had devised a peace plan that would divide Bosnia into a number of regions, each with a high degree of autonomy. The guiding idea was that there would be decentralization of power but not along ethnic lines. This arrangement was acceptable to the Bosnian Muslims at that time, but not to the Bosnian Croats or Serbs. Tudjman manifested his support for the Bosnian Croats by advising the Bosnian Muslims to accept the ethnic partitioning of Bosnia. Karadzic presented a peace plan that basically ratified the battlefield territorial acquisitions. At this stage the Bosnian Serbs, constituting about one-third of the population, held about 70 percent of Bosnian territory and were supported by the Croats, who were then implicitly (and later overtly) allied with them against the Muslims; thus, acceptance of ethnic partitioning would have left the Muslims in a weak and untenable position. Most of the remaining territory was in Bosnian Croat hands, and Serbia was trying to get sanctions imposed on Croatia, claiming that it was supporting the Bosnian Croats.

At the continuing Geneva peace conference in early 1993, Owen and Vance unveiled a new ten-point plan. Bosnia was to be divided into ten regions, three for each of the warring factions and one, Sarajevo, mixed. The Croats were pleased with the plan since it gave them more territory than they had at that time; the Serbs were displeased since they would lose some territory and not obtain the sovereignty they desired; and the Muslims were the real losers, since a great deal of the territory they had possessed before the war would be relinquished. The Bosnian Serb leader initially rejected the plan, but under pressure from Milosevic he dropped the demand for a separate Bosnian Serb state. Just as in Croatia, Milosevic, sensing that the Serbs in Bosnia had gotten most of what they wanted, urged them toward a peace settlement.

However, although both the Croats and the Muslims signed the agreement, it was not ratified by the Bosnian Serb "parliament." Further negotiations were then described as futile by Izetbegovic, who also rejected a further peace plan proposed by the United States (though he was later to withdraw his rejection in the light of the partition proposals that emerged in June). The U.S. proposals were also rejected by the Bosnian Serbs on the ground that the peacekeeping and monitoring provisions would violate the future sovereignty of the state of Bosnian Serbia.

With the collapse of the Geneva proposals and the rejection of the U.S. plan, yet another attempt at mediation was made by Lord Owen and Thorvald Stoltenberg, who had replaced Vance as the UN mediator. The Owen-Stoltenberg plan basically accepted the political, military, and physical reality of the situation and proposed a three-way partition of Bosnia. Each group would obtain an ethnic state, initially joined in a weak confederation but with the Bosnian Croats and Serbs free to hold a plebiscite to decide whether they would join Croatia and Serbia. The Muslims were parceled out into four separate landlocked territories with complicated arrangements for access to the sea and other amenities. Sarejevo would be demilitarized and administered for two years by the UN.

The warring parties' reaction to these proposals was weak and non-committal. By autumn, the international impetus was showing signs of fatigue and the media and public opinion had begun turning to other international issues, so that the Bosnian peace process stagnated for several months. It was only on November 21, 1993, with a hard winter looming for the hundreds of thousands of displaced persons in former Yugoslavia and aid supplies already being constantly interrupted, that the French and German governments launched a new joint initiative to revive the Geneva talks.

ASSESSING THE UTILITY OF THE CONTINGENCY APPROACH

The Balance of Subjective and Objective Factors

In intense conflict of any duration, subjective factors will increase. The peacemaking process is thus not a mere reversal of the warmaking process, since warmaking creates factors that were not there, or not in such intensity, before the war. Such factors are emotions of hatred and revenge, the group adoption or heightening of a common definition and history of the situation, the demand for security at a higher level, and the intensification of moral justification for action. Coser (1956) stresses, in such situations, the "unrealistic" aspects of conflict; Simmel (1955) notes the role of hostility as a psychological reinforcement. Many of the dynamic changes noted by Fisher and Keashly as typical in conflict as it moves from one stage to another can be observed in the Yugoslavian situation. For example, often parties would not meet or talk to one another or would deny the utility of any such contact. But sometimes this refusal was not the expression of a psychological state but was in itself a strategic part of the negotiating process.

Furthermore, according to Fisher and Keashly objective interests are related to resource scarcity and subjective elements to "misperception, miscommunication, or the differential valuing of objective interests" (p. 34), with the latter becoming more important as the conflict escalates. I contend, however, that while there were unrealistic elements in the conflict in Coser's sense, the level of communication between the parties was at all times extremely high, particularly in the case of the respective leaderships. This high level of communication was in part a result of the density and intensity of the mediation process. Positions hardened and also changed in response to the battlefield situation or international pressure, but there was rarely evidence that any one party was not acutely aware of the positions and demands of the others. It is true that there was movement and change in valuing as a function of the conflict—though it should also be noted that conflict is sometimes *about* differential valuing—but this change was a reflection of the parties' "real" interests as they perceived them. For the Croats in Bosnia to move from acceptance of an independent Bosnia to acceptance of partition did not involve a change in subjective factors, but rather a recognition and response to the perceived realities of the situation.

The Levels of Conflict and the Mediation Process

Although the contingency model is a useful guide to conflict analysis, care should be taken not to apply it too rigidly. Fisher and Keashly acknowledge this point when they note that conflict is a dynamic process. In the Yugoslavian conflict, the shifting of positions was sometimes very rapid and what might be true at one level of the conflict (such as the leadership level) was frequently not true at others (such as subleadership levels). Similarly, in a "rolling conflict" of this sort the degree of contagion is high and the kind and level of conflict are not the same for all parties at any one time. Even where direct communication ceased between the parties—as predicted by the Fisher and Keashly model—it was not so much a result of the level of conflict per se as a tactical ploy in the negotiating process. Again, although there was (and is) hatred between the parties, it is clear that this hatred did not rule them out as negotiating partners either within the mediation process or when a shift in alliance was demanded by the strategic situation. Moreover, in the negotiating process levels of violence do not necessarily indicate the level of conflict; as van der Merwe (1988) points out, it is often the case that the level of violence escalates before negotiation merely to strengthen the negotiating position; a bomb, in this context, can be a message. What this combination of strategic and psychological levels, ambiguity, complexity of motives, and so on implies for the mediation process is that rather than restricting it to particular kinds of intervention, care should be taken to maintain all kinds of intervention at all times.

The Sequencing and Coordination of Third-Party Intervention

Fisher and Keashly suggest that insofar as there are particular strategies of intervention suitable for different levels of conflict, intervention should be coordinated so that the appropriate strategy is used at the right time. The mediation in former Yugoslavia has indeed been atypical of international third-party interventions in that it has been far more coordinated than in many other such situations, largely because of the EC's proximity to the conflict and the increased authority and activity of the UN since the end of the Cold War. Even in this case, however, the impossibility of coordinating the activity of states with different interests in the conflict has emerged clearly and sometimes dramatically. States may intervene for a number of reasons, such as the perception of a role, the defense of material interests, the acquisition of prestige, for humanitarian considerations, on behalf of one or more of the participants, or for reasons of national security. But whatever the particular motives of a state, the nature of the international system is such that excluding interventions (which sometimes itself motivates an intervention) is often impossible, so that the coordination of mediatory activity is limited.

The largely chimerical nature of sequencing and coordination in international mediation is attributable to the nature of the international system itself, which although not wholly unordered lacks any overarching authority and hence has anarchic characteristics. To sequence and coordinate implies a degree of control over the activities of numerous actors that is simply unattainable in the international system. A brief look at some of the actors' interests and interventions in the Yugoslavian conflict should bear this out.

Germany has had religious and political ties with Croatia ever since the time of the Austro-Hungarian Empire, as well as evolving economic interests and a potential for political influence in the East European region. Despite Germany's calls for recognition of Croatia and Slovenia after they declared independence in June 1991, the EC maintained caution regarding the disintegration of Yugoslavia and declared that it would only consider recognizing the breakaway republics if a negotiated settlement to the conflict were reached. On December 17, 1991, the EC foreign ministers agreed to recognize on January 15, 1992, any Yugoslavian republic that met a series of conditions, including human rights guarantees for minorities within its borders.[3] Germany, however, went ahead and recognized Croatia and Slovenia immediately, claiming that it had received satisfactory assurances from the two republics concerning the fulfillment of the conditions. Thus Germany deliberately defied the EC's attempt to present a common front.

Because of their religious affiliation with the Bosnian Muslims, Turkey and the Arab world have pledged their total support to Izetbegovic and have consistently tried to induce clandestine international intervention in the Bosnian crisis. Turkey in particular has unsuccessfully lobbied its Western allies for limited military intervention to end the Serbian attacks on the Muslims in Bosnia. The OIC has repeatedly attempted to pressure the Security Council to intervene militarily to stop the fighting in Bosnia, lift the arms embargo, and allow the Muslims to arm themselves; the OIC has even suggested it might consider intervening to support the Bosnian Muslims unilaterally, regardless of the UN embargo. Indeed, Turkey, Iran, and several Arab countries are alleged to have been secretly sending Mujahedeen fighters as well as arms and resources to the Bosnian Muslims throughout the conflict, although none of these countries has as yet openly defied the UN embargo.

Russia has traditional ties with Serbia, partly stemming from its common ground of Orthodox Christian religion and Slavic culture, and has had an alliance with Serbia since before the seventy-year period of Soviet domination of the Eastern bloc. With its present weak political position and substantial economic dependence on the United States and Western Europe, Russia has unreservedly backed the EC- and UN-led peace process and the specific proposals made by the official mediators. Yet although it has not justified Serbian expansion and has condemned atrocities, Russia has steadily, albeit cautiously, voiced its support for Serbian positions. This support has usually been expressed in separate consultations between Russian officials (including Gorbachev) and representatives of the former Yugoslavian republics, heads of Arab organizations such as the OIC, international mediators, and representatives of other permanent members of the Security Council such as the United States and China. Foreign Minister Andrei Kozyrev has staunchly warned against U.S. and NATO suggestions of military intervention in Bosnia. When the negotiations on the Vance-Owen peace plan broke down in January 1993 amid continued fierce fighting, he warded off proposals for the imposition of tougher sanctions on Serbia or the lifting of the arms embargo. Moreover, Deputy Foreign Minister Vitaly Churkin advocated sanctions against Croatia as well, when by December 1992 it became obvious that Croats were equally responsible for instigating cease-fire breakdowns and unwarranted expansionist attacks in Bosnia. Although Russia has generally gone along with U.S. and European demands for sanctions against Serbia, both Russia and the Ukraine are alleged to have occasionally and indirectly given Serbia military supplies, whether for economic or ideological reasons. Indeed, during 1993 pressures on Yeltsin's government from hard-liners mounted as retired Russian generals appeared on television, trying to mobilize public opinion in favor of what they perceived as Russia's moral and military duty to its old ally Serbia, and Russian volunteers started coming to the aid of Serb fighters. Recently, as moderates vie for power with hard-liners in Russia, there have been indications of a pro-Serbian shift. Russia's role in any Security Council vote is, of course, key, since as one of the five permanent members it has the power of veto, the use of which it has not ruled out. Thus, this war near the geographical heart of Europe could conceivably spark the first crisis between Washington and Moscow since the collapse of communism.

It was in late 1992 that the United States first started pressing for some form of military intervention in Bosnia. The United States has no express interests in Yugoslavia, but as the sole big power remaining in the international arena it was expected to adopt a stance toward the crisis.

The Clinton administration was pressured by both international and regional organizations and lobbies to formulate a decisive policy on the issues involved. The U.S. proposals for a no-fly zone encountered some opposition but were eventually adopted and enforced by the Security Council. At that stage, British Foreign Secretary Douglas Hurd favored a tough stance toward Serbia as well, and did not exclude military intervention. His European counterparts also favored sanctions, albeit to varying degrees, but still concentrated on humanitarian aid and on the mediation process, which began in 1991 with Lord Carrington's involvement in the Croatian issue and continued in 1992 with a succession of mediators in the Bosnian crisis.

Beginning in December 1992, however, the United States increasingly expressed disillusionment with the peacemaking efforts up to that point, and began to speak of arming the Muslims and/or intervening militarily with U.S.-led air raids. Leaving aside the question of the appropriateness of these measures, the timing was very unfortunate, as for the first time since the conflict had begun some concrete proposals, encapsulated by the Vance-Owen ten-point plan, were being placed on the table and the opposing sides were showing an interest in compromise. It is worth noting that the United States has not participated in the UN's peacekeeping operations in Yugoslavia. It is reluctant to relinquish control of U.S. troops to UN (non-U.S.) commanders, and although promoting the idea of military intervention, Secretary of State Warren Christopher only spoke of air raids and denied having contemplated the use of ground forces. His lukewarm support for the negotiating process and skepticism, verging on hostility, toward the Vance-Owen plan were revealed by his statements that some "tough and searching questions" had to be asked about "the fairness and feasibility" of the peace plan. The Clinton administration indeed felt that the plan gave the Serbs too much, thus rewarding aggression, and took a decidedly pro-Muslim stance.

With the failure of the talks in Geneva and then in New York in January 1993, U.S. pressure only intensified, despite pleas by Boutros-Ghali to give political means and the peace plan a chance and despite Lord Owen's criticism that the United States was effectively sabotaging the peace process. Owen suggested that U.S. troops participate as a possible NATO contingent within the UN peacekeeping effort, an idea that was predictably rejected by the United States, which strongly feared becoming caught in another Vietnam-like quagmire. Meanwhile, representatives of EC countries such as Danish Foreign Minister Niels Helveg Petersen and German Foreign Minister Klaus Kinkel urged President Clinton to back the UN-EC-brokered peace process. The United States dismissed the accusations of undermining the peace process, but also gradually bowed to West European and Russian opposition. In the meantime, however, its stance had so frustrated the mediators, angered the Serbs, and encouraged the Bosnian Muslims in their hope for greater military gains that a negotiated agreement became a good deal more remote.

Finally, Greece has been a traditional ally of Serbia and up to the time of the EC's recognition of the breakaway republics had campaigned for a rescue of the ideal of united Yugoslavia. It has also operated as a go-between with Serbia and the EC, trying unsuccesfully to moderate EC sanctions against Yugoslavia and also to make more palatable the EC demands to the Serb and Bosnian Serb leaderships. Partly because of the Greek government's mediating efforts, Milosevic realized that continuing Bosnian Serb defiance of the peace process was creating a more substantial economic liability for Serbia than were any further small territorial restraints, and together Milosevic and the Greeks influenced Bosnian Serb leader Karadjic to accept the mediators' proposals at least as a basis for negotiation. Greece, indeed, has vital geopolitical interests in the region; the Balkans are generally a sensitive area and Serbian support helps Greece to contain the perceived expansionist tendencies of the former Yugoslavian republic of Macedonia. Greece has vital economic interests in the region as well; the majority of its trade with Europe used to be conducted via Macedonia, and when the economic sanctions forced it to divert its trade to the longer and more expensive Italian route, Greece had to be compensated. Greece was, however, committed to the UN-EC-sponsored peace process and strongly opposed to suggestions of military intervention or the further fueling of the war by lifting the arms embargo.

This overview demonstrates that there is little possibility of coordinating mediation in complex international situations such as in the former Yugoslavia. If a day were ever to arrive when the UN had an overarching moral status, perhaps such coordination would be possible; but given the welter of conflicting interests among sovereign states, even then it seems unlikely. Indeed, it may well be that the growing interdependency in international relations will bring an increase in the complexity and number of separate interests involved and further diminish any possibility of control.

CONCLUSION

If it is to be useful at the level of international conflict, the contingency model of mediation must be considerably developed. In its present simple form, which was derived largely from domestic conflict, it is an inappropriate guide to mediatory action in the international arena. Excessively rigid and formulaic adherence to the model can even have deleterious consequences. For example, the perception that particular kinds of mediation are appropriate for particular stages of a conflict might prevent possibly beneficial actions from being taken had the mediation activity been perceived more flexibly. It is implicit in Fisher and Keashly's model that the failure rate of mediation is a function of the applied techniques of mediation, and that if mediation were done differently more favorable outcomes would be probable. This is an untested (and possibly untestable) proposition. In an area where we know so little about the effects of mediatory style, it makes far more sense at any particular stage of conflict to rule out no particular type of mediation.

NOTES

1. For an extended discussion of this point, see Eberwein, Girard, and Webb (1994).

2. Sources for this section include the Associated Press, BBC News, *The Economist,* European News, *German Brief, Les Echoes,* Reuters, TASS, *The Times* (London), the *Sunday Times* (London), the *Washington Post,* and *Keesing's Contemporary Archives.*

3. For an interesting discussion of the problems of European cooperation, see Salmon (1992).

REFERENCES

Coser, L. A. (1956). *The Functions of Social Conflict.* London: Routledge & Kegan Paul.

Eberwein, W. D., Girard, M., and Webb, K., eds. (1994). *Perspectives on Academics and Professionals in International Relations.* London: Francis Pinter.

Fisher, R. J. (1972). "Third Party Consultation: A Method for the Study and Resolution of Conflict." *Journal of Conflict Resolution* 16, 1: 67–94.

Fisher, R. J. (1986). "Third Party Consultation: A Problem Solving Approach for De-escalating International Conflict." In J. P. Maas and R. A. C. Stewart, eds., *Towards a World of Peace: People Create Alternatives.* Fiji: University of the South Pacific, 18–32.

Fisher, R. J., and Keashly, L. (1991). "The Potential Complementarity of Mediation and Consultation Within a Contingency Model of Third Party Consultation." *Journal of Peace Research* 28, 1: 29–42.

Glasl, F. (1982). "The Process of Conflict Escalation and Roles of Third Parties." In G. B. H. Bomers and R. B. Peterson, eds., *Conflict Management and Industrial Relations.* Boston: Kluwer-Nijhoff, 119–140.

Jabri, V. (1988). "The Western Contact Group as Intermediary in the Conflict Over Namibia." In C. R. Mitchell and K. Webb, eds., *New Approaches to International Mediation.* New York: Greenwood 102–131.

Jabri, V. (1990). *Mediating Conflict: Decision Making and Western Intervention in Namibia.* Manchester, U.K.: Manchester University Press.

Mitchell, C. R. (1988). "The Motives for Mediation." In Mitchell and Webb, *New Approaches,* 29–51.

Nicholson, M. (1992). "Prediction, Structures, and Chaos Theory in International Relations." *Kent Papers in Politics and International Relations,* no. 8. Kent, U.K.: University of Kent.

Prein, H. (1984). "A Contingency Approach for Conflict Resolution." *Group and Organization Studies* 9, 1: 81–102.
Ramet, S. P. (1992). *Nationalism and Federalism in Yugoslavia, 1962–1991*. Bloomington and Indianapolis: Indiana University Press.
Salmon, T. C. (1992). "Testing Times for European Political Cooperation: The Gulf and Yugoslavia, 1990–1992." *International Affairs* 68, 2: 233–253.
Sheppard, B. H. (1984). "Third Party Conflict Intervention: A Procedural Framework." *Research in Organizational Behaviour* 6: 141–190.
Simmel, G. (1955). *Conflict and the Web of Group Affiliations*. Glencoe, Ill.: Free Press.
Sword, K., ed. (1991). *The Times Guide to Eastern Europe: Inside the Other Europe*. London: Times Books.
van der Merwe, Hendrik W. (1988). "South African Initiatives: Contrasting Options in the Mediation Process." In Mitchell and Webb, *New Approaches,* 180–194.
Webb, K. (1992). "Prediction in International Relations: The Role of Power Interest and Trust." *Kent Papers in Politics and International Relations*, no. 11. Kent, U.K.: University of Kent.
Wright, Q. (1965). "The Escalation of International Conflicts." *Journal of Conflict Resolution* 9, 4: 434–449.

CHAPTER NINE

Environmental Mediation in International Relations

Deborah Shmueli and Ariella Vranesky

> Only within the moment of time represented by the present century has one species—man—acquired significant power to alter the nature of his world. . . . The most alarming of all man's assaults upon the environment is the contamination of air, earth, rivers, and sea with dangerous and even lethal materials.
>
> —*Rachel Carson*

Rachel Carson's message becomes even more compelling as worldwide data accumulate to substantiate the dangers about which she warned, and scientific studies confirm her prophecies. The time has long since come for humankind to use that power she refers to, which has dangerously altered the nature of our world, in ways that will foster healing and amelioration.

International environmental mediation constitutes the intersection of three fields: international relations, environmental studies, and conflict resolution (Figure 9.1).

Much is known about mediation in international relations, and a substantial literature addresses the strengths and weaknesses of environmental mediation; but experience with international environmental mediation is minimal. In this chapter, we will focus on what are known to be common elements of mediation in international relations and intranational environmental mediation, and will also refer to the smaller body of international environmental experience. Recommendations are made concerning the importance, indeed the urgency, of applying alternative dispute resolution techniques to the very pressing international environmental threats.

We begin by looking at the environmental problems that are demanding attention on the international and global levels. The next section focuses on environmental conflict resolution on both the intranational and international levels. It starts with a consideration of general theory and

Figure 9.1 Intersection of Three Fields Constituting International Mediation

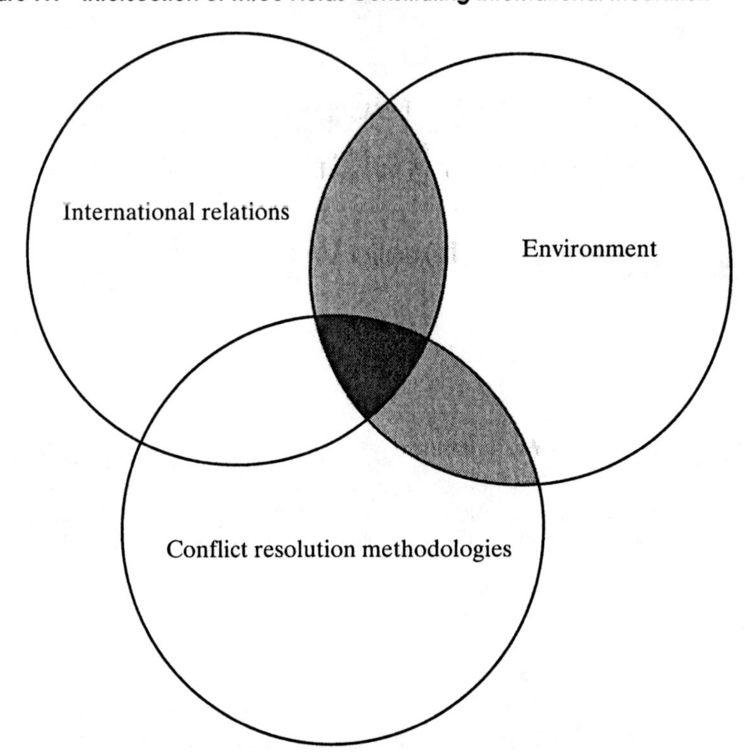

methodologies that relate to alternative dispute resolution (ADR). We portray the use of conflict resolution approaches—in particular ADR methodologies with their interdisciplinary applications—focusing on their role in resolving environmental issues. To clarify the potential for international environmental mediation, the concluding section presents the challenges, selected approaches to coping with them, and a research agenda.

THE ENVIRONMENT

A Progressively Global Perspective

The Cold War has ended but many dangers to world peace persist. The threats to our physical environment both cause and result from political upheaval, starvation, and mass migrations, as well as struggles over water and other resources. National security no longer involves only weapons and borders but also watersheds, croplands, and erosion of topsoil. New and ominous enemies are global warming, thinning of the ozone layer, desertification, deforestation, pollution of irreplaceable resources, and the alarming effects of overpopulation.

Because environmental threats cannot be contained within politically drawn boundaries, we must set our sights differently and find new techniques for coping with these problems.

It is much easier, of course, to state the problem than to find solutions. The issues of the global environmental movement range from the protection of wildflowers to the protection of whales, from the urgent problem of toxic wastes to the dangers of global warming, and from the effects of affluence to the effects of poverty. Approaches range from balancing the needs of development and economic growth to uncompromising antigrowth stances and "deep ecology." One of the most difficult problems faced by environmentalists is the conflict between development goals and sustainable environmental management in the developing world, where national interests often conflict with international and global environmental well-being.

From 1962 to 1972, a "new environmentalism" emerged in industrialized countries in response to a variety of events (McCormick, 1989). The roots of this movement include the influence of Rachel Carson, whose classic *Silent Spring* sounded the alarm about pesticide dangers; the reaction to affluence and the growing awareness of the long-term effects of development; the fear of nuclear fallout; and the impact of environmental disasters. More recent awareness can be attributed to the greater scope for other issues in public discourse made possible by the waning of the Cold War, as well as a genuine shift in the scientific community's perception of global environmental problems (Gleick, 1987).

The 1970s and 1980s saw several environmental incidents that had major repercussions. The partial core melt at the Three Mile Island power station in Harrisburg, Pennsylvania, in March 1978 gave substance to the warnings of opponents of nuclear power. Their fears materialized on April 26, 1986, when as a result of the deliberate shutdown of safety systems a reactor exploded at the Chernobyl nuclear power station, fifty miles from Kiev in the then-Soviet Ukraine. In addition to local fatalities, the impact of that explosion was felt over great geographical distances—for example, winds carrying the radiation caused contamination of milk products and vegetables in Scandinavia and other parts of Europe. A scientific consensus (Hohenemser et al., 1986) regarding the long-term health effects of Chernobyl predicts that thousands of people will suffer radiation-related illnesses.

This accident was a dramatic example of how mismanaged technology can cause sudden and extreme environmental contamination. However, most man-made environmental change is much slower, less blatant, and more difficult to detect and measure. In 1988, for example, biologists dredged a small lake on Isle Royale, a remote island in Lake Superior, the cleanest of the Great Lakes, and discovered significant traces of chemically fresh DDT (Rosenbaum, 1991), a substance that had been banned for agricultural use in the United States since 1972. Had the DDT traveled on tiny atmospheric particles from Central and South America, where it is still widely used in agriculture, as scientists have suggested? If so, the causation of that process spanned years or even decades and great geographic distances—a reminder that ecology is a science rife with uncertainty and surprise.

International Relations

Governments are increasingly aware of domestic and international ecological dangers, and have become more aggressive in seeking international solutions to global degradation. Their efforts are supported by the growing availability of global environmental trend data provided by international organizations such as the United Nations Environment Programme and the Worldwatch Institute, as well as by the scientific community.

Is the environment fundamentally a scientific, economic, or political issue? Science provides some understanding of the mechanics of environmental problems, but the causes as well as solutions of those problems are ultimately a question of human behavior and values. Economic growth and development often come at the expense of increased environmental degradation. A step toward coping with this problem is the adoption of environmental mandates by some multilateral development banks.

In the final analysis, the environment is indeed a political issue. Whether or not solutions are effectively applied will continue to depend on politics and policy and on the attitudes and capacities of leaders, parties, and constituents. Solutions to these transnational problems increasingly depend on a system involving international agencies and conventions and on agreements that are often nonbinding, as well as national environmental agencies and nongovernmental organizations.

The Salience of International Environmental Issues

"International" environmental issues can be grouped into three categories—transboundary, regional, and global. Although it overlaps with these three categories, we will consider the question of resource allocation separately for purposes of clarity.

Transboundary Issues

Wherever boundaries between countries exist, site-specific local environmental problems such as air, water, or ground pollution affect the nation across the border, often without affecting the source nation. From the point of view of the national capitals, the management of such problems is often considered to be successful as long as bilateral diplomatic relations are not damaged (Carroll, 1990). However, people living in border regions who suffer the effects of pollution, as well as environmental cleanup crews on either side of the border, often regard the matter quite differently.

Regional Issues

Natural systems may absorb stress for long periods without overt signs of damage. "A point comes, however, when suddenly conditions worsen rapidly. . . . Scientists may anticipate such sudden changes . . . but rarely can they predict when they occur. As the scale and pace of human activities intensify, the risk of overstepping such thresholds increases" (Postel, 1986).

In the late 1970s, a new international environmental issue emerged. The world first became aware of acid rain through the broad dissemination of scientific findings and the very vocal complaints of people in Sweden, Canada, and other nations. Anti-acid rain activism ushered in the new era of large-scale international regional problems. Incomparably more grave than the transboundary environmental problems that preceded them, international regional problems include nuclear contamination, toxic wastes, the overuse and pollution of water supplies, the ecological decline of oceans, deforestation, and the killing of wildlife.

Global Issues

Nature continually surprises science. In the late 1970s, two problems that affect the planet as a whole emerged concurrently: the threats to the ozone layer, and the warming of the global climate known as the greenhouse effect. Agreement on the issue of the ozone layer—which protects life on our planet from the sun's harmful ultraviolet light—was reached remarkably quickly. The question of how to deal with the greenhouse effect is still being considered.

Chlorofluorocarbon (CFC) gases used in air conditioners, refrigerators, and aerosol containers destroy ozone and prevent it from re-forming. Because CFCs linger from fifty to one hundred or more years in the atmosphere, it is difficult to reverse damage already done. In 1988, many of the more developed countries, including the United States and Canada, signed the Montreal Protocol, an agreement to freeze production of all CFCs and other pollutants at their existing levels and to reduce their amounts by 50 percent by the year 2000 (Granda, 1990). In 1989, over eighty countries signed the Helsinki Declaration, which declared the objective of phasing out by the year 2000 all CFCs and other pollutants believed responsible for global ozone depletion.

The greenhouse effect, however, is far more intractable (McCormick, 1989). The increased use of coal, oil, and natural gas since the Industrial Revolution has caused the concentration of carbon dioxide in the earth's atmosphere to rise steadily. This carbon dioxide has been trapping solar radiation in the earth's atmosphere, creating a "greenhouse." The resulting climatic changes threaten to alter crop production patterns and wind patterns and velocities, and to cause melting of the polar ice caps that will raise global sea levels and lead to inundation of many coastal areas.

The scientific community disagrees about many aspects of the climate warming issue. Scientists concur that as greenhouse gases such as carbon dioxide, methane, and nitrous oxide accumulate in the atmosphere they will make the world warmer, but they disagree about the magnitude of the warming and the damage it will cause. This uncertainty makes it difficult to decide how much money and effort to invest in reducing greenhouse gas emissions.

Resource Allocation

Another environmental concern of international proportions involves resource allocations—the use of water and energy, and the growing inequities in use of such resources among nations. Rees (1991) has grouped resource problems into four categories: physical, geopolitical, economic, and problems involving environmental and renewable scarcities.

Experts have noted the risks to international security from ongoing environmental degradation and the nonsustainable use of living natural resources. Attention to peace and security implications is being drawn at many levels—military and political, local and global. In 1987, the Brundtland Report noted:

> conflicts over natural resources are likely to increase as competition for them increases, and . . . such conflicts could be expected to arise from the marginalization of sectors of the population and from ensuing violence that occurs when political processes are unable to handle the effects of environmental stress. (Report of the World Commission on Environment and Development, 1987; quoted in Scott and Trolldalen, 1993:44)

This statement implies that local or regional instability arising from environmental, resource, and political factors may escalate to the international level. Governments must, therefore, identify and address cases in which environmental variables threaten security.

Homer-Dixon offers a series of examples of how environmental change may lead to acute conflict:

> environmental change may shift the balance of power between states either regionally or globally, producing instabilities that could lead to war. Warmer temperatures could lead to contention over new ice-free sea-lanes in the Arctic or more accessible resources in the Antarctic. Or as global environmental damage increases the disparity between the North and South, poor nations may militarily confront the rich for a greater share of the world's wealth. . . . Bulging populations and land stress may produce waves of environmental refugees that spill across borders with destabilizing effects on the recipient's domestic order and on international security. Countries may fight over dwindling supplies of water and the effects of upstream pollution. In developing countries, a sharp drop in food crop production could lead to internal strife across urban-rural and nomadic-sedentary cleavages. (1991:77)

Fundamentally nonmilitary resource scarcities and ecological stresses, then, constitute real and imminent challenges to peace.

Difficulties in Addressing the Issues

National jurisdiction cannot encompass such issues as protection of rain forests, genetic diversity, migratory animals, soil erosion, or long-range atmospheric transport of pollutants. It cannot extend to policies on international common spaces, notably the high seas and deep seabed, extraterrestrial space, and Antarctica. Such large-scale environmental problems threaten the survival of mankind and must assume a place on the international agenda.

Such international environmental issues are usually intrusive and extensive, involving deep-rooted demographic and economic behaviors. Matters regarded as strictly national in one country may have negative consequences that are deeply resented elsewhere. There are many current examples of such situations. Heavy use of irrigation and fertilizers by U.S. farmers in the valley of the Colorado River causes its waters to be saline and chemically polluted when they reach Mexico. Land development and deforestation in Nepal has allegedly increased the severity of floods in India and Bangladesh. Caldwell (1990) discusses Haiti and El Salvador, whose internal environmental problems impoverish their people and impair the economic infrastructure (such as roads and dams), in turn aggravating social and political instability. Such problems not only make international cooperation difficult but stimulate emigration that is unwelcome in the receiving countries.

Despite the increased public awareness of these critical international and global environmental issues, the problems persist or worsen. The following factors indicate the dimensions of the problem.

1. Most ecological ills have multiple causes. Such "synergy" arises when "two or more environmental processes interact in such a manner that the joint product of their interactions is not merely additive but multiplicative.... One problem combines with another, and the upshot is not a double problem but a super-problem" (Myers, 1993:205).

2. The existence of a problem of regional or global magnitude is a relatively new concept (in the context of a public agenda). It is only three decades since the publication of *Silent Spring,* which was the first such work to reach a wide audience.

3. National governments are reluctant to initiate proposals for international environmental cooperation because such issues often extend geographically beyond any one nation's borders, and beyond the tenure of political office-holders and even the lifetimes of their constituents.

4. Although important environmental ills have been targeted by international agreements, delay and difficulty in program implementation are common. Within nations, citizens can go to court to address environmental conflicts, but on the international level there is no central government or international court with power and authority for enforcement.

5. Conflict between the developed and developing world on who should pay for cleaning up the planet and for population control policies proves to be a major barrier. These are politically very sensitive issues. Economic growth and employment appear to be in jeopardy, at least in the short run, if environmental protection receives too much attention and resources. In many developing countries, the options are often brutal. Who would sacrifice the economic progress or even survival of perhaps millions of people to safeguard a sustainable natural resource base for future generations?

6. Economic growth and population expansion often diminish the effectiveness of pollution controls over time. Cost-benefit analyses of proposed environmental measures are hard to carry out, and balancing short-term costs and long-term benefits is also difficult (see Fouere, 1990; Rosenbaum, 1991).

7. Accurate scientific data on the nature, causes, and consequences of long-term environmental effects are difficult and expensive to obtain, a problem that is complicated by differences among scientific schools of thought as to what is really happening to the biosphere. Competition among the many views about what should be done to redress environmental problems leads governments to adopt a dangerous wait-and-see attitude.

8. These difficulties are compounded by continuing scientific and technical innovations that contribute to environmental problems by creating new substances or technologies with potentially serious or unpredictable environmental risks.

ALTERNATIVE DISPUTE RESOLUTION AND ENVIRONMENTAL MEDIATION

Theory and Approaches

Conflicts within and between tribes, religious sects, ethnic groups, and nations have been handled both peacefully and otherwise from the beginning of history. Conventional dispute resolution, on the intranational level, is often entrusted to the legislative branch (by vote) or the judicial system (by law), or to an administrative arena where decisions are made according to some technical expertise. Because of the severe drawbacks of time and money and the frequent dissatisfaction of the parties when disputes are resolved through these traditional channels, researchers and practitioners have explored alternative dispute resolution methodologies to supplement conventional systems.

Over the past thirty years, public awareness of intergroup conflicts in almost all social areas has grown substantially (Fink, 1968; Crozier, 1974; Deutsch, 1973; Hocker and Wilmot, 1985). In recent years, scholarly attention has begun to focus on the use of social scientific knowledge to develop methods for resolving conflicts (Rubin, 1980; Fisher and Ury, 1981; Raiffa, 1982; Shea, 1983; Bercovitch, 1984; Lewicki and Litterer, 1985; Lax and Sebenius, 1986; Ury, Brett, and Goldberg, 1988; Gray, 1989; Hall, 1993).

Researchers generally agree on the following basic points (Vranesky, 1992):

1. Conflict is a powerful and ubiquitous social force.
2. Conflict can have both socially destructive and constructive functions.
3. Although conflicts appear in varying areas, they have enough in common to warrant a unified theoretical approach and the development of cross-substantive methods of resolution.
4. The approach to conflict management should relate to the particular characteristics of each case.
5. Dispute resolution techniques may lead to socially unjust outcomes; hence conflict managers should be trained to be aware of social-justice aspects of conflict resolution and the ethical dilemmas that arise.
6. Application of conflict resolution processes can improve the functioning of the system in which they are implemented.
7. Conflict resolution processes should aim to increase the gains for all the groups involved in the conflict, rather than only for some as with solutions likely to be reached through traditional means.

Methodologies of conflict resolution include negotiation, mediation (in some form of nonbinding third-party intervention), and arbitration. Researchers emphasize the importance of good, sound process, improving the dispute's outcomes, mutual gains, and, when possible, reaching consensus. Our focus is on the spectrum of methodologies referred to as mediation.

Mediation

Mediation is one of the oldest informal modes of conflict resolution. In this chapter, mediation refers to a broad range of methodologies including all types of assisted negotiations. Mediation has been described (for example, by Bercovitch, 1984; Susskind and Cruikshank, 1987) as a goal-directed, problem-solving intervention. As a process, it educates the participants about each other's needs and potentially provides a model for settling the current and future disputes between them. Mediation explicitly aims to resolve the dispute to the satisfaction of all participants to the issue. This outcome, of course, is not guaranteed, but mediation seeks to increase the chances of its realization. It attempts to fashion "mutual gain" solutions, as opposed to the traditional adversarial approaches that result in zero-sum agreements.

Analysts vary in their perception of the role of the mediator. Some assume a neutral mediator who remains impartial throughout (Raiffa, 1982); others see the mediator as part of the negotiating system (Kolb, 1989; Bercovitch, 1991; Kriesberg, 1991). Susskind describes the mediator's involvement as nonpartisan, but not neutral with respect to outcome (quoted in Forester, 1994). All regard the mediator's role as flexible in accordance with the characteristics of the dispute.

ENVIRONMENTAL MEDIATION

Environmental mediation is an informal, voluntary process in which a mediator facilitates the resolution of an environmental dispute. Proponents claim that when the parties can be convinced to accept environmental mediation as an alternative, the result is a more cooperative process whose aim is to achieve a more fair and timely, and far less costly resolution. We will first examine the intranational experience with environmental mediation; many of the insights gained from this experience can be adapted to the even more complex arena of international environmental conflicts.

The Intranational Sphere

Approaches to environmental conflicts have claimed the attention of researchers and practitioners alike, especially in the United States. Numerous applications and analyses, primarily within national borders, have been made over the past decade and a half (Bacow and Wheeler, 1984; Bingham, 1986; Amy, 1987; Susskind and Cruikshank, 1987; Rabe, 1988). Most of these analyses have focused more generally on the environmental dispute resolution process than on the evaluation of outcomes.

Drawbacks of Judicial and Legislative Solutions

Environmental dispute resolution has evolved out of the growing concern in the United States that environmental policy, which is riddled with conflict, is dependent on the judiciary for direction, given the incapacity of the executive and legislative branches of government to resolve fundamental disputes. The liabilities of court-shaped policy include its inability to protect human health, to limit interference with development, and to stimulate more innovative methods of environmental policy and regulation, as well as more creative solutions. Litigation generally is costly in both time and money, and often the remedies do not meet the needs of all (or any) of the sides. Litigation often causes environmental disputants to focus on technicalities of law and procedure rather than addressing substantive issues.

Concern over these drawbacks led to the exploration of alternative approaches to resolving environmental conflicts. These approaches include mediation, negotiation, and policy dialogue. In many cases, environmental mediation is a more cooperative and also more effective process. Susskind and Cruikshank (1987) identify four characteristics of good negotiated settlements: fairness, efficiency, wisdom, and stability; they contend that often outcomes produced by negotiated settlements satisfy these conditions better than those reached via litigation or political compromise.

Early Environmental Mediation Experience

Experiments with environmental mediation began in the United States in the mid-1970s, as an extension of techniques that were being used successfully in community disputes. In one of the first test cases, Gerald Cormick and Jane McCarthy of the University of Washington's Environmental Mediation Project were appointed by the governor of Washington State to serve as mediators in a dispute between environmentalists, farmers, developers, and public officials over the damming of the Snoqualmie River. The resulting agreement illustrated one of mediation's main assets—its capacity to generate creative solutions that satisfy the interests of all parties involved.

Sullivan (1979) notes:

> Although the original conflict arose over the single issue of dam construction, the communication required in bargaining helped change the

> shape of the conflict. The negotiation changed from a yes/no dam issue into a search for environmentally acceptable flood control measures. Both dam proponents and opponents moved beyond their original misconceptions of the other side and dealt with each other's real needs and concerns.

Following the success of Cormick and McCarthy, an increasing number of academics, environmentalists, developers, and practitioners began to explore environmental mediation. There were further experiments and successes in such areas as power plant siting, pollution abatement, land use preservation of parklands, and transportation planning (Bacow and Wheeler, 1984; Bingham, 1986; Amy, 1987).

Environmental mediation has taken many different forms. Not only is it used in local, site-specific disputes such as the Snoqualmie dam, but also for basic environmental policy issues on the national level such as the National Coal Policy Project (Amy, 1987). Mediation has gradually become an official part of environmental policymaking. For example, several states in the United States now have laws that allow or even require mediation in disputes over the location of hazardous waste disposal facilities. One of them, the Massachusetts Hazardous Waste Siting Act (1980), empowers a local assessment committee—serving as a mediation council—to negotiate a binding contract with the developer. The developer must submit an environmental impact report and a socioeconomic appendix, which can include analyses of the anticipated effects on property values and of possible psychological effects on local residents (Shmueli, 1979).

Although it holds considerable promise as one approach to environmental regulatory reform, environmental dispute resolution is not an all-encompassing remedy that can be applied to every type of environmental dispute. Alternative methodologies are more appropriate in environmental disputes that focus on achieving a solution when there is agreement about the necessity of a course of action, as opposed to disputes about rights. The latter may well be cases in which a middle ground should not be sought, or for which establishing precedent is important, so that the traditional judicial setting may be more appropriate. Unfortunately, the distinction between these two categories of conflict is not always clear. Dam/no dam may be only the beginning. Overall, mediation can be an effective process for resolving or managing certain disputes, at times as a replacement for or in combination with the more traditional conflict resolution processes.

Environmental disputes are usually multilateral, and it is often unclear who should be a party to the negotiations. A major risk is the exclusion of certain groups or an imbalance in negotiation strength that might be lessened in a more adversarial context. For example, it has been very difficult to bring about bring about broad participation in the institutionalization of the Massachusetts Hazardous Waste Siting Act because of a perceived power imbalance that enables siting opponents to dominate the negotiation process (Provost, 1982–1983).

Thus, important tasks of mediation in environmental disputes are to identify who has a stake in the outcome and who can speak for the groups involved, and to assure the representation of different interests. Other tasks include: narrowing the agenda of issues to be negotiated; ensuring that the incentives to bargain are substantial; creating situations in which the bargains that are made can be held secure; defining timetables and deadlines; and participating in the development of, or even suggesting, creative solutions. The nonadversarial, participatory nature of environmental mediation accounts for much of its capacity to resolve environmental disputes where other approaches have failed.

The International Sphere

International environmental conflict resolution often begins through diplomacy. Diplomacy includes different methodologies within the spectrum of mediation. Relatively little has been written on environmental diplomacy, however, and even less on international environmental mediation, which is new and which frequently occurs behind closed doors. But such mediation is an important supplement to the more common conflict-resolution techniques now used in the international environmental arena, and will undoubtedly receive more varied use and greater documentation.

Environmental problems are linked to the gamut of human activities. The handling of environmental issues on the national level is complicated by the diversity of agencies that may be involved, such as those responsible for industry, physical planning, agriculture, energy, and finance. This nonsectoral character of environmental problems makes diplomacy particularly difficult. Environmental legislation and management require complex coordinating processes, which in the international arena are only compounded by multiple governments with varying levels of commitment to the stated objectives.

Environmental Diplomacy

Environmental diplomacy is a relatively recent concept. To promote it, special organizations have been created with their supporting governing boards, secretariats, and international legal conventions (Bjorkbom, 1990). We will outline the existing official and nonofficial structures, and explore the potential role of environmental nongovernmental organizations in international conflict resolution.

International agreements concerning the environment are not a new phenomenon; the first one was signed in 1886. Today they number more than 250, three-fourths of which were signed after 1960, although many of these agreements have not been implemented. The difficulties that environmental regulation poses on the national level are compounded on the international level.

Official structure. The following noninclusive, general listing of the institutional creations in the international environmental arena indicates the dynamics and complexity of the existing structure (for greater detail, see Wilson, 1971; Bjorkbom, 1990):

- UNESCO's Biosphere Conference in 1968 might be identified as the first sign of an environmental point of view emerging within the community of transnational organizations.
- The Swedish Resolution, passed unanimously by the UN General Assembly, triggered a new international awareness of an environmental crisis. That resolution was authorized at the 1972 UN World Conference on the Human Environment in Stockholm. Much of the current institution building is descended from that conference, although there were some earlier international environmental committees and conventions.
- The most conspicuous of the multilateral organizations is the United Nations Environment Programme (UNEP) based in Nairobi. UNEP is the coordinating and motivating body that draws attention to the environmental aspects of the operational activities of the UN Secretariat and the Specialized Agencies. Only UNEP handles environmental issues of a global character. The Specialized Agencies include: Food and Agriculture Organization (FAO), International Maritime Organization (IMO), United Nations Development Program (UNDP), United Nations Educational, Scientific and Cultural Organization (UNESCO), World Health Organization (WHO), and World Meteorological Organization (WMO).
- All UN Regional Economic Commissions include subsidiary bodies whose task is to cope with environmental problems of regional scope.
- Other bodies outside the UN system that have created intergovernmental institutions to deal with environmental issues include: European Bank for Reconstruction and Development (EBRD), European Economic Community, Global Environmental Facility (GEF), Nordic Council of Ministers, Organization for Economic Cooperation and Development (OECD), and the World Bank.

Perhaps the most ambitious international conference ever convened to address any subject, the 1992 Rio de Janeiro Conference on Environment and Development (UNCED), clearly acknowledged the scientific, economic, and political linkages between international environment and development issues. Delegates signed two general conventions regarding biodiversity and climate change. Delegates also accepted a nonbinding "declaration of concern," the Rio Declaration; as well as an unfunded set of ambitious goals, a statement of principles, and a list of hundreds of potential projects known as Agenda 21 (that is, the environmental agenda for the twenty-first century). The ultimate success of the conference is uncertain, but it clearly highlighted the environment as a key international and indeed very multilateral issue.

One significant outcome of UNCED is the creation of the United Nations Commission on Sustainable Development (CSD), whose broad mandate is still being formulated.

These bodies have negotiated and adopted international agreements to promote multilateral cooperation in resolving the environmental problems common to the respective parties. A full list of the multilateral agreements already in force or pending is published annually by UNEP in its *Register of International Treaties and Other Agreements in the Field of the Environment.*

This system can function only if the governments taking part in the governing council of UNEP support its environmental programs not only in the UN General Assembly but also in the various governing boards of the relevant operative agencies. To do so requires that governments coordinate domestically their conduct in all the concerned spheres, a rarity in multilateral environmental conflict resolution.

Unofficial structure: environmental nongovernmental organizations. Parallel to this official structure, an unofficial, nongovernmental structure carries on independent but often coordinated activities. With these nongovernmental organizations taking on more and more mediating functions, it is here in particular that we see roles for international environmental mediation.

International cooperation is strongly influenced by environmental nongovernmental organizations (ENGOs) that operate across political and bureaucratic boundaries and form networks of influence on policy decisions. By bearing directly on national governments and intergovernmental organizations, ENGOs have promoted the institutionalization of international cooperation. In 1982, an estimated 2,230 ENGOs existed in developing countries and 13,000 in developed countries (Caldwell, 1990). Since 1945, the number of ENGOs with permanent UN accreditation has risen from 41 to 928 (Lindborg, 1992). Hence, the strength and potential influence of ENGOs are considerable.

ENGOs include philanthropic, scientific, educational, and economic associations, as well as multinational corporations. They have vastly different goals and ideologies. Groups such as the National Resources Defense Council (NRDC) provide legal and policy expertise; Greenpeace focuses on public education and involvement and makes skillful use of media. Some multilateral organizations, including the World Bank, have been examining ways to incorporate community and ENGO participation in project planning, and particularly in environmental assessments. An example of an apolitical (or perceived as such) ENGO is the World Wildlife Fund (WWF), which specializes in ecological projects in less-developed countries (McMahon, 1993; Scott and Trolldalen, 1993).

Although supranational and nongovernmental, this unofficial structure of ENGOs has a public and official character. Its purposes resemble those of national and intergovernmental agencies, and ENGOs have played a significant part in the development of both national and international environmental policy and law.

While much has been written on ENGOs at the national level, there is little on the international organizations, about which more research is needed. Indeed, on the international level the role of ENGOs has been critical, but it needs to be more clearly defined in order to augment its effectiveness.

The increasing influence of environmental organizations that have international concerns is manifested in the following ways:

- The ENGOs provide continuity in international environmental policy not obtainable through periodic international conferences.
- Resources of money and skilled personnel have increased the ability of ENGOs to influence the policy agendas of governments and to encourage action and implement international commitments.
- ENGOs serve as unhampered advocates, and as mobilizers of public opinion.
- ENGOs currently play a significant role in initiating proposals for international environmental cooperation, and often the strategies used by these groups at intergovernmental negotiations directly influence outcomes.

For example, ENGOs in a number of countries have played a leading role in mobilizing the public and governmental support necessary to establish the Montreal Protocol on substances that deplete the ozone layer (Granda, 1990). Another instance is the preparatory process for the Rio conference, when hundreds of ENGOs participated in the negotiations concerning the Climate Change Convention, the Biodiversity Convention, and the two documents produced by the conference delegates, the Rio Declaration and Agenda 21 (McMahon, 1993).

Some limits to ENGOs' effectiveness stem from territoriality and competition with each other. The immense diversity of ENGOs also hampers coordination and communication, and for many, inadequate financial resources and manpower undermine the capacity to pursue more comprehensive coordinating efforts.

Negotiations on the Environment

In recent years, assisted negotiations on the environment within the framework of international organizations have become more common. Only a few such negotiations, however, have been well documented. These include the Basel Convention on transboundary movement of hazardous wastes and their disposal (Hilz and Radka, 1990); a moratorium on whaling (Stedman, 1990); the Antarctic minerals regime treaties (Laws, 1990); and the issue of transferring of the African elephant (Arend, 1990). In each of the negotiations, a mediating party can be identified.

Lang (1991) investigates three multilateral assisted negotiations—on air pollution, nuclear accidents, and the depletion of the ozone layer. The origin of the air pollution negotiation was the acidification of inland waters in Scandinavia, which was traced back to sulfur emissions in East Germany, West Germany, Poland, and the United Kingdom. The negotiations began in 1978 and continued into the present decade. Here the Economic Commission for Europe (ECE), a regional body of the UN covering all states in Europe as well as Canada and the United States, dominated the process and became the guardian of the resulting convention on sulfur emissions and nitrous oxide.

The nuclear accidents negotiation was triggered by the Chernobyl tragedy. The International Atomic Energy Organization (IAEO) provided mediation in the form of technical and legal services. A six-month negotiating process culminated in a treaty that established a system of ecological crisis management by respective governments.

In the ozone depletion negotiation discussed previously, UNEP was the international organization in charge, although it relied on the services of other UN organizations during different stages of the process. This three-phase negotiation ran from the early 1980s to 1989, but the process remains open-ended because reductions agreed upon, and even realized, may quickly be overtaken by new evidence requiring more stringent cuts in the production and use of chlorofluorocarbons.

In all of these negotiations, Lang describes conference officers as

> playing an active role . . . that went far beyond their formal duties laid down in the rules of procedure of the respective conference; these offic-

> ers were mediating, animating, advancing the process, preventing confrontations to the extent possible, and briefing the media. (Lang, 1991)

All formal actions taken by the multilateral negotiations mentioned are regulated by rules of procedure of which the public is apprised. These actions are paralleled by informal actions. Decisions are reached in the formal settings by vote or consensus, but are preceded by agreements on substance concluded informally among a very limited number of actors.

Obstacles to Environmental Conflict Resolution

Although sometimes perceived by policy elites as a threat to national sovereignty, ENGOs often interact with official governmental authorities when programs are initiated and developed. A qualitatively new institutional structure has emerged from this interaction for initiating and negotiating international environmental relationships.

However impressive in apparent size and diversity, the current international institutional framework is not yet satisfactory as a tool for environmental conflict resolution. The existing treaty-making system has produced several notable agreements over the past twenty years but it is not sufficient for the enormous challenges that lie ahead. Critics often cite the shortcomings of the current system: it is very time-consuming and because of its nonsectoral nature requires tremendous coordination; it ignores important scientific findings, encourages "lowest common denominator" solutions, encounters great difficulties with effective implementation, and not least, allows the most powerful nations to dominate (Babbit, 1990; Bjorkbom, 1990; Salzburg Initiative, cited in Babbit, 1990:Appendix C).

Even in the aftermath of Rio, no overarching global environmental agenda exists to which the nations of the world have committed themselves. Nor has there been much progress in building a long-term institutional capacity for effective global environmental management. The situation, indeed, begs for supplemental alternative dispute resolution tools.

One of the fundamental conditions for international cooperation within the framework of the sovereignty of nations is the willingness and ability of national governments to make and honor agreements. In some cases, governments are asked or pressured to cooperate in the implementation of international agreements whose effect on their interests may be unclear or even adverse.

There are also a number of obstacles to genuine implementation of even those policies to which nations may formally agree:

1. A nation may be pressured to give the appearance of consent by a more powerful participant, international opinion, allies in other endeav-

ors, or public opinion resulting from highly publicized conferences or, alternatively, disasters.

2. Readiness to cooperate may vary with changes in national government. One example is the U.S. government's environmental policy reversals during the Reagan administration in the early 1980s.

3. Negotiators and implementers may represent different constituencies, and the officials or agencies negotiating the agreements may be unauthorized to implement them.

4. Intentions may be genuine, but administrative and/or financial capabilities inadequate.

Indeed, a general and fundamental issue is the inadequacy of most official environmental agencies. The human and material resources allotted to dealing with environmental threats are limited, and offices are small, understaffed, and often merely subdivisions of departments whose main attention is directed elsewhere. Moreover, the capacity of governments to participate in cooperative programs is unequal. Many programs require scientific-technical as well as financial capabilities that only a few nations possess, and in those cases the nominal participants can contribute neither skilled personnel nor effective administration of their obligations at home.

The emergence of environmental issues on the international agenda poses new problems of cooperation for national governments and challenges to international diplomacy. Many environmental problems transcend the traditional boundaries of national interest and responsibility. Although international cooperation is impossible without national concurrence, formal agreement is insufficient to ensure effective cooperation and implementation. What clearly emerges from the immense complexity of environmental issues is the need for supplemental and integrative approaches.

CONCLUSIONS: CHALLENGES OF INTERNATIONAL ENVIRONMENTAL MEDIATION

Strengthening the Chances of Success

We have seen that environmental problems are severe, and that neither conventional conflict-resolution techniques nor the existing international organizational structure provide the necessary solutions. Mediation methodologies, however, can be a significant supplemental tool for coping with international environmental conflicts, for several reasons: (1) stakeholders can gain integrative and creative solutions for mutual benefit; (2) there are better chances of implementation because all stakeholders have something to lose should an agreement not be implemented; and (3) the outcomes of a voluntary process have a greater chance of implementation, given that the International Court of Justice has a very limited mandate with respect to environmental issues (Johnson, 1993) and is not the equivalent of national court systems.

The following are some important points that emerge from this chapter and from empirical as well as theoretical research.

ENGOs

Existing ENGOs should be assigned a more defined mediating role in initiating proposals for international environmental cooperation and ensuring implementation. Participation of ENGOs in future environmental negotiations should be increased to include mediator roles, representation at the negotiation table, and development of scientific expertise.

For example, the United Nations Commission on Sustainable Development should include in its mandate the identification of an ENGO to act as mediator in each specific dispute. Together the Commission and that ENGO should identify the parties to be involved in the negotiation, trying to consider balances of power and to ensure that those with the authority to implement are represented at the bargaining table. At the same time, however, it is essential that to maintain credibility the ENGOs preserve independent, outside status.

Attainable Objectives and Linkages

It is important to set objectives that are attainable, which sometimes requires advancing in smaller, but achievable, steps; for example, by shifting the primary objective of environmental regulation to reduction of risk, rather than elimination of all pollutants.

The issue of linkage in international negotiations must be considered carefully. Breaking an issue into smaller pieces or adding issues to the agenda can help parties to construct an agreement. Often the linkage between environmental issues and critical development issues is central to negotiations. Analysis of the linkage between environment and trade, for instance, can contribute to implementing stronger environmental treaties. Currently, the objectives of the world trade system and of most international environmental agreements are at odds. Free trade fails to recognize the limits of the planet's natural resources and actually promotes their unsustainable consumption. We join Winden and Matza (1993) in arguing that international trade regimes must be realigned to support "fair trade" based on the principle of sustainability.

Science and Politics

Scientific discourse about international environmental problems must be integrated into policy negotiations. Scientific uncertainty and lack of consensus characterize several environmental conflicts. But the Montreal Protocol demonstrates that despite these problems, politicians can act forcefully and quickly (Granda, 1990). The interrelationship between politics and science must be such that their agreements are flexible enough to accommodate environmental "surprises." ENGOs can be used to promote the long-term emergence of groups of scientific experts whose conclusions are considered authoritative.

Mutual-Gain Strategies

Conflict resolution theory should be called upon to develop more pragmatic and "mutual gain" strategies for approaching the dilemmas of environment-development conflicts. The gap between the developed and developing countries has only worsened. Environmental treaties are threatened and weakened by the clash of two competing demands—the call for "reparations" for environmental damage caused by the industrial countries and the unsustainable development path of the developed nations. There does seem, however, to be a growing recognition by developed nations that the world's natural resources must be managed in a sustainable way, and that therefore development of mutual-gain strategies is particularly urgent.

Success Indicators

Prime targets for international mediation are those issues for which intensity has not yet heightened. Findings indicate that disputes of relatively low intensity are much more amenable to mediation than more intense disputes (Bercovitch, Anagnoson, and Wille, 1991; several of the chapters in Kressel and Pruitt, 1989, also strengthen this conclusion).

Another prerequisite for resolution that many environmental issues satisfy is a situation that Touval and Zartman (1989) call a "hurting stalemate." When prior attempts to resolve the dispute through other means have failed, there develops an especially strong commitment to mediation.

The management of environmental conflicts can have a positive influence on other areas of conflict among the same stakeholders, and serve as a basis for changing and building their relations. We can learn more about this influence by examining the ongoing Middle Eastern multilateral and bilateral negotiations. As yet undocumented, these talks will provide an opportunity to examine various roles of environmental dialogue.

Participants report (Prujinen, interview, November 1993) that the environmental negotiations served as confidence-building measures for the more publicized negotiations on the area's security problems and geopolitical future. Although priorities differed, the environmental issues were of interest to all parties and helped to establish their common ground.

Future Research Agenda

There is a need for better analytical work that will reveal the crucial links between environmental degradation on the one hand and social, economic, and political destabilization on the other. A major, concerted research effort of ecologists, economists, sociologists, political scientists, and conflict researchers should be directed toward such analytical work, and the results should be presented in terms accessible to politicians and experts on international issues. Such joint research might help governments to perceive more clearly the role that forceful efforts to redress the ongoing environmental destruction could play in preventing international crises. Most of these efforts should combine conceptual schemes with data from the real world.

There is no overall solution to the complex issues that characterize international environmental conflict, and mediation is but one approach. But environmental degradation has become such an overwhelming problem that an approach like mediation, which does offer considerable promise, should be advanced on as wide a scale as possible.

NOTE

We thank John Forester for his careful reading of an earlier draft of this chapter and for his most helpful comments and suggestions.

REFERENCES

Amy, D. (1987). *The Politics of Environmental Mediation.* New York: Columbia University Press.

Arend, T., Jr. (1990). "Ivory, Elephants—Or Both: Negotiating the Transfer of the African Elephant to an Appendix II Within CITES." In Susskind, Siskind, and Breslin, *Nine Case Studies,* 103–124.

Babbit, E., (1990). "Negotiation Theory and Practice: International Environmental Disputes." Program on Negotiation Working Paper Series (90–19), Cambridge, Mass.

Bacow, L., and Wheeler, M. (1984). *Environmental Dispute Resolution.* New York: Plenum.

Bercovitch, J. (1984). *Social Conflicts and Third Parties: Strategies of Conflict Resolution.* Boulder, Colo.: Westview.

Bercovitch, J., guest ed. (1991). "International Mediation." Special Issue, *Journal of Peace Research* 28, 1.

Bercovitch, J., Anagnoson, J. T., and Wille, D. (1991). "Conceptual Issues and Empirical Trends in the Study of Successful Mediation in International Relations." In Bercovitch, "International Mediation," 7–18.

Bingham, G. (1986). *Resolving Environmental Disputes: A Decade of Experience.* Washington, D.C.: Conservation Foundation.

Bjorkbom, L. (1990). "Resolution of Environmental Problems: The Use of Diplomacy." In Carroll, *International Environmental Diplomacy,* 123–137.

Blackburn, J. W. (1990). "Theoretical Dimensions of Environmental Mediation." In M. A. Rahim, ed., *Theory and Research in Conflict Management.* New York: Praeger, 151–169.

Caldwell, L. (1990). "Beyond Environmental Diplomacy: The Changing Institutional Structure of International Cooperation." In Carroll, *International Environmental Diplomacy,* 13–27.

Carroll, J., ed. (1990). *International Environmental Diplomacy: The Management and Resolution of Transfrontier Environmental Problems.* Cambridge: Cambridge University Press.

Carson, R. (1962). *Silent Spring.* Boston: Houghton Mifflin.

Commoner, B. (1971). *The Closing Circle: Nature, Man and Technology.* New York: Alfred A. Knopf.

Crozier, B. (1974). *A Theory of Conflict.* London: Hamish Hamilton.

Deutsch, M. (1973). *The Resolution of Conflict: Constructive and Destructive Processes.* New Haven: Yale University Press.

Fink, C. (1968). "Some Conceptual Difficulties in the Theory of Social Conflict." *Journal of Conflict Resolution* 12, 4: 412–460.

Fisher, R., and Ury, W. (1981). *Getting to Yes.* New York: Houghton Mifflin.

Forester, J. (1994). "Politics, Pragmatism, Vision." In D. Kolb, ed., *When Talk Works.* San Francisco: Jossey-Bass.

Fouere, E. (1990). "Emerging Trends in International Environmental Agreements." In Carroll, *International Environmental Diplomacy,* 29–44.

Gleick, J. (1987). *Chaos: Making of a New Science.* New York: Viking.

Granda, C. (1990). "The Montreal Protocol on Substances That Deplete the Ozone Layer." In Susskind, Siskind, and Breslin, eds., *Nine Case Studies,* 27–47.

Gray, B. (1989). *Collaborating: Finding Common Ground for Multiparty Problems.* San Francisco: Jossey-Bass.

Hall, L. (1993). *Negotiation: Strategies for Mutual Gain.* Beverly Hills, Calif.: Sage.

Hilz, C., and Radka, M. (1990). "The Basel Convention on Transboundary Movement of Hazardous Wastes and Their Disposal." In Susskind, Siskind, and Breslin, *Nine Case Studies,* 79–102.

Hocker, J., and Wilmot, W. (1985). *Interpersonal Conflict.* Dubuque, Iowa: William C. Brown.

Hohenemser, C., Deicher, M., Ernst, A., Hofsass, H., Lindner, G., and Recknagel, E. (1986). "Chernobyl: An Early Report." *Environment* 28, 5: 6–13, 30–43.

Homer-Dixon, T. (1991). "On the Threshold: Environmental Changes as Causes of Acute Conflict." *International Security* 16, 2: 76–116.

Johnson, T. (1993). "Mediating Environmental Treaty Disputes and the International Court of Justice." In Susskind, Moomaw, and Najam, *Papers,* 231–254.

Kolb, D. (1989). "Labor Mediators, Managers, and Ombudsmen: Roles Mediators Play in Different Contexts." In Kressel and Pruit, *Mediation Research,* 91–114.

Kressel, K., and Pruitt, D., eds. (1989). *Mediation Research: The Process and Effectiveness of Third-Party Intervention.* San Francisco: Jossey-Bass.
Kriesberg, L. (1991). "Formal and Quasi-Mediators in International Disputes: An Exploratory Analysis." In Bercovitch, "International Mediation," 19–27.
Lang, W. (1991). "Negotiations on the Environment." In V. Kremenyuk, ed., *International Negotiation: Analysis, Approaches, Issues.* San Francisco: Jossey-Bass, 343–656.
Laws, D. (1990). "The Antarctic Minerals Regime Negotiations." In Susskind, Siskind, and Breslin, *Nine Working Papers,* 125–154.
Lax, D., and Sebenius, J. (1986). *The Manager as Negotiator.* New York: Free Press.
Lewicki, R., and Litterer, J. (1985). *Negotiation.* Homewood, Ill.: Richard Irwin.
Lindborg, N. (1992). "Nongovernmental Organizations: Their Past, Present, and Future Role in International Environmental Negotiations." In L. Susskind, E. Dolin, and J. W. Breslin, eds., *International Environmental Treaty Making.* Cambridge, Mass.: Program on Negotiation Books.
McCormick, J. (1989). *The Global Environmental Movement.* London: Belhaven.
McMahon, V. (1993). "Environmental Nongovernmental Organizations at Intergovernmental Negotiations." In Susskind, Moomaw, and Najam, *Papers,* 1–21.
Myers, N. (1993). *The Environmental Basis of Political Stability.* New York: W. W. Norton.
Postel, S. (1986). *Altering the Earth's Chemistry: Assessing the Risks.* Washington, D.C.: Worldwatch Institute.
Provost, D. (1982–1983). "The Massachusetts Hazardous Waste Facility Siting Act: What Impact on Municipal Power to Exclude and Regulate?" *Environmental Affairs* 10: 715–793.
Prujinen, A. (Israeli representative to the Middle East environmental negotiations from 1989 to 1991, former deputy CEO for the Israeli Ministry of Environment). Interview, November 1993.
Rabe, B. (1988). "The Politics of Environmental Dispute Resolution." *Policy Studies Journal* 16, 3: 585–601.
Raiffa, H. (1982). *The Art and Science of Negotiation.* Cambridge: Harvard University Press.
Rees, J. (1991). "Resources and the Environment: Scarcity and Sustainability." In R. Bennett and R. Estall, eds., *Global Change and Challenge: Geography for the 1990's.* London: Routledge.
Report of the World Commission on Environment and Development (The Brundtland Report) (1987). Norwegian Prime Minister Gro Harlem Brundtland, Chair.
Rosenbaum, W. (1991). *Environmental Politics and Policy.* Washington, D.C.: Congressional Quarterly.
Rubin, J. (1980). "Experimental Research on Third-Party Intervention in Conflict: Toward Some Generalizations." *Psychology Bulletin* 87: 379–391.
Scott, P., and Trolldalen, J. (1993). "International Environmental Conflict Resolution: Moving Beyond Rio." *International Perspectives on Dispute Resolution Forum* (Winter). Washington, D.C.: National Institute for Dispute Resolution.
Shea, F. G. (1983). *Creative Negotiating.* Boston: CBI Books.
Shmueli, D. (1979). "A New Process for Energy Facility Siting." Unpublished master's thesis. Massachusetts Institute of Technology, Cambridge.
Stedman, B. (1990). "The International Whaling Commission and Negotiation for a Moratorium on Whaling." In Susskind, Siskind, and Breslin, *Nine Case Studies,* 155–182.

Sullivan, T. (1979). "Negotiation-Based Review Processes for Facility Siting." Unpublished doctoral dissertation. Harvard University, Cambridge.

Susskind, L., and Cruikshank, J. (1987). *Breaking the Impasse: Consensual Approaches to Resolving Public Disputes.* New York: Basic Books.

Susskind, L., Moomaw, W., and Najam, A., eds. (1993). *Papers on International Environmental Mediation,* vol. 3. Cambridge, Mass.: Program on Negotiation Books.

Susskind, L., Siskind, E., and Breslin, J. W., eds. (1990). *Nine Case Studies in International Environmental Negotiation.* Cambridge: MIT-Harvard Public Disputes Program.

Touval, S., and Zartman, W. (1989). "Mediation in International Conflicts." In Kressel and Pruit, *Mediation Research,* 115–137.

Ury, W., Brett, J., and Goldberg, S. (1988). *Getting Disputes Resolved.* San Francisco: Jossey-Bass.

Vranesky, A. (1992). *Conflict Management in Urban and Regional Planning.* Haifa: Center for Urban and Regional Studies, Technion. (Hebrew)

Wilson, T., Jr. (1971). *International Environmental Action: A Global Survey.* Cambridge, Mass.: Dunellen.

Winden, A., and Matza, A. (1993). "Free Trade, Fair Trade, and Environmental Treaty Making." In Susskind, Moomaw, and Najam, *Papers,* 37–68.

PART FOUR

EXTENDING THE RANGE OF INTERNATIONAL MEDIATION

CHAPTER TEN

Varieties of Mediating Activities and Mediators in International Relations

Louis Kriesberg

Mediation is usually identified as a set of activities that a mediator performs to facilitate settling a conflict. That concept is appropriate when we are discussing institutionalized mediator roles, as in collective bargaining in domestic labor disputes. In international affairs, however, the mediator roles usually are not as highly institutionalized (Bercovitch, 1984).

It is useful to distinguish between the roles of those who perform the variety of mediating services provided in international conflicts. Some mediating services are provided by a person or group designated as a mediator. But some are provided by a representative or member of one side in the dispute, referred to here as quasi-mediators; for example, ambassadors and negotiators sometimes mediate between the government they represent and its adversaries. The contributions of official and nonofficial quasi-mediators to peacemaking are not adequately recognized and understood. Comparing the mediating activities of formal and quasi-mediators will advance our understanding of each.

EFFECTIVENESS

The effectiveness of mediating actions is usually discussed in terms of success and failure. The definition of success in a mediating effort, however, is nearly always obscure. Even if the mediating activity is followed by movement toward accommodation, it is not necessarily valid to credit such progress to the mediating effort. Failure is usually easier to recognize than success, but even the constitution of failure is unclear and disputed in actuality. Failure is always relative to the goal that was sought and not attained. Various parties to a fight have different objectives and those objectives shift in the course of a conflict and its settlement.

In this chapter, I focus on one set of developments that would generally be regarded as success (Ross, 1993). This set includes de-escalation in the means of struggle, negotiations that move toward an agreed-upon settlement, and a settlement that contributes to an enduring resolution.

There is no consensus, however, that such developments can always be considered successful. For example, some may think that a move toward a settlement between one set of parties that occurs at the expense of other important parties is not a success. Most observers would label the 1938 settlement reached in Munich, where representatives of Germany, Italy, France, and the United Kingdom appeased Germany at the expense of Czechoslovakia, a dreadful failure.

There is another problem in characterizing a particular outcome as either a success or a failure. While the process of mediation may have been excellent, the background circumstances may have prevented the conflict from moving toward mutual accommodation. Conversely, the mediation may have been conducted clumsily, but because the time was ripe the conflict may have moved toward resolution anyway (Kriesberg, 1987).

In assessing efforts to mediate, I consider the general background conditions affecting movement toward conflict reduction. An agent providing mediating services should be aware of those conditions and construct a set of activities appropriate to them. Not doing so may cause the conflict to escalate and persist in violence, constituting a failed mediation effort. The mediation is successful insofar as it contributes significantly to a de-escalating movement, to mutually acceptable agreement, or to reconciliation, and is responsive to the prevailing conditions.

THE CONTEXT OF MEDIATION ACTIVITIES

Three sets of conditions are relevant for the appropriate timing of effective mediating activity (Kriesberg and Thorson, 1991): (1) the international context, (2) the support of the constituency for either de-escalation or escalation, and (3) the relations between the adversaries. I discuss aspects of each kind of condition, noting their relevance to the mediation of international conflicts.

International Context

Three features of the international context are especially relevant to mediating activities. First, the availability of international bodies for intermediary action has varied over time. Currently there are a great many such bodies, including universal organizations such as the United Nations Security Council (Claude, 1971). In many parts of the world, regional organizations such as the Organization of American States are available to provide mediating services (Dreier, 1962). International bodies available for some kinds of mediation also include nongovernmental actors; for example, church-based organizations such as the American Friends Service Committee (Berman and Johnson, 1977).

Second, the world structure of relative power and of alliances gives some governments the appropriate status to provide mediating activities. This may be true for disputes among members of the same alliance or among parties who are not members of any alliance.

Third, in considering the possibility of mediation in a given dispute, the potential mediator is selecting that dispute as the focal conflict. But in actuality each such fight is linked with many others (Kriesberg, 1980), and as those others increase or decrease in salience the focal conflict is likely to decrease or increase in significance. Insofar as its salience declines as other fights take on greater importance for one or more of the adversaries, de-escalation of a conflict is likely to occur.

Constituency

Public pressure expressed through public opinion surveys, social movements, or elections varies greatly in its impact on movement toward accommodation. Public pressure is generally more relevant for policies made over a period of years rather than a brief span of days or weeks (Hughes, 1978). Its impact among countries with different governmental systems varies relative to their responsiveness to elections, public opinion, and other manifestations of popular attitudes.

In addition to the public, the constituency affecting leaders' policies includes various subelites executing policies, counterelites presenting challenges, intellectuals offering alternatives, and media personnel transmitting information (Sanders, 1983).

The visibility of constituency support for de-escalation contributes a great deal to the timing of de-escalating initiatives by adversaries and by potential mediators. For example, public support for a de-escalating move, even if contrary to prevailing government policy, often encourages the adversary to make peacemaking overtures. Such overtures, however, may be treated by the government of the recipient country as efforts to undermine its popular support and therefore be resented and rejected. A mediator can take advantage of such opportunities without incurring the same risk (Kriesberg, 1992).

Adversary Relations

A specific dispute is only one aspect of the relationship between adversaries. Major adversaries have a variety of interactions, not only other disputes but also cooperative efforts based on complementary and common interests, and the relative importance of these relations affects the likelihood that any specific conflict can be reduced through intermediary action.

Parity of power is often stressed as a requisite for mutual accommodation and conflict resolution (Touval and Zartman, 1985). That is an important truth, but it is far from the whole truth. Power is always relative to what is being sought. It takes little power to induce an adversary to yield something that is unimportant to it and great power to win something it regards as vital. Power, then, is not independent of the goals for which it is being exercised. Furthermore, the many forms of power are not obviously commensurate. To calibrate parity simply by counting military hardware is certainly inadequate, and even factoring in geopolitical considerations and military organization is not enough. Economic, ideological, social, and cultural resources can provide noncoercive as well as coercive inducements.

When adversaries do not recognize each other as legitimate, a negotiated ending to any conflict between them is most difficult. This denial of legitimacy arises particularly in relations between state and nonstate actors, but often the major parties in a conflict are both challengers to a state. The recent upsurge in conflicts based on ethnic and other communal differences means there is an increase in situations in which parties deny each other's legitimacy.

Adversaries may contend with each other about a wide range of matters, and the nature of the issue in contention significantly affects the likelihood of a contribution by various intermediary activities. For example, the adversaries may be contending about matters that are largely dissensual, where they differ about their values. On the other hand, they may differ about largely consensual matters, where they both value the same resources. Dissensual issues are often difficult for adversaries to recognize and fully appreciate, and mediators can be especially helpful in clarifying differences in values and world views.

Of particular interest in this chapter is the course of a specific conflict between adversaries and the role of mediation at different stages of the conflict. I assume that for analytic purposes it is possible to treat a conflict as if it followed a course of emergence, escalation, de-escalation, and settlement (Kriesberg, 1982). Of course, new conflict can emerge out of the settlement of a previous one, and each specific conflict may be part of others with longer and shorter cycles of change. The sequence of stages is not to be applied rigidly; for example, a conflict can begin to de-escalate and not reach a settlement before it escalates again. The point of noting a sequence is to emphasize that conflicts evolve and mediation is likely to take different forms at different stages in their evolution.

KINDS OF MEDIATING ACTIVITY

Mediating activities vary in many ways (Moore, 1987; Mitchell and Webb, 1988) and in this section I identify major mediating strategies and techniques. In subsequent sections, I discuss who performs the activities and then the conflict stages at which the activities generally occur. In short, I consider what is done by whom, and when. In Table 10.1, a wide variety of mediating activities are listed and examples of each are identified.

Some mediating actions involve strategic choices; for example, selecting the parties and the issues for de-escalating efforts. Any person or group seeking to foster de-escalation must first consider the parties among whom the de-escalation is to be sought, and the parties to be included are never wholly clear and uncontested. In the Arab-Israeli conflict, for example, the choice of parties to be included in a de-escalating effort has always been a matter of dispute (Gazit, 1983; Touval, 1982). Even in the Argentina-United Kingdom conflict about the Falkland/Malvinas Islands, the British and Argentinean governments may not be regarded as the only parties to the dispute, as the residents of the islands may or may not be included in negotiations.

The choice of issues is also part of the mediating strategy, particularly in the prenegotiation stage (Stein, 1989). Does the effort involve many issues or a few, and does it concern peripheral or core matters in dispute? Of course, the issues in a de-escalating effort are selected relative to the parties included or excluded from such efforts. Setting the agenda also includes the number of issues to be discussed and how they are linked for possible trade-offs.

Most attention in the conflict resolution field, however, is given to mediating tactics rather than to strategic choices. The many specific short-term functions traditionally performed as part of mediation include providing good offices, communicating each side's views to the others, suggesting new options, and giving some solutions legitimacy and visibility.

Other actions that are increasingly emphasized in de-escalation include reframing the conflict so that it can be seen as a problem to be solved (Burton, 1969; Pruitt and Rubin, 1986). Intermediary parties can also contribute by adding resources to compensate one or another of the disputants for at least some of the losses that a settlement would involve, a move that has frequently been made in the U.S. mediation of the Israeli-Egyptian conflict. Resources can also be either added or withdrawn to approach parity between the adversaries or to increase the costs of not reaching a de-escalating agreement.

PROVIDERS OF MEDIATING SERVICES

Usually we think of persons or organizations who are formally designated as mediators as the ones who will provide mediating services, although sometimes such services are provided by nongovernmental actors. Mediators fulfill a social role that is shaped by the social conventions and

Table 10.1 Selected Mediation Cases by Mediating Activities and Stages of Conflicts

Mediating Activities	Preparing to De-escalate	Initiating Negotiations	Conducting Negotiations	Implementing Agreements
1. Selecting issues		Eric Johnson re Kissinger and bilateral shuttles, 1974, 1975		
2. Selecting parties	Cordovez (UN) re Afghanistan, 1983		U.S. re Israel-Lebanon, 1983	
3. Providing good offices	French government re U.S.-N. Vietnam			
4. Communicating each side's views	**American Friends Service Committee in SE Asia:** ***Track II; Dialog Groups***	***Cousins re U.S.-USSR, 1963***	*Weizman at Camp David, 1978; Carter in Korea, 1994*	
5. Reframing conflict to problem	***Middle East Problem-Solving Workshop;*** Haig in Middle East, 1981	***Problem-Solving Workshop***		
6. Suggesting new options	**AFSC re Middle East; Dartmouth Conferences**	*Rapacki Plan 1957; Macmillan and Limited Test Ban, 1959, 1962*	**Pugwash** 1960s; *Nitze and Kvitsinsky "walk in the woods";* Peru, UN, and Haig re Argentina-U.K., 1982; Jarring, Rogers re Israel-Egypt, 1969–1970;	
7. Raising costs of failing to de-escalate			Carter at Camp David 1978	
8. Adding resources for settlement			Carter at Camp David 1978; Rogers re Egypt-Israel 1970	U.S. Peacekeeping Forces in Sinai 1974; Syrian forces in Lebanon
9. Helping to create parity	U.S. government meets with PLO, 1988; US re Egypt-Israel 1973 war			
10. Building trust and credibility			*Weizman at Camp David 1978*	

Mediating Activities	Preparing to De-escalate	Initiating Negotiations	Conducting Negotiations	Implementing Agreements
11. Fostering reconciliation	**Dialogue Groups**			
12. Legitimating and helping to implement proposal or agreement	***U.S.-Soviet People-to-People Dialogue, 1980s;*** **U.S. Jews and PLO December, 1988;** ***Community Dialogue Groups***		Carter and ceremonial signing of Egyptian-Israeli Peace Treaty	

Note: Cases in bold are examples of nonofficial mediating activities; cases in italics are examples of quasi-mediators.

expectations of the parties with whom they interact. There are many social conventions about mediators but within the role there are also wide variations, some of which are cultural and others situational; for example, in the domain of how actively the mediator offers options or intervention. Certain roles are circumscribed by rules embodied in international law and treaty obligations. The UN Secretary-General, for example, may not seek or receive instructions from any government (Bailey, 1962).

A mediator may be a government that is not regarded as a party to the conflict, or it may be an agent for an international governmental organization. Some mediating services also may be provided by nongovernmental individuals or groups who are not clearly seen as mediators; these include church officials, journalists, and academics representing constituencies that are not primary adversaries in the dispute (Berman and Johnson, 1977; McDonald and Bendahmane, 1987). In Table 10.1, the variety of mediators is illustrated.

Nongovernmental actors may be able to perform mediating activities especially well when one or more of the conflicting parties are themselves nonstate actors, because actors in this same category can more easily understand each other. On the other hand, as an intergovernmental organization the United Nations is often unable to engage in mediating activities when one or more of the adversary parties is not a state, as it is better equipped and oriented to deal with governments. Nongovernmental organizations that have a single, enduring constituency are sometimes able to pursue a consistent policy for a longer period of time than governments that are subject to electoral change.

Some mediating activities are provided by members of one of the adversary parties, who act as quasi-mediators between, for example, their government and their government's adversary. In this dual role, it is not always clear when such a person or organization is serving only the adversary party and when he or she is acting as a quasi-mediator. Someone acting under instructions from the formal head of an adversary party is not acting as a quasi-mediator but as an agent for that party. On the other hand, someone who is not in accord with the leaders of his or her own community is not in a position to contribute as a quasi-mediator with the adversary community once negotiations between official negotiators are under way.

Quasi-mediators can be members of factions or even of political parties within the governing coalitions of one of the adversaries. They also can be unofficial persons who have close ties with officials and act as agents for them, conducting inquiries or testing responses to possible official proposals. In some cases, quasi-mediators may be nonofficial groups without close ties to any government representatives. Track 2 diplomacy (nonofficial), people-to-people meetings, dialogue groups, and problem-solving workshops are types of such quasi-mediator functions.

Even officials of the disputing parties may occasionally act as quasi-mediators and provide some mediating services. For example, members of negotiating teams usually vary in what they expect and want from the negotiations and in how they perceive the adversary. In the 1978 Camp David negotiations between Israel and Egypt, for instance, Israeli defense minister Ezer Weizman performed important mediating services between President Sadat and Prime Minister Begin (Quandt, 1986; Weizman, 1981), helping to convey the trustworthiness of the Egyptians to the Israelis.

Another notable illustration of the services of quasi-mediators is the "walk in the woods" proposal developed by Paul Nitze and Uyli Kvitsinski, the U.S. and Soviet negotiators at the talks on intermediate-range nuclear forces in Geneva (Talbott, 1984). Acting without instructions from above, the two negotiators developed a joint proposal and each presented it to his government. After deliberation, however, both governments rejected the proposal, and the negotiations failed at that time.

Persons and groups differ greatly in the resources they can bring to their mediating work. Formal and informal mediators and quasi-mediators have varying capacities to offer compensations and guarantees, provide legitimacy to options, and make suggestions that demand attention.

An official member of one of the partisan groups generally has more credibility and is accorded more trust by his or her own colleagues than is a formal mediator. For example, although effective in many ways in his 1974–1975 shuttle diplomacy between Israel and Egypt and Syria, Secretary of State Henry Kissinger came to be viewed as untrustworthy by some Israelis (Golan, 1976). But on the other hand, a member of a partisan group is less likely to be viewed as trustworthy by his or her adversary than is a formal mediator.

A proposal from a member of one of the adversary parties is also more likely to be considered by his or her own colleagues than a proposal from a formal mediator. For example, the Nitze-Kvitsinski "walk in the woods" proposal would probably not have been considered if it had been developed by a formal mediator. In general, quasi-mediators are less constrained by the mediator's social role than formal mediators are.

CONFLICT STAGES AND MEDIATING ACTIVITIES

Each kind of mediating activity can occur at every stage of a conflict, but the specific content, form, and significance of the activities vary at different stages. In this section, I consider how mediators and quasi-mediators differ in the services they provide and in the effectiveness of those services, in the context of four major stages of de-escalation: preparation, initiation, negotiation, and implementation. The possibilities for success and for failure differ at each stage of the effort, with each kind of mediating activity, and with the agent providing the mediating service.

Preparation

The prenegotiation stage is increasingly recognized as an important one (Stein, 1989). Mediating activity at this stage includes exploring which parties are ready to discuss de-escalation and which can be excluded without undermining a possible agreement. A formal mediator is freer to explore alternative agendas and sets of partners than is a member of one of the adversary parties, and nonofficial mediators may be particularly free to explore and communicate views among possible de-escalation partners. Adversary parties may request an unofficial person or organization to conduct informal conversations in order to determine the likelihood of particular responses to a de-escalating initiative.

Quasi-mediators can convey certain kinds of information in a particularly compelling way. By demonstrating flexibility in their party, they can raise the expectation in the other side that its de-escalating initiatives will be reciprocated. Furthermore, they can suggest how such initiatives might be articulated so that they will be credible and therefore effective. Finally, they can provide some assurance that even risky de-escalating initiatives will not be exploited.

Quasi-mediators can also play an important role in helping to develop constituency support for peace efforts (Saunders, 1985). International nongovernmental agencies, especially those focusing on relations between adversaries, are in a position to foster understandings and interpersonal relationships that support de-escalating initiatives and responses. The Dartmouth conference involving U.S. and Soviet citizens is an example of such an organization.[1]

The breakthrough agreement reached by the leaders of Israel and the Palestine Liberation Organization in 1993 was preceded by many years of unofficial meetings between Israeli Jews and PLO members. In those discussions, both sides exchanged concerns and suggestions for solutions, so that when conditions became propitious for a settlement the knowledge had been gained that made undertaking negotiation seem possible.

Initiation

At the initiating stage, the mediating activity entails helping to undertake discussions among the parties. Inadequate exploration and preparation may lead to initiating proposals that fail to open up de-escalating exchanges. The dramatic 1977 offer by President Sadat to go to Jerusalem, for example, might not have been responded to as quickly and clearly as it was had no prior explorations been conducted at the highest levels. Indeed, Israeli officials who had not been informed of some of the prior moves were skeptical of President Sadat's initiative (Stein, 1989).

Quasi-mediators can be particularly helpful at this stage. Thus Norman Cousins, as a private U.S. citizen, was invited by Premier Khrushchev to visit him in Moscow in 1963. Cousins returned with the suggestion that President Kennedy make some sort of gesture to reopen negotiations regarding a nuclear test ban (Cousins, 1972). The American University speech followed in June and the Partial Nuclear Weapons Test Ban was signed shortly thereafter.

The strategic choices made in the initiating stage regarding parties, issues, and format may be inappropriate for the prevailing conditions, such as the severity of the conflict and the deep distrust between the parties, and therefore fail. For example, UN resolutions calling for a comprehensive peace conference and settlement of the Israeli-Arab conflict repeatedly failed to lead to such an event until the Madrid Conference in 1991.

Negotiation

The primary mediating activity in the negotiating stage is making more acceptable the adversaries' negotiations. This includes giving legitimacy to offers and to options for settlement. A proposal made by one of the adversaries may be easier to accept if it is presented by a mediator, so parties in the negotiations may request that a mediator perform this function. In this situation, the formal role of the mediator is crucial.

At this stage also, mediating activity includes managing relations with the parties who are not directly involved in the negotiations. A quasi-mediator is especially useful in this function. Mediating activity might also involve helping the adversaries to take into account the interests and concerns of conflict parties not represented in the discussions. A formal mediator is much more likely than a quasi-mediator to be effective in this service; for example, the concerns of Afghan refugees were represented to some extent by the formal UN mediator.

During negotiations, intermediaries with great power and resources relative to the adversaries may try to impose a settlement and find that they are unable to do so. The hubris of mediators is dangerous, as is that of an apparently winning adversary. For example, the Syrian government intervened in the complex internecine struggles in Lebanon, but only recently was able to attain the settlement it preferred. By not taking Syrian interests adequately into account, the U.S. government's mediation between the Lebanese and Israeli governments in 1983 also failed to forge an agreement that could be ratified and sustained (Young, 1987; Khouri, 1985). Quasi-mediators are less likely to suffer from the same sort of hubris.

Implementation

In implementing an agreement, mediating services may include seeking to win support for the settlement by the negotiating parties' constituencies. Formal mediators can do much in this regard by providing legitimacy and credibility to an agreement. They can help stage traditional and symbolic rituals that make the agreement more visible and more obligatory. They also improve the likelihood of compliance because the adversaries have developed an obligation to them.

The stage of implementing a de-escalation is often inadequately considered in planning for and negotiating agreements. Powerful mediators can be important sustainers, if not enforcers, of an agreement. Adversaries have an obligation to those helping them to reach an agreement, while the mediators have an interest in sustaining a settlement that they helped bring about, and may provide resources to do so. For example, in mediating various Israeli-Egyptian agreements the U.S. government has frequently provided monitoring and other services to ensure the fulfillment of an agreement. International governmental organizations (IGOs) are frequently useful intermediaries at this stage—by providing peacekeeping forces, for example—but quasi-mediators are less able to provide such services.

Although their contributions are more limited at the de-escalation stage, quasi-mediators can help to sustain an agreement. They can provide independent verification of the agreement, monitoring their own government, and can communicate convincingly to the adversary that members of their side accept responsibility for having done harm in the past. They may also express an acceptance of the other side, despite the harm that side has done to them. Expressions of sorrow, apology, forgiveness, and irretrievable loss can contribute to a process of reconciliation.

CONCLUSIONS

Making distinctions within the categories of mediation activities, actors, and stages of conflict de-escalation is useful. It offers a sound basis for assessing what kinds of action contribute to movement toward mutual accommodation and what kinds do not. In drawing attention to the wide variety of persons and groups who are involved in such movements, it performs the social service of demonstrating how many different kinds of people can contribute to peacemaking. Furthermore, attention to mediating services provided by adversaries can suggest new or alternative ways to provide such services. This chapter has explored differences between the activities of formal and quasi-mediators.

Intermediary activities have been discussed in relationship to preparing for negotiations, starting and conducting them, reaching mutual accommodative agreements, and sustaining those agreements. Such movement is regarded here as success, but assessing whether or not any particular mediating behavior contributes to such movement is another matter. Success in mediation is never attributable to a single cause or factor, and consequently no one mediating activity can be the sufficient cause for the movement; it may, however, add a necessary or critical element. A mediating activity may contribute to the de-escalation movement even without being necessary, however—for instance, by improving the quality or the speed of the de-escalation.

There are also varying degrees to which mediating efforts contribute to failure. A mediating activity may simply contribute nothing to ending an ongoing struggle; it may be essentially irrelevant. Or it may be one of the factors that impedes a de-escalating process from making progress by, for instance, allowing one party to appear to be seeking a settlement while it holds out for better terms in the future. The introduction of the mediator's own interests may also disrupt an accommodation.

The contributions of mediating efforts to failure have several sources; I cite only a few here. The very fact that many different persons and groups are engaged in mediating activities may mean that they interfere with rather than complement and supplement each other, a difficulty that has been suggested as arising when UN special representative Jarring and U.S. secretary of state Rogers sought to mediate the conflict between the Israeli and Egyptian governments between 1969 and 1971 (Gazit, 1983; Touval, 1982).

Some persons or groups try to carry out mediating activities for which they lack the resources—for example, acting as if they had the capacity to impose a settlement. The hubris of mediators can be dangerous, as illustrated by the failed mediation efforts of both the Syrian and the U.S. governments in regard to Lebanon.

There are many ways to fail. Relative to the circumstances and the stage of the conflict, failures basically result from one or both of the following: the application of an inappropriate strategy, and the application of a strategy by an inappropriate person or group.

Many conditions must be present if a mediation effort is to contribute to progress toward mutual accommodation. Formal mediators certainly have made vital contributions, as President Jimmy Carter did at Camp David in 1978. Quasi-mediators also have made important contributions, as did Ezer Weizman at those same negotiations. Quasi-mediators can be particularly effective in the early stages of de-escalating movements because although they may lack the resources available to the formal mediators, they can provide useful supplementary or even essential services when no formal mediator is deemed acceptable.

In the case of large-scale, intractable conflicts, formal mediators have played critical roles once the parties have already come close to reaching some de-escalating agreements. And quasi-mediators, by making probes, offering suggestions, and providing reassuring information to their constituency and to the adversary, have often played crucial roles in moving adversaries into position for such agreements.

NOTES

An earlier version of this chapter was published in the *Journal of Peace Research*, vol. 28, no. 1 (1991). I want to thank Herbert Kelman, Carolyn Stephenson, Nils Peter Gleditsch, and Jacob Bercovitch for their comments on earlier versions.

1. The Dartmouth conferences began at Hanover, New Hampshire in 1960. The conferences have been meeting regularly, bringing together academicians, scientists, and writers from the United States and former Soviet Union. Problems facing government officials of both countries are explored and initial approaches that government leaders might undertake to reduce the problems are sought.

REFERENCES

Bailey, S. D. (1962). *The Secretariat of the United Nations*. New York: Carnegie Endowment for International Peace.

Bercovitch, J. (1984). *Social Conflict and Third Parties: Strategies of Conflict Resolution*. Boulder, Colo.: Westview.

Berman, M. R., and Johnson, J. E., eds. (1977). *Unofficial Diplomats*. New York: Columbia University Press.

Burton, J. W. (1969). *Conflict and Communication: The Use of Controlled Communication in International Relations*. London: Macmillan.

Claude, I. L., Jr. (1971). *Swords Into Plowshares*. 4th ed. New York: Random House.

Cousins, N. (1972). *The Improbable Triumvirate*. New York: Norton.

Dreier, J. C. (1962). *The Organization of American States and the Hemisphere Crisis*. New York: Harper & Row.

Gazit, M. (1983). "The Peace Process 1969–1973: Efforts and Contacts." Jerusalem Papers on Peace Problems, no. 35. Jerusalem: Leonard Davis Institute of International Relations/Magnes Press.

Golan, M. (1976). *The Secret Conversations of Henry Kissinger: Step-by-Step Diplomacy in the Middle East*. Trans. R. G. Stern and S. Stern. New York: Bantam Books.

Hughes, B. B. (1978). *The Democratic Context of American Foreign Policy*. San Francisco: Freeman.

Khouri, F. J. (1985). *The Arab-Israeli Dilemma*. 3rd ed. Syracuse: Syracuse University Press.

Kriesberg, L. (1980). "Interlocking Conflicts in the Middle East." In L. Kriesberg, ed., *Research in Social Movements, Conflicts and Change*, vol. 3. Greenwich, Conn.: JAI, 99–118.

Kriesberg, L. (1982). *Social Conflicts*. 2nd ed. Englewood Cliffs, N.J.: Prentice-Hall.

Kriesberg, L. (1987). "Timing and the Initiation of De-Escalation Moves." *Negotiation Journal* 3, 4: 375–384.

Kriesberg, L. (1992). *International Conflict Resolution: The U.S.-USSR and Middle East Cases*. New Haven: Yale University Press.

Kriesberg, L., and Thorson, S., eds. (1991). *Timing the De-escalation of International Conflict.* Syracuse: Syracuse University Press.
McDonald, J. W., and Bendahmane, D. B., eds. (1987). *Conflict Resolution: Track Two Diplomacy.* Foreign Service Institute, U.S. Department of State. Washington, D.C.: U.S. Government Printing Office.
Mitchell, C. R., and Webb, K., eds. (1988). *New Approaches to International Mediation.* Westport, Conn.: Greenwood.
Moore, C. W. (1987). *The Mediation Process: Practical Strategies for Resolving Conflict.* San Francisco: Jossey-Bass.
Pruitt, D. G., and Rubin, J. Z. (1986). *Social Conflict: Escalation, Stalemate, and Settlement.* New York: Random House.
Quandt, W. B. (1986). *Camp David: Peacemaking and Politics.* Washington, D.C.: Brookings Institution.
Ross, M. H. (1993). *The Management of Conflict.* New Haven: Yale University Press.
Sanders, J. W. (1983). *Peddlers of Crisis.* Boston: South End.
Saunders, H. H. (1985). *The Other Walls: The Politics of the Arab-Israeli Peace Process.* Washington, D.C.: American Enterprise Institute.
Stein, J. G., ed. (1989). *Getting to the Table: The Processes of International Prenegotiation.* Baltimore: Johns Hopkins University Press.
Talbott, S. (1984). *Deadly Gambits.* New York: Knopf.
Touval, S. (1982). *The Peace Brokers: Mediators in the Arab-Israeli Conflict, 1948–1979.* Princeton, N.J.: Princeton University Press.
Touval, S., and Zartman, I. W., eds. (1985). *International Mediation in Theory and Practice.* Boulder, Colo.: Westview.
Weizman, E. (1981). *The Battle for Peace.* New York: Bantam Books.
Young, R. J. (1987). *Missed Opportunities for Peace: U.S. Middle East Policy 1981–1986.* Philadelphia: American Friends Service Committee.

CHAPTER ELEVEN

A Contingency Perspective on Conflict Interventions: Theoretical and Practical Considerations

Loraleigh Keashly and Ronald J. Fisher

The involvement of impartial third parties has a long and honorable history in the domain of human social conflict (Mitchell and Webb, 1988; Rubin, 1981). In the field of international relations, the longstanding role of third parties has only recently begun to receive frequent attention, with the work by Young (1967) leading the way to further developments. In the current decade, third-party interventions, particularly in the form of mediation, have become the focus of a considerable amount of scholarly activity (for example, Bercovitch and Rubin, 1992; Carnevale, 1985; Touval and Zartman, 1985). This growing emphasis reflects the current reality of international relations, in which the pacific intervention of third parties in conflicts is a common occurrence (see Bercovitch, 1984). As expected, the most frequent form of intervention is that of mediation, with fact-finding, good offices, and arbitration also being much in evidence.

In addition to traditional third-party roles, scholar-practitioners have recently developed an innovative third-party method in the form of problem-solving workshops directed toward intergroup and international conflict resolution (Burton, 1969; Doob, 1970; Kelman, 1972). These various developments can be subsumed under a model of *third-party consultation* that emphasizes the facilitative and diagnostic role played by knowledgeable and skilled intermediaries who assist the parties in analyzing their conflict and searching for mutually acceptable solutions (Fisher, 1972). A comprehensive, evaluative review of such efforts at the community, organizational, and international levels is provided by Fisher (1983).

Third-party consultation involves interventions, often in the form of problem-solving workshops, in which a team of consultants works with the parties to improve communication, diagnose underlying relationship issues, and facilitate the search toward creative resolution of the conflict. In contrast, mediation at the international level involves interventions by credible and competent intermediaries who assist the parties in working toward a negotiated settlement on substantive issues through persuasion, the control of information, the suggestion of alternatives, and, in some cases, the application of leverage. Although this distinction seems clear-cut, there has been an unfortunate blurring of the boundaries between mediation and consultation in some of the recent literature, which essentially attempts to subsume consultation as a form of mediation (Bercovitch, 1992; Fisher and Keashly, 1988; Kelman, 1992; Kressel and Pruitt, 1985). This is especially surprising in that a number of the seminal writers on problem solving took pains to distinguish their approach from mediation. Fisher and Keashly (1988) challenged this blurring with a detailed discussion demonstrating meaningful differences between traditional mediation and consultation in terms of underlying assumptions, third-party identity, role, functions and tactics, and overall objectives. They argued that by articulating and understanding the unique strengths and limitations of each approach and the conditions under which each method is initially effective, a fuller range of "intervention tools" becomes available for dealing with particularly complex disputes.

Once the distinctions are clear, it becomes apparent that mediation and consultation have a high degree of potential complementarity (Fisher, 1986). At the international level in particular, consultation might be used to analyze and de-escalate need and interest conflicts to the point where mediation of interests would more likely be successful. In other words, it is likely that consultation might serve a premediation or prenegotiation function, enhancing the chances of acceptable settlement of substantive issues within the context of an overall resolution of the conflict (Fisher, 1989). These ideas presage the possibility of a contingency approach in which the various forms of pacific third-party intervention would be sequenced and coordinated in the most efficacious manner to control, de-escalate, settle, and resolve destructive international conflict.

The purpose of this chapter is to discuss the potential complementarity of international mediation and consultation within a contingency approach to third-party intervention. Some examples of complementarity exist at the organizational level (for example, Birnbaum, 1984; Brett et al., 1980), and initial explorations of a contingency approach have been undertaken (for example, Prein, 1984). At the international level, these areas offer fruitful ground for development as there is little indication of coordination among third-party interventions (Ury, 1987). The conceptual task will be approached by briefly describing the method of third-party consultation, followed by the rationale for and an initial model of the contingency approach. Examples of current conceptual and practical work that examine and elaborate on various linkages of the contingency model will be presented. The conclusion will stress that the complementarity of mediation and consultation (and, by extension, other interventions) within a contingency approach is deserving of further elaboration both conceptually and practically, work which may ultimately have important implications for practitioners of conflict management and resolution.

THIRD-PARTY CONSULTATION

Fisher (1972) developed an initial model of third-party consultation by drawing on seminal contributions at the interpersonal, intergroup, and international levels (Blake and Mouton, 1964; Burton, 1969; Doob, 1970; Walton, 1969). As opposed to highlighting the problem-solving aspect of the method, the model emphasizes the unique and essential role played by the impartial team of facilitators or consultants who enter directly into the field of the conflict and assist the antagonists in analyzing the underlying issues and searching for creative solutions. The rationale of third-party consultation is largely based on a social-psychological perspective that sees conflict at least partly and at times predominantly as a subjective social process (Fisher, 1989). This rationale does not deny the objective approach to conflict. Indeed, it accepts the tenet of realistic conflict theory that real differences in interests cause intergroup conflict (Campbell, 1965). However, once a conflict is initiated the perceptions, attitudes, and interaction of the parties become crucial elements in determining its further course. Typically, there is an escalating spiral of intensity in which the relationship between the parties moves toward destructive competition and finally to a "malignant social process" from which the parties are unable or unwilling to extricate themselves (Deutsch, 1973). The rationale of consultation thus draws on a variety of concepts at the individual, the interpersonal, the group, the intergroup, and the system levels to explain why the method may have some potential utility for understanding and resolving protracted intergroup and international conflict (Fisher, 1989). Figure 11.1 provides a revised version of the model (Fisher, 1976) in which each circle represents a major component of the method.

In terms of identity, the model prescribes that the third-party consultants should be knowledgeable and skilled scholar-practitioners whose background, attitudes, and behavior engender impartiality or, at least, balance, and whose training and expertise enable them to facilitate productive confrontation between the parties. Thus, in addition to the demanding array of skills required for success in informal diplomatic activity, third-party consultants uniquely require extensive knowledge and sensitivity regarding the social processes of human interaction, in much the same vein as a human-relations trainer and group/organizational consultant. At the international level, consultants also require an understanding of cultural differences since these differences influence interactions

Figure 11.1 A Model of Third-Party Consultation

Third-party identity: Skilled and impartial consultant

Situation: Small-group discussions in a neutral and informal setting

Third-party functions: Induce positive motivation. Improve communication. Diagnose the conflict. Regulate the interaction

Objectives: Improved attitudes. Improved relationship. Conflict resolution

Program of third-party consultation

Trusting, respectful, and empathic helping relationship

Facilitative and diagnostic third-party role

Third-party tactics and procedures: To carry out the role and the functions

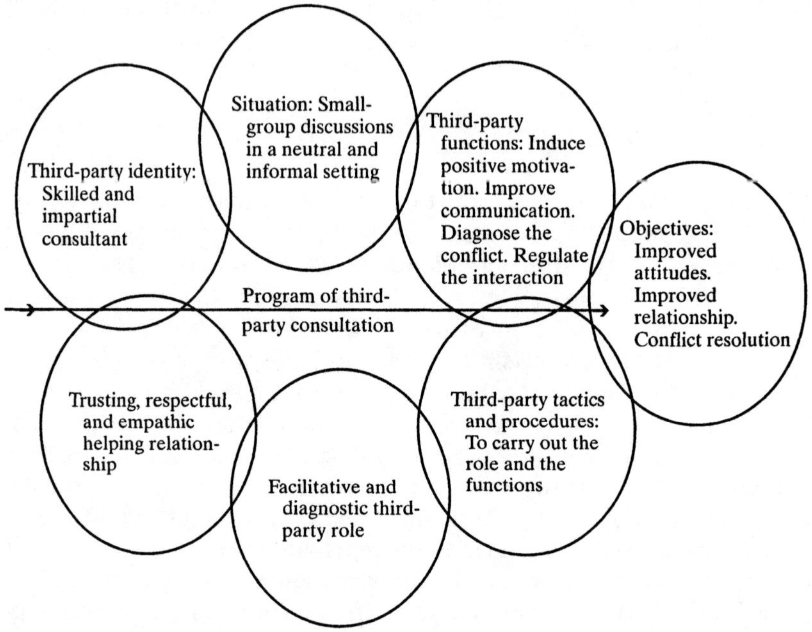

Source: Reprinted, by permission, from Fisher, 1976, p. 345; © 1976 by the American Psychological Association.

and an appreciation of the broader structures and processes of the global system in which their interventions are embedded.

An adequate identity provides the foundation for an effective helping or consulting relationship with the parties that involves trust and respect and encourages the movement toward an open and constructive problem-solving process. The necessary physical and social arrangements of the method are captured by the term *situation*. Typically, the third-party consultant designs and arranges a series of informal and flexible small-group discussions, not unlike academic seminars, in a neutral and isolated setting. The rationale is to provide a relaxed and supportive atmosphere in which the participants will undertake the demanding task of confrontation, wherein they focus directly on the basic perceptions, attitudes, and issues involved in the conflict. The third-party role is seen as primarily facilitative and diagnostic, but also nonevaluative, noncoercive, and nondirective over outcomes. The consultants draw on their social-scientific knowledge of conflict to further the parties' analysis and use their social skills to facilitate the problem-solving process. The role blends into the third-party functions, the core strategies of the method, which include inducing mutual motivation for problem solving, improving the openness and accuracy of communication, diagnosing the processes and issues of the conflict, and regulating the interaction among the participants.

The functions are put into practice through specific behavioral tactics (for example, controlling a disruptive interchange) and procedures that involve structured exercises (for example, the development and exchange of perceptions of an ideal relationship). The objectives of the method include improved (that is, more complex, veridical, and positive) attitudes, an improved (less destructive, more cooperative) relationship, a resolution of the conflict (innovative solutions freely and mutually agreed upon), and increased knowledge about conflict for both the participants and the consultants. The initial presentation of the model (Fisher, 1972) also noted that a variety of supportive activities are required for implementation, and discussed the important aspect of the identity and role of participants in the problem-solving discussions. On the latter point, participants in actual sessions have ranged from interested and representative groups or countries to appointed yet informal influentials who have direct input into decisionmaking. The identity of participants is significant, since it relates directly to the difficult question of transfer of outcomes back to the actual relationship between the parties (see Bloomfield, 1993, for further discussion of this point).

A CONTINGENCY MODEL OF THIRD-PARTY INTERVENTION

The idea of a contingency approach to third-party intervention in intergroup and international conflict is gaining increasing currency (Bercovitch, 1991; Bloomfield, 1992; Keashly and Fisher, 1990; Kriesberg, 1989). Basically, a contingency approach would work to match the type of third-party intervention to certain characteristics of the conflict in question. Work at the organizational level is beginning to make a strong conceptual and empirical case for a contingency approach. Sheppard (1984), for example, developed a complex procedural framework, covering conflict in a variety of settings, that in part describes different interventions in terms of the form of control exercised by the third party as well as the timing of entry in relation to stages of the conflict. Prein (1984) provides a simpler conceptual scheme that relates the choice among mediation and two forms of consultation to the characteristics and context of the conflict. Based on an analysis of sixty-nine cases of organizational conflict, Prein finds in part that consultation is more effective when miscommunication and mistrust are high whereas mediation is more successful when substantive issues are at the fore of the conflict.

Glasl (1982) outlines a nine-stage model of conflict escalation to which he matches the most common forms of third-party intervention. His contingency model is noteworthy for three reasons. First, this model brings together a diverse range of interventions that have typically been developed in isolation from one another, from the traditional substantive and structural approaches of mediation and arbitration to the newer relationship-building approaches of consultation and problem solving. Second, all forms of intervention are acknowledged as having utility if applied at the appropriate level of escalation. Thus, instead of arguing for the ultimate superiority of one approach, scholars' and practitioners' attention is refocused on effectiveness relative to the conflict as it is manifested at a particular point in time. This notion of relative effectiveness leads to the third noteworthy and perhaps most unique aspect of Glasl's model, which is the raising of the possibility of coordination and sequencing of (sometimes qualitatively) different interventions over the course of a conflict-management initiative. The present analysis follows most strongly the approach outlined by Glasl, in that different types of third-party intervention, particularly mediation and consultation, are linked to the stage of escalation to which they seem most applicable and are sequenced within stages when most appropriate.

The presentation of the contingency model will proceed with a brief discussion of the basic assumptions of the model. Subsequently, the two main components of the model (intervention typology and stages of escalation) will be described. Finally, the notions of complementarity and sequencing of the interventions will be explored within this context.

Basic Assumptions of the Model

A contingency approach to third-party intervention is based on the assessment that social conflict involves a dynamic process in which objective and subjective elements interact over time as the conflict escalates and de-escalates. Depending on the objective-subjective mix, different interventions will be appropriate at different stages of the conflict. If objective elements linked to resource scarcity are predominant at a given point, then third-party methods that facilitate a compromise or provide a judgment are appropriate. If subjective elements such as misperception, miscommunication, and the differential valuing of objective interests are much in evidence, then third-party activities that improve the relationship and induce problem solving are indicated. In all cases, the beliefs held about the nature of social conflict (that is, objective vs. subjective) by the parties (and any third parties) will have an effect on perceptions about what type of interventions are realistic (Keashly and Fisher, 1990). Rather than being limited to particular strategies by the assumptions that are made, the contingency approach challenges all parties to entertain a complex view of conflict, and to develop and adapt strategies from a range of options.

There are two additional assumptions related to the objective-subjective mix in conflict. The first is that as the conflict escalates, the subjective elements become predominant in fueling the conflict. The other is that focusing on either the subjective or objective aspect exclusive of the other aspect may result in short-term or medium-term settlement, but for long-term resolution to occur both objective and subjective elements must be addressed. Since third-party interventions differ in the emphases they give to objective and subjective aspects, the potential of matching the type of intervention to the level of escalation (that is, to the objective-subjective mix) becomes apparent (Keashly and Fisher, 1990). It also becomes conceivable to engage in sequencing and coordinating different third-party interventions in any one conflict in order to de-escalate and resolve it beginning at any specific stage. In line with a complex conceptualization of social conflict, this approach acknowledges that no one third-party method should be expected to deal with all or even most elements of a given conflict. Furthermore, it highlights the need to clearly articulate the strengths and limitations of a variety of approaches in order to facilitate such coordination. In fact, the considerable potential of a contingency approach is based on an acknowledgment of the limitations of all approaches and the realization that they are at present seldom if ever coordinated in the real world of conflict management.

Types of Intervention

There is unfortunately no agreed-upon typology for classifying third-party interventions in intergroup and international conflict. In some contexts, terms are used interchangeably (for example, conciliation and mediation), and in some cases a single term, usually mediation, is used to refer to a wide range of third-party interventions in which the third party does not have the power to impose a settlement (Bercovitch, 1992; Sheppard, 1984). As argued earlier, this labeling may obscure the unique strengths and limitations of these interventions, effectively limiting the possibilities for contingent and coordinated action. To more fully acknowledge the diversity of intervention, this discussion will use a typology consisting of conciliation, consultation, pure mediation, power mediation, arbitration, and peacekeeping.

Conciliation involves a trusted third party providing an informal communication link between the antagonists for the purposes of identifying the major issues, lowering tension, and encouraging them to move toward direct interaction such as negotiation to deal with their differences. The important distinction is that the third party does not propose alternatives for settling the dispute. Related forms of limited third-party intervention include good offices, wherein the intermediary acts simply as a go-between, and fact-finding, wherein a third party assesses the situation and provides a statement back to the parties. *Consultation* (also referred to as problem solving) involves the intervention of a skilled and knowledgeable third party (usually a team) who attempts to facilitate creative problem solving through communication and analysis using social-scientific understanding of conflict etiology and processes. An attempt is made to confront the opposing perceptions and attitudes and to reveal the underlying affective and relationship issues. It is assumed that an increase in understanding and trust will enable the parties to settle their differences on substantive issues, either through negotiation or as part of the creative problem solving within consultation itself. *Pure mediation* involves the intervention of a skilled and experienced intermediary who attempts to facilitate a negotiated settlement to the dispute on a set of specific substantive issues. The mediator usually combines individual meetings involving each party's representatives with joint negotiating sessions, and uses reasoning, persuasion, the control of information, and the suggestion of alternatives to assist the antagonists in finding an acceptable agreement. *Power mediation* builds on these functions, but also includes the use of leverage or coercion by the third party in the form of promised rewards or threatened punishments. In a very real sense, the third party becomes a member of a negotiating triad and bargains with each party, using carrots and sticks, to move them toward a settlement. This form of mediation often leads to settlements that have future implications for the third party as a provider of continuing benefits and/or the guarantor of the agreement. *Arbitration* involves a legitimate and authoritative third party providing a binding judgment to the parties that is arrived at by considering the merits of the opposing positions and imposing a settlement deemed to be fair and just. In social systems where legitimate authorities and the rule of law are well institutionalized, arbitration usually carries penalties for noncompliance. In the relative anarchy of the international system, submission to forms of arbitration or adjudication and compliance with the outcomes are largely voluntary. *Peacekeeping* involves the provision of military personnel by an outside party (often the United Nations) to supervise and monitor a cease-fire between antagonists. The third-party forces may also engage in a variety of humanitarian activities in addition to their basic function of securing the peace. Although third-party personnel often engage in day-to-day mediatory activities around particular incidents or situations, their role is not designed to move the parties toward a political settlement.

Stage Model of Escalation

The second major component of a contingency approach concerns the identification of characteristics of conflict that can provide the cues for the implementation of particular strategies. As noted earlier, the stage of escalation and de-escalation stands out as the critical cue for the adoption of one strategy over another (Glasl, 1982; Prein, 1984; Wright, 1965). Wright's model of escalation in international conflict identifies four stages according to the increasingly overt actions of violence. Unfortunately, Wright (1965) says little about the subjective aspects of conflict such as perceptions, attitudes, and patterns of interaction. This deficit is partly counterbalanced by Prein (1984), who identifies communication difficulties and relationship issues along with substantive issues as key elements in conflict to be considered in adopting the appropriate third-party strategy.

Glasl's (1982) contingency model delineates nine stages of conflict escalation by changes in perceptions, attitudes, overt behavior, and patterns of interaction. The nine stages are then combined into three main phases based on particularly significant shifts in cognitions and interactions. Glasl then presents six common strategies of third-party intervention (moderation, process consultation, sociotherapeutic process consultation, mediation, arbitration, and power intervention) and discusses each strategy in terms of its relevance to selected stages of escalation. Finally, Glasl (1982) notes that over the long-term course of conflict handling, a third party may begin with one strategy, achieve the appropriate results, and then move to another strategy. Kriesberg (1989) also relates a broad set of "mediating activities" to the stages of de-escalation, thus producing a description of international mediation with some elements of a contingency approach built in.

Building on the formative work of Prein, Glasl, and Kriesberg, with particular attention paid to incorporating both subjective and objective indicators of escalation, the present stage model identifies four stages of conflict escalation: (1) discussion, (2) polarization, (3) segregation, and (4) destruction. The stages are distinguished by noticeable changes in the nature of communication between the parties, their perceptions and images of each other and their relationship, the overt issues at the fore of the dispute, the perceived possible outcomes, and the preferred strategy for handling the conflict. Described in these terms, the reverse order of the stages provides for the occurrence of de-escalation, although other elements specific to de-escalation may need to be added for a fully comprehensive description.

Briefly, as intergroup and international conflict escalates, communication and interaction move from discussion and debate (stage 1) to a reliance on the interpretation (often the misinterpretation) of actions with less direct interchange (2), to the use of threats (3), and finally to an absence of direct communication combined with violent attacks on the adversary (4). With respect to perceptions and images, these change from being relatively accurate, or at least benign (1), to rigid and simplified negative stereotypes (2) that become cast in terms of good versus evil (3), to an ultimate view of the other party as nonhuman (4). Concurrently, the relationship moves from one of trust, respect, and commitment (1) to one wherein the other party is seen as difficult yet remains important in its own right (2), to one of mistrust and disrespect (3), to one of complete hopelessness in terms of any possible improvements (4). In terms of issues fueling the conflict, the emphasis shifts from substantive interests and related positions (1), to concerns regarding the relationship (2), to fundamental needs or core values such as identity and security (3), to the question of the ultimate survival of one or both parties (4). In concert with these changes, the perceived possible outcomes begin with joint gain or win-win options (1), move to mutual compromise (2), then to win-lose possibilities (3), and finally to lose-lose alternatives wherein the objective is to minimize one's own losses while inflicting maximum costs on the other party (4). In attempting to achieve these kinds of outcome, the parties' preferred methods of conflict management shift from joint decisionmaking (1), to negotiation (2), to defensive competition (3), to outright attempts at destruction (4).

To the extent that this stage model represents a valid, albeit simplified, picture of the escalation process, it is immediately apparent that different management or intervention strategies would be appropriate and effective at different points. In fact, it is likely that one of the reasons for the "failure" of particular interventions in particular conflicts may be inappropriate application with respect to the stage of escalation (Bercovitch and Langley, 1993; Rubin, 1980). Given that most intervenors rely predominantly or solely on one type of intervention and attempt to apply it to a variety of conflicts at different stages of escalation, it is not surprising that frustration and failure are often the result. An additional reason for failure in the longer term may be the lack of coordinated follow-up interventions to deal with elements not addressed by the initial intervention.

Complementarity and Sequencing of Interventions

The overall strategy of the contingency approach, then, is to intervene with the appropriate third-party method at the appropriate time in order to de-escalate the conflict back down through the stages identified above. This is potentially accomplished by initially matching a particular intervention to a specific stage and then by combining further interventions, if necessary, in appropriate sequences to further de-escalate the conflict. The initial contingency model that relates the stage of conflict to the prescribed intervention sequence is given in Figure 11.2.

In stage 1, the key dimension of concern is the quality of communication between the parties, since the relationship is still in relatively good shape in terms of trust and commitment and perceptions, and images are relatively accurate and positive. The primary issues derive from substantive concerns and the parties believe that joint gain is possible. However,

Figure 11.2 A Contingency Model of Third-Party Intervention

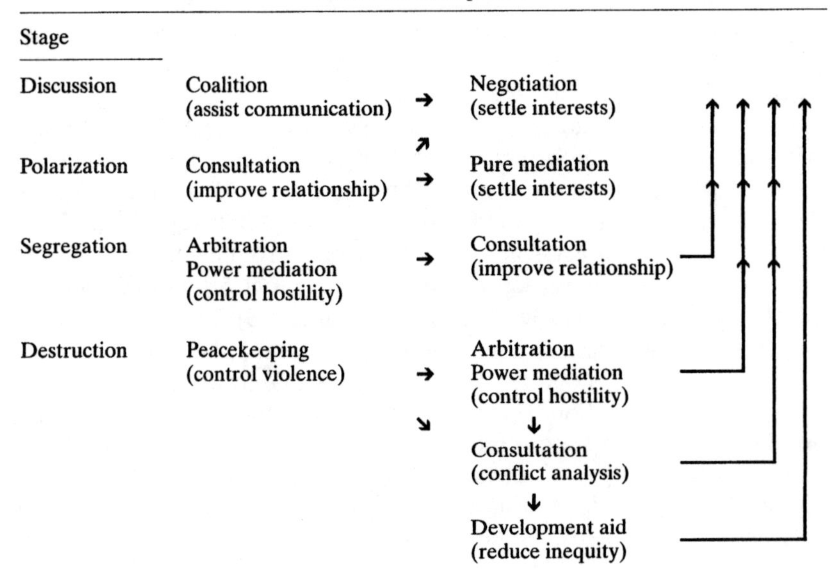

Source: Revisions from Ronald J. Fisher, *The Social Psychology of Intergroup and International Conflict Resolution,* New York, Springer-Verlag, 1990.

for whatever reasons, communication difficulties may occur as the interaction moves from discussion to a debate involving adversarial behavior. Particularly if the parties are having difficulty talking constructively or directly about the issues in dispute, the intervention of a third party may be useful. The prescribed intervention would be that of conciliation, in order to facilitate clear and open communication on interests and related positions. The hope would be that this conciliation would clear the way toward direct negotiations between the parties that would settle the dispute before any damage was done to the underlying relationship.

In stage 2 of conflict escalation, relationship issues become the focus of concern as trust and respect are threatened and distorted perceptions and simplified images in the form of negative stereotypes begin to emerge. At this point, consultation is the most appropriate intervention, since it uniquely deals with relationship issues such as mistrust, distorted perceptions, and negative attitudes. Once these issues are addressed and a cooperative relationship is established or reestablished, the parties are in a more efficacious position to handle the substantive issues in the dispute. Thus, consultation could pave the way for direct negotiation between the parties. However, given that the particular substantive issues led to escalation of the conflict in the first instance, it is likely that they are contentious and difficult and not readily settled by direct negotiation. It is in this instance that mediation in its pure form becomes the preferred third-party intervention to follow consultation. Rather than having to work around relationship issues, as is typical in mediation practice, the mediator would be in the relatively advantageous position of focusing on substantive issues without the typical interference of distorted perceptions, negative attitudes, considerable mistrust, and so on. It is of course also possible that successful mediation may restore trust, build more positive attitudes, and improve other important qualities of the relationship. It should be noted, however, that there is very little empirical evidence for the positive influence of successful mediation on relationship variables (see Wall and Lynn, 1993). In fact, some recent evidence from a complex laboratory simulation of intergroup conflict indicates that mediation does not have these effects (Keashly, Fisher, and Grant, 1993).

Thus, the first point of potential complementarity between consultation and mediation is that the former may be able to serve a very useful "premediation" function. This is similar to the emerging realization that problem-solving workshops may be able to serve as an important technology in the prenegotiation phase of conflict management (Fisher, 1989). This linkage is provided for in the contingency model, where consultation is successfully followed by direct negotiation between the parties (see Figure 11.2).

Prenegotiation as an emerging focus in the study of international conflict management is defined as the process that begins when one or more parties considers negotiation as an option and communicates this intention to other parties. Prenegotiation ends when one party abandons negotiation as a policy option or when the parties agree to formal negotiations (Stein, 1989). In recent work on a prescriptive theory of prenegotiation, Rothman (1989) identifies three stages of prenegotiation: the diagnostic, the procedural, and agenda setting. In the diagnostic phase, parties are encouraged to jointly articulate their underlying concerns (such as basic needs for security, identity, and so on) along with the substantive issues (such as territory, economic resources, and so on) in order to move toward a shared definition and analysis of the conflict. The procedural phase then provides a bridge for moving these two sets of issues into the agenda-setting process. The third-party intervention appropriate to the diagnostic phase of prenegotiation is that of consultation, again primarily in the form of problem-solving workshops. Indeed, linking consultation to negotiation in this direct manner may help overcome one of the central issues in consultation, that of transferring the effects of workshops back to the decisionmaking process, in this case, that of negotiation.

To return to the contingency model, the prescription is that consultation has a useful role to play during "premediation," in which the parties are going through a decisionmaking process very similar to that of prenegotiation. Used in this way, consultation would allow the parties to work on relationship issues (that are not the focus in mediation) and would provide the parties with a low-risk forum in which to consider the merits of and the potential agenda for mediation (Kelman and Cohen, 1986). The desired outcome would be that mediation would have a much greater chance of success if the parties *chose* to move in that direction.

It is apparent that the scenario described above is at odds with existing practice and reality in contemporary conflict management, where consultation is not readily available and not seriously considered by parties to disputes. Mediation is typically the third-party intervention of choice when the parties have exhausted the possibilities of negotiation as well as themselves. Unfortunately, this may be one of the prime reasons why mediation is as likely to fail as to succeed—the relationship between the parties has deteriorated significantly, interests are often interfused with needs and appear nonnegotiable, and the respective positions have become intransigent through a series of past commitments.

By suggesting consultation as the lead intervention in moderately escalated conflict, the contingency model may provide an avenue for significantly increasing the success rate of mediation. This form of "preventative consultation" has occurred at times in industrial relations (for example, Birnbaum, 1984; Brett et al., 1980), but appears to occur only informally and partially, if at all, in international relations. However, recent empirical work by Druckman and his colleagues (for example, Druckman, Broome, and Korper, 1988; Druckman and Broome, 1991) using intergroup conflict simulations that mirror current regional disputes provides evidence that, at least with respect to negotiation, problem-solving workshops enhanced parties' expectations and guided subsequent negotiation behaviors in productive directions. Extending these results to third-party intervention, the appeal of using consultation at this stage is that it may prevent the conflict from escalating further and from rendering future efforts at resolution much more difficult. In line with the contingency model, successful mediation would then de-escalate the conflict back down to stage 1, wherein the parties could handle future disputes through bilateral interaction.

In stage 3 of conflict escalation, defensive competition and hostility become main themes. More important, the conflict is now seen as threatening basic needs such as those for security and identity. Therefore, some form of immediate control is necessary to halt the spiral and to show the parties that agreement is still possible on substantive issues. Thus, in situations where it is appropriate, arbitration would be the third-party intervention of choice. A second alternative, which can be seen as midway between arbitration and pure mediation, is power mediation. In this form of intervention, the third party has the power to influence the parties toward agreement through inducing costs, present or future, or providing positive inducements such as military or development aid (Stein, 1985;

Touval and Zartman, 1985). The result of this power is that the mediator is able to go beyond persuasion to coerce the parties toward a settlement that will temporarily halt the escalatory spiral. This creates the second point of complementarity between mediation and consultation. Consultation could immediately be used to improve the relationship between the parties and de-escalate the conflict to stage 2 (where pure mediation could be instituted to deal with further substantive issues—the first point of complementarity noted above) or to stage 1 (where the parties could negotiate directly—the prenegotiation function of consultation). Thus, consultation, typically in the form of problem-solving workshops, could serve as a potential follow-up intervention to power mediation, rather than assuming that settlement of substantive issues will by itself improve the relationship between the parties—an assumption that is not supported by empirical evidence (see Wall and Lynn, 1993).

In stage 4, the conflict has escalated to the point where the parties attempt to destroy each other through the use of various forms of violence, expressed as war at the international level. The third-party strategy of choice at this point is that of peacekeeping, a power intervention designed to assist in the separation of the parties and the control of violence. This pacific and impartial intervention typically follows a diplomatic agreement on a cease-fire, and provides for the monitoring of the cease-fire and the restoration of some normality of living by forces under the control of the third party, most commonly the United Nations. When the interaction between the parties can be stabilized and some initial commitment to joint effort can be obtained, the path is cleared for other third-party interventions, depending on the receptivity of the parties and their sense of the critical issues. In line with other elements of the contingency model, the first possibility is that arbitration or power mediation might be implemented to further control hostility and demonstrate that at least a partial agreement is possible. As in stage 3, this could be followed by consultation to improve the relationship, but more broadly to provide a full analysis of the conflict and its escalation. This broader goal recognizes that it will be more difficult to de-escalate the conflict from stage 4 than stage 3, and therefore a more intensive and comprehensive problem-solving effort will be required. It is also conceivable that this form of consultation could follow peacekeeping directly in order to identify key elements and issues in the conflict; some might be handled by pure mediation and some by continuing consultation. Finally, the provision of development aid by third parties could be one outcome of consultation. This form of intervention could be designed to deal with the structural inequalities that are often part and parcel of protracted intercommunal and international conflict. The need and focus for such efforts would be identified in the consultation process through dealing with basic needs relating to equality and justice. Indeed, in this scenario, consultation with its focus on interactive activities directed at meeting basic needs, decreasing hostility, and improving the parties' relationship can be viewed as an important peacebuilding effort (Fisher, 1993a). Thus, combined efforts on a number of fronts would be required to eventually de-escalate a stage 4 conflict back down to a manageable and productive relationship. The role and utility of third-party interventions in this process could be maximized through the matching, coordination, and sequencing envisaged in the contingency model.

CURRENT CONCEPTUAL AND PRACTICAL WORK

The contingency model presented and discussed here is part of a movement that recognizes the need for a more holistic approach to the study of conflict intervention generally and, more particularly, to dealing with specific conflicts (for example, Bloomfield, 1992; Hadjipavlou-Trigeorgis and Trigeorgis, 1993). The recognition of intractable social conflicts that appear to be resistant to many traditional efforts has challenged scholars and practitioners to expand their conceptualizations of the nature of conflict to include both objective aspects and more subjective or social-psychological elements. The acknowledgment of this objective-subjective mix and its changing composition as a conflict escalates requires the recognition and development of a broader range of management and resolution strategies. This contingency model has highlighted the need for articulating the variety and diversity of approaches as well as exploring the possibility of a conflict-management initiative that is multilevel and multi-intervention in nature. In this chapter, we have focused on the potential complementarity of mediation and consultation, but these arguments can be extended to include other forms of intervention.

Although the development of this contingency model was based on careful integration and consideration of the available theoretical and empirical literatures and of discussions with various scholars and practitioners, the validity of the model needs to be tested in both the conceptual and practical arenas. In this section, recent conceptual and empirical work related to the concepts and assumptions presented in this model will be identified and discussed. Based on this discussion, future directions for this model specifically and the contingency approach more generally will be identified.

Empirical Research

To this point, there have been two types of empirical research undertaken regarding the contingency model and its component parts: (1) intergroup conflict simulations and (2) retrospective case studies. The former has focused on testing specific components of the model and their connections; the latter has applied the model as a whole to the intervention history of ongoing regional conflicts.

Basic to the contingency model is the assumption that distinctions between different interventions can be made and that these distinctions have implications for differential effects of these interventions in a conflict situation. Contrasting traditional mediation and consultation, Fisher and Keashly (1988) argued for meaningful conceptual differences between these two types of "nonbinding settlement" intervention approaches. Based on these differences, the authors hypothesized that although both interventions were likely to result in settlement on substantive issues, only consultation would result in significant positive changes in intergroup attitudes and affect subsequent behaviors. These proposed differential effects were subsequently tested within the context of a complex intergroup conflict simulation concerning a land dispute (see Keashly, Fisher, and Grant, 1993). As predicted, though all groups came to similar agreement on the division of land, only groups exposed to consultation showed marked positive changes in attitudes toward the other groups and an enhanced desire to work with the other groups on future efforts. These results are supportive of the distinction between mediation and consultation and of the presence and importance of the social-psychological or subjective aspects of conflict interaction.

Druckman and his colleagues (Druckman, Broome, and Korper, 1988; Druckman and Broome, 1991) have examined the proposed prenegotiation function of problem-solving workshops. Using a simulation of intergroup relations resembling the conflict between the Greek-Cypriot and Turkish-Cypriot communities in Cyprus, these researchers found that the prenegotiation sessions resulted in positive change in negotiators' expectations (for example, viewed situation as more collaborative, expressed greater willingness to compromise, saw other as more friendly and cooperative) and subsequent negotiation behavior (more movement from initial positions and more compromise on desired outcomes). These results provide empirical support for the role of consultation as preparation for subsequent negotiation and thereby mediation on substantive issues. In addition, the changes in expectations and behavior were found to be due to a combination of enhanced positive affect (liking) and understanding (familiarity) between negotiators that was created within the interactive context of the problem-solving workshop. Thus, effective strategies for positively influencing negotiators' behavior need to affect both affective and cognitive processes. These findings are supportive of the value of attending to social-psychological or subjective aspects of the conflict and highlight the value of coordinating different strategies to deal with the subjective and objective elements of the conflict. Although extrapolation of these findings requires recognition of the specificity of the conflict situation examined, Druckman and Broome (1991) suggest that:

> as groups and nations begin to concentrate more on lasting relationships than on short-term agreements, prenegotiation processes take on increasing importance both as a prelude to later negotiations and as a form of interaction that can influence intergroup relations in ways that differ from the effects of formal agreements. (p. 591)

The other arena for testing the contingency model and the notion of complementarity has been case studies of various regional conflicts (for example, Bloomfield, 1992; Dawson, 1991; Keashly and Fisher, 1990). In their consideration of the model, Keashly and Fisher (1990) examined the history of third-party interventions in the Cyprus conflict, comparing the success of these efforts with what would have been predicted by the model. The stage model of escalation proved useful in providing a rationale for the success and the failure of different interventions and in the identification of points in the management process where different approaches might have been more constructive.

In a related vein, Hadjipavlou-Trigeorgis and Trigeorgis (1993) call for an "evolutionary and cooperative approach" to the Cyprus situation. In their analysis, they argue that past intervention efforts (primarily mediation) have focused on developing a compromise among the official positions. Although recognizing the need for such work, the authors assert that an emphasis on common interests and needs in the form of a shared definition of the problem is necessary to develop the will and confidence of the parties to negotiate. To balance the objective-subjective mix, they propose a multiphase incremental solution that involves coordinated action of more structural and substantive elements (for example, a third joint federated area contributed to by both communities) with the more subjective, relationship-building efforts (for example, confidence and trust-building efforts such as joint projects on education and economic development). Although addressing the validity of the current contingency model was not the purpose of their analysis, the proposed solution is consistent with the propositions and assumptions of the model.

Application of the model to the ongoing Northern Ireland conflict (Bloomfield, 1992; Dawson, 1991) has provided support for the basic premise of considering subjective or social-psychological elements of the conflict and the notion of coordinated action. These analyses, however, have also revealed some implicit assumptions of the model that may limit its conceptual and practical usefulness to the Northern Ireland situation. Specifically, the sequential nature of conflict development, the assumption of intraparty cohesion, and the proposed cues of escalation are argued not to hold in this conflict. Regarding the first point, though this model is presented as a linear progression, it is important to acknowledge that conflicts (particularly intractable ones; see Azar, 1983) may move back and forth or very rapidly through stages. This may be a result of a number of factors, such as different attempts to manage the conflict that result in apparent or temporary de-escalation, the surfacing of "new" issues or additional parties that were not considered in previous management attempts, and/or strategic management of conflict behavior by the parties to meet other goals (for example, the lifting of economic sanctions). Thus, in agreement with the concern expressed, analysis of a conflict using these stages as indicators of escalation needs to be coupled with an extensive consideration, both at the manifest and less overt levels, of the issues and the parties involved (Bercovitch, 1991; Glasl, 1982).

The issue of intraparty cohesion speaks to concerns about identifying and addressing the needs of all relevant parties and stakeholders to the conflict. Of necessity and partly as an artifact of using interventions in isolation of one another, limited numbers and types of parties are involved, often with the assumption that these "representatives" do speak for the larger constituent group. As has been witnessed in the Arab-Israeli peace agreements and peace initiatives in other conflicts, the concern about intraparty cohesion is a critical one. Although not explicitly addressed in the current discussion of the contingency model, consultation and problem-solving approaches often include intraparty "teambuilding" as a preliminary step in the intervention process (for example, Kelman and Cohen, 1986). Indeed, these approaches deliberately seek intraparty diversity on the premise that such diversity is a requirement for representation and a resource for creative solution development (for example, Burton, 1968). In addition, it is believed that any solution developed that recognizes this diversity will have an enhanced probability of being acceptable to those who were not directly involved in the process. Using consultation to facilitate intraparty cohesion and support, then, is a form of the premediation or prenegotiation complementarity described earlier. Thus, while not explicitly addressed in the model, the inclusion of consultation and the notion of the need for coordinated action permit consideration of issues of intraparty cohesion.

With respect to escalation, Dawson (1991) notes that attempting to identify the stages of the Northern Ireland conflict was difficult, particularly insofar as cues of parties' perceptions and attitudes were concerned. That is, to what documents or to whom does one look for this information? Bloomfield (1993), while arguing that the social-psychological cues for escalation are generally useful, suggests that a more applicable contingency model needs to recognize context specificity of escalation cues by incorporating "embedded" criteria that would be identified through an analysis of the specific conflict itself. Thus, although the value of escalation as a means to identify appropriate intervention strategies is supported by these authors, they challenge the sensitivity, practicality, and specificity of the model's escalation cues.

Dawson's Northern Ireland case analysis also provides a challenge to the model regarding how success and failure are defined, an issue that plagues the field of conflict intervention generally. Dawson (1991) judged the success (failure) of the four interventions proposed for stage 4 in terms of short-term impact and long-term endurance (twelve months) of these short-term results. She noted that peacekeeping, power mediation, and developmental aid had impact but only peacekeeping was successful in terms of endurance. Consultation was found not to demonstrate either impact or endurance. Although these findings could be challenged on the operationalization of the measures of impact and endurance as well as the nature of the different interventions, there are two more important concerns to address. The first is that success and failure have not been clearly articulated in this model, but only indirectly through de-escalation. It may well be that "success" will occur for those elements on which the intervention focuses and "failure" for those elements that are not attended to directly (Bartunek, Benton, and Keys, 1975). That is, relationship change would occur with consultation, and settlement on substantive issues would occur with mediation, but the reverse (that is, substantive settlement with consultation and relationship change with mediation) would not necessarily occur. In fact, such specificity of impact makes the case stronger for the value of coordinating strategies. Thus, in order to fully examine this model and the effectiveness of any intervention approach, a multidimensional definition of success is required that incorporates these different aspects of change and recognizes time as an element.

The second important point raised by Dawson (1991; and Bloomfield, 1992) relates to more pragmatic concerns. The apparent lack of success of efforts at consultation may not only be related to what is meant by success/failure but may also be a reflection of comparing and, indeed, explicitly coordinating interventions that operate at informal (consultation) and formal (power mediation, peacekeeping, developmental aid) levels of public and political awareness. If, as Bercovitch (1992) argues, the form of intervention practiced is affected by the resources that a particular third party has and the parties involved in the intervention (for example, the public, private individuals, political figures or groups), then consultants, mediators, arbitrators, and peacekeepers are not only different actors operating in different spheres but work with qualitatively different people or groups. Although the model suggests a sequence of interventions, an important question is, who will take on the task of identifying and coordinating the interventions and what is their agenda? At the international level, there are few persons or groups/nations with the legitimacy to play the coordinator role. Although the UN, under the leadership of Boutros-Ghali, seems a likely choice for this role, it is clear from recent UN efforts that the energy and effort required are beyond the resources and perhaps the will of member states. In addition, the success of any intervention depends on the acceptability of that intervention to the parties involved. As noted earlier in this chapter, consultation has not traditionally been perceived as among the alternatives by virtue of its relatively recent development and its informal, nonpublic nature. No matter how conceptually sound and internally consistent the contingency model may be or how intuitively appealing the notion of coordinated action is, the possibilities and prescriptions of this model will not be fully realized unless these implementation challenges are explicitly acknowledged and addressed. In essence, consultation is so underdeveloped and underutilized that attempted analyses and evaluations such as Dawson's are rather questionable.

In sum, the research discussed above is generally supportive of and consistent with the rationale of the contingency model, the value of social-psychological processes, and the complementarity of interventions. The potential power of sequencing interventions for greater effectiveness in de-escalating the conflict received some limited support from the simulations and the case studies. The case studies on Northern Ireland have identified specific areas, both conceptually and practically, that require further consideration and elaboration. The challenge regarding the research reported here, particularly the case studies, is that the model has been assessed in a postdictive manner relying on co-occurrence of interventions rather than coordinated intervention. The necessity of selectively interpreting complex histories and the paucity of certain third-party interventions (conciliation, consultation, arbitration) does not permit an adequate test of the model. Given the phenomenon the model deals with (that is, social conflict), there are severe and understandable constraints on implementing and evaluating this model in a controlled and rigorous manner. However, there are examples of past and current situations in which consultation efforts have likely influenced the substance and outcomes of subsequent formal efforts.

Practical Examples of Complementarity

In the practice domain of international conflict management, there are a number of instances where consultation efforts have most likely played a useful role at the first point of complementarity with mediation or negotiation. However, these instances are very difficult to document for at least three reasons. First, the professional scholar-practitioners who carry out consultation interventions restrict themselves on ethical grounds from identifying their participants and their contacts and influences that may have affected the policymaking process. Not only do they initially guarantee the anonymity and confidentiality of the participants and their interactions, but they are also restricted from engaging in follow-up activities that might identify and place participants at risk in situations of intense conflict. Second, even if consultants were in a position to engage in research to assess the effects of their interventions, they would face severe methodological and practical constraints. Tracing the transfer effects of consultation discussions on subsequent decisionmaking and negotiating behavior would require an expensive, large-scale research effort involving multiple methods (interviewing, observation, content analysis) and would face the many restrictions on access to information that exist for official and sensitive material dealing with matters of security. Third, even if one could gather some of the relevant data, placing and evaluating the effects of consultation within the complexity of multiple factors that influence policy formation and execution in international relations would be an immense task, both conceptually and in operational terms. There is no conceptual model of the transfer process itself, let alone a comprehensive model of political decisionmaking and interstate relations into which it could be integrated. Similarly, there are no multiple regression equations or structural equation models that capture the variables, processes, and relationships that contribute to the resolution of an international conflict. The field is basically in its infancy in identifying and sorting out what interventions have what influences on what outcomes.

Given this daunting situation, what is possible is to identify points of transfer where consultation may have had a beneficial effect on subsequent mediation and/or negotiation efforts. These cases are based on a review of the scholarly literature on consultation over the past twenty-five years, combined with the results of semistructured personal interviews held with almost all of the leading scholar-practitioners in the field, focusing in part on their contributions (Fisher, 1993b). In most cases, the perceived effects of the interventions are based on more than one source of information, thus adding some credence to their anecdotal nature.

The two very first consultation interventions by John Burton (1969) and his colleagues at University College London were deemed to have positive influences on the conflicts in question. The first series of meetings focused on the Indonesia-Malaysia conflict of the mid-1960s and allowed the parties to correct mutual misperceptions, redefine the conflict, reassess the costs of their objectives, and envisage new policy options (de Reuck, 1974). The representatives were able to reach an understanding on the overall framework of a resolution, and following the 1966 coup in Indonesia, the new government adopted the basic elements that were subsequently reflected in the Manila peace agreement. The second initiative was a workshop involving high-level, unofficial representatives from the Greek and Turkish Cypriot communities in Cyprus (Mitchell, 1981). The conflict was deadlocked and the UN mediation efforts at an impasse, with both parties insisting on incompatible preconditions. The discussions allowed for the sharing of differing perceptions and an exploration of the possibilities of resuming negotiations, which the parties subsequently did under UN auspices. Follow-up investigations indicated that some of the insights gained at the workshop had been communicated to the decisionmaking elites of the two communities and had assisted in the resumption of mediation.

The work of Herbert Kelman and his colleagues over the past two decades has most likely had positive effects on the reduction of the Middle East conflict at a number of points. Kelman, along with Stephen Cohen, Edward Azar, and others, has engaged in a long-term program of action research involving problem-solving workshops, meetings with various influentials, contacts with decisionmakers, and policy analyses of the conflict. In this context, Cohen and Azar (1981) served as third-party facilitators for problem-solving discussions with Egyptian and Israeli intellectuals in 1976 and held in-depth interviews with members of the two decisionmaking elites. These activities provided some impetus and input into the peace process that culminated in the successful mediation by U.S. president Carter at Camp David and the peace treaty between Egypt and Israel.

Following his collaboration with Kelman, Azar joined forces with Burton and completed a number of problem-solving forums on different conflicts, including the seemingly intractable situation in Lebanon (Azar, 1990). Two forums were held in 1984, bringing together influential representatives of the various religious and political groupings to share the fears and goals of each and to outline the principles for movement toward a united Lebanon. As a result of the workshops, the participants established an informal network for ongoing discussion that produced a "National Covenant Document" in 1988, outlining the steps for reunification that were integrated into the 1989 Taif agreement that brought peace to Lebanon.

Kelman has focused his consultation work on the Israeli-Palestinian conflict and has increasingly come to see the problem-solving approach as a prenegotiation process that can assist in creating the psychological and political conditions necessary for negotiations (Fisher, 1989). Thus, he has provided analyses of the psychological prerequisites for mutual acceptance by Israelis and Palestinians, has identified the barriers to negotiation, and has proposed a prenegotiation process of successive approximations that differentiates the enemy image and offers mutual reassurance (Kelman, 1978, 1982, 1987). Through his workshop initiatives over the past twenty years, Kelman has built up a large network of increasingly influential participants in both communities, many of whom hold or have gained important positions in community leadership, political activism, policy formation, and decisionmaking. It is likely that the efforts of Kelman and his many collaborators have made contributions to a constructive political dialogue, the humanization of the enemy, and a sense of possibility that the conflict is resolvable. Among the many learnings from workshops that have been communicated to political elites are insights into the other side's priorities and areas of flexibility, signs of readiness for negotiation and the availability of negotiating partners, and ideas for confidence-building measures and ways of moving to the table (Kelman, 1992). These efforts are now coming to fruition, along with the effects of many other influences, in the initiation of formal peace talks between the various parties in the Middle East conflict under U.S. auspices, the breakthrough achieved through the "back channel" meetings in Norway, and the resulting formal recognition and initiation of a peace process between Israelis and Palestinians. Kelman and his colleagues are now engaged in a continuing workshop on the Israeli-Palestinian conflict, which brings together the same participants in a series of sessions for sustained dialogue and the creation of joint proposals for de-escalating the conflict and transforming the relationship between the two communities (Kelman, 1992; Rouhana and Kelman, 1994). It is unlikely that without such informal efforts focusing on the human dimension, peace can be achieved in the Middle East (Rothman, 1994).

These few examples and others awaiting documentation indicate that consultation and related problem-solving approaches have value as prenegotiation and peacebuilding mechanisms that help to prepare the ground for formal discussions and agreements. It is incumbent on the scholar-practitioners engaged in such work to document their activities and the effects as best they can within the constraints of ethical principles and pragmatic limitations. In this way, it will be possible to build a repository of at least descriptive evidence that will support the potential complementarity of consultation and mediation at the international level.

CONCLUSION

The continuing popularity of third-party intervention in protracted conflicts demands that our understanding and skill be substantially increased. The overreliance on one or another method needs to be reexamined. In both theoretical work and practical application, a healthy eclecticism should be encouraged, with, of course, all due caution exercised in regard to ethical and professional concerns. Within this context, the appeal of a coordinated sequenced approach is increasingly apparent. The contingency model provides an initial picture of such an approach based on a rationale that accepts the objective and subjective mix that underlies most conflicts. The model also provides for the complementarity of a variety of third-party methods, as opposed to seeing these as competing or contradictory. Both research studies and practical examples, while limited, provide some support for the basic propositions of the model and some challenges for further elaboration. The contingency model, therefore, provides a useful point of departure for further understanding pacific third-party intervention and for ultimately increasing its efficacy in dealing with protracted social conflict.

NOTE

The authors made equal contributions to this chapter, so coauthorship is claimed with the order of names determined by alternation. Portions of this chapter appear in Fisher and Keashly (1991).

REFERENCES

Azar, E. E. (1983). "The Theory of Protracted Social Conflict and the Challenge of Transforming Conflict Situations." *Monograph Series in World Affairs* 20, 2: 81–99.

Azar, E. E. (1990). *The Management of Protracted Social Conflict.* Hampshire, U.K.: Dartmouth.

Bartenuk, J. M., Benton, A. A., and Keys, C. B. (1975). "Third Party Intervention and the Bargaining Behavior of Group Representatives." *Journal of Conflict Resolution* 19: 532–557.

Bercovitch, J. (1984). *Social Conflict and Third Parties: Strategies of Conflict Resolution.* Boulder, Colo.: Westview.

Bercovitch, J. (1991). "International Mediation and Dispute Settlement: Evaluating the Conditions for Successful Mediation." *Negotiation Journal* 7, 1: 17–30.

Bercovitch, J. (1992). "Mediators and Mediation Strategies in International Relations." *Negotiation Journal* 8, 2: 99–112.

Bercovitch, J., and Rubin, J. Z., eds. (1992). *International Mediation: A Multi-Level Approach to Conflict Management.* London: Macmillan; New York: St. Martin's.

Bercovitch, J., and Langley, J. (1993). "The Nature of the Dispute and the Effectiveness of International Mediation." *Journal of Conflict Resolution* 37, 4: 670–691.

Birnbaum, R. (1984). "The Effects of a Neutral Third Party on Academic Bargaining Relationships and Campus Climate." *Journal of Higher Education* 55, 6: 719–734.

Blake, R. R., and Mouton, J. S. (1964). *The Managerial Grid.* Houston: Gulf Publishing.

Bloomfield, D. P. (1993). "Towards a Model of Complementarity in Conflict Management Theory: The Practice of Resolution and Settlement in Northern Ireland." Unpublished manuscript, University of Bradford, U.K.

Brett, J. M., Goldberg, S. B., and Ury, W. (1980). "Mediation and Organization Development." *Proceedings of the Thirty-Third Annual Meeting of the Industrial Relations Association.* Madison, Wisc.: Industrial Relations Research Associates, 195–202.

Burton, J. W. (1968). *Conflict and Communication: The Use of Controlled Communication in International Relations.* London: Macmillan.

Campbell, D. T. (1965). "Ethnocentrism and Other Altruistic Motives." In D. Levine, ed., *Nebraska Symposium on Motivation,* vol. 13. Lincoln: University of Nebraska Press, 283–311.

Carnevale, P. J. (1985). "Mediation of International Conflict." In S. Oskamp, ed., *International Conflict and National Public Policy Issues. Applied Social Psychology Annual,* vol. 6. Beverly Hills, Calif.: Sage.

Cohen, S. P., and Azar, E. E. (1981). "From War to Peace: The Transition Between Egypt and Israel." *Journal of Conflict Resolution* 25: 87–114.

Dawson, G. E. (1991). "Third Party Intervention in Northern Ireland: Assessing the Value of a Contingency Model Approach." Unpublished master's thesis. Carleton University of Ottawa.

de Reuck, A. V. S. (1974). "Controlled Communication: Rationale and Dynamics." *The Human Context* 6, 1: 64–80.

Deutsch, M. (1973). *The Resolution of Conflict.* New Haven: Yale University Press.

Doob, L. W., ed. (1970). *Resolving Conflict in Africa: The Fermeda Workshop.* New Haven: Yale University Press.

Druckman, D., Broome, B. J., and Korper, S. H. (1988). "Value Differences and Conflict Resolution: Facilitation or Delinking?" *Journal of Conflict Resolution* 32, 4: 489–510.

Druckman, D., and Broome, B. J. (1991). "Value Differences and Conflict Resolution: Familiarity or Liking?" *Journal of Conflict Resolution* 35, 4: 571–593.

Fisher, R. J. (1972). "Third Party Consultation: A Method for the Study and Resolution of Conflict." *Journal of Conflict Resolution* 16, 1: 67–94.

Fisher, R. J. (1976). "Third Party Consultation: A Skill for Professional Psychologists in Community Practice." *Professional Psychology* 7 (August): 344–351.

Fisher, R. J. (1983). "Third Party Consultation as a Method of Intergroup Conflict Resolution: A Review of Studies." *Journal of Conflict Resolution* 27, 2: 301–334.

Fisher, R. J. (1986). "Third Party Consultation: A Problem Solving Approach for De-escalating International Conflict." In J. P. Maas and R.A.C. Stewart, eds., *Toward a World of Peace: People Create Alternatives.* Fiji: University of the South Pacific, 18–32.

Fisher, R. J. (1989). "Pre-negotiation Problem-solving Discussions: Enhancing the Potential for Successful Negotiation." *International Journal* 64 (Spring): 442–474.

Fisher, R. J., and Keashly, L. (1988). "Distinguishing Third Party Interventions in Intergroup Conflict: Consultation Is *Not* Mediation." *Negotiation Journal* 4, 4: 381–393.

Fisher, R. J., and Keashly, L. (1991). "The Potential Complementarity of Mediation and Consultation Within a Contingency Model of Third Party Consultation." *Journal of Peace Research* 28, 1: 29–42.

Fisher, R. J. (1993a). "The Potential for Peacebuilding: Forging a Bridge From Peacekeeping to Peacemaking." *Peace & Change* 18, 3: 247–266.

Fisher, R. J. (1993b). "Developing the Field of Interactive Conflict Resolution: Issues in Training, Funding and Institutionalization." *Political Psychology* 14: 123–138.

Glasl, F. (1982). "The Process of Conflict Escalation and Roles of Third Parties." In G. B. J. Bomers and R. B. Peterson, eds., *Conflict Management and Industrial Relations.* Boston: Kluwer-Nijhoff, 119–140.

Hadjipavlou-Trigeorgis, M., and Trigeorgis, L. (1993). "Cyprus: An Evolutionary Approach to Conflict Resolution." *Journal of Conflict Resolution* 37, 2: 340–360.

Keashly, L., and Fisher, R. J. (1990). "Toward a Contingency Approach to Conflict Resolution: A Cyprus Illustration." *International Journal* 43, 2: 424–453.

Keashly, L., Fisher, R. J., and Grant, P. R. (1993). "The Comparative Effectiveness of Third Party Consultation Versus Mediation Within a Complex Simulation of Intergroup Conflict." *Human Relations* 46, 3: 371–393.

Kelman, H. C. (1972). "The Problem Solving Workshop in Conflict Resolution." In R. Merritt, ed., *Communication in International Politics*. Urbana: University of Illinois Press, 168–204.

Kelman, H. C. (1978). "Israelis and Palestinians: Psychological Prerequisites for Mutual Acceptance." *International Security* 3, 1: 162–186.

Kelman, H. C. (1982). "Creating the Conditions for Israeli-Palestinian Negotiations." *Journal of Conflict Resolution* 26: 39–75.

Kelman, H. C., and Cohen, S. P. (1986). "Resolution of International Conflict: An Interactional Approach." In S. Worchel and W. G. Austin, eds., *The Psychology of Intergroup Relations*. 2nd ed. Chicago: Nelson-Hall, 323–342.

Kelman, H. C. (1987). "The Political Psychology of the Israeli-Palestinian Conflict: How Can We Overcome the Barriers to a Negotiated Solution?" *Political Psychology* 8: 347–363.

Kelman, H. C. (1992). "Informal Mediation by the Scholar/Practitioner." In J. Bercovitch and J. Z. Rubin, eds., *Mediation in International Relations*. New York: St. Martin's; London: Macmillan.

Kressel, K., and Pruitt, D., eds. (1985). "Social Conflict." *Journal of Social Issues* 41 (special issue).

Kriesberg, L. (1989). "Varieties of Mediation Activities." Paper presented at the annual meeting of the International Society of Political Psychology, Tel Aviv, June.

Mitchell, C. R. (1981). *Peacemaking and the Consultant's Role*. Westmead, U.K.: Gower.

Mitchell, C. R., and Webb, K. (1988). *New Approaches to International Mediation*. New York: Greenwood.

Prein, H. (1984). "A Contingency Approach for Conflict Intervention." *Group and Organization Studies* 9, 1: 81–102.

Rothman, J. (1989). "Developing Pre-negotiation Theory and Practice." Policy Studies, no. 29. Jerusalem: Leonard Davis Institute for International Relations, The Hebrew University of Jerusalem.

Rothman, J. (1994). "Unofficial Talks Yielded Mideast Peace." *Philadelphia Inquirer,* September 1.

Rouhana, N. N., and Kelman, H. C. (1994). "Promoting Joint Thinking in International Conflicts: An Israeli-Palestinian Continuing Workshop." *Journal of Social Issues*.

Rubin, J. Z. (1980). "Experimental Research on Third-Party Intervention in Conflict: Toward Some Generalizations." *Psychological Bulletin* 87, 2: 379–391.

Rubin, J. Z., ed. (1981). *Dynamics of Third Party Intervention: Kissinger in the Middle East*. New York: Praeger.

Sheppard, B. H. (1984). "Third Party Conflict Intervention: A Procedural Framework." *Research in Organizational Behaviour* 6: 141–190.

Stein, J. G. (1985). "Structures, Strategies and Tactics of Mediation: Kissinger and Carter in the Middle East." *Negotiation Journal* 1, 4: 331–347.

Stein, J. G., ed. (1989). *Getting to the Table: The Processes of International Prenegotiation.* Baltimore: Johns Hopkins University Press.

Touval, S., and Zartman, I. W., eds. (1985). *International Mediation in Theory and Practice.* Boulder, Colo.: Westview.

Touval, S., and Zartman, I. W. (1989). "Mediation in International Conflicts." In K. Kressel and D. P. Pruitt, eds., *Mediation Research: The Process and Effectiveness of Third Party Intervention.* San Francisco: Jossey-Bass, 115–137.

Ury, W. L. (1987). "Strengthening International Mediation." *Negotiation Journal* 3, 3: 225–229.

Wall, J. A., and Lynn, A. (1993). "Mediation: A Current Review." *Journal of Conflict Resolution* 37, 1: 160–194.

Walton, R. E. (1969). *Interpersonal Peacemaking: Confrontations and Third Consultation.* Reading, Mass.: Addison-Wesley.

Wright, Q. (1965). "The Escalation of International Conflicts." *Journal of Conflict Resolution* 9, 4: 434–449.

Young, O. R. (1967). *The Intermediaries: Third Parties in International Crises.* Princeton: Princeton University Press.

The Contributors

Sharon Arad's research interests include fairness and trust issues in conflict resolution, empowerment processes in organizations, and leadership assessment. She has recently published in the *Journal of Conflict Resolution*.

Jacob Bercovitch is a senior lecturer at the University of Canterbury in Christchurch, New Zealand. His most recent book is *Mediation in International Relations* (with Jeffrey Z. Rubin).

Peter J. Carnevale is associate professor of psychology at the University of Illinois at Urbana-Champaign. His most recent book is *Negotiation in Social Conflict* (with Dean G. Pruitt).

Raymond Cohen is associate professor in the Department of International Relations at the Hebrew University of Jerusalem. His publications include the book *Culture and Conflict in Egyptian-Israeli Relations*.

Gunnar Fermann is a research fellow at the Fridtjof Nansen Institute in Norway. His most recent book is *Bibliography on International Peacekeeping*.

Ronald J. Fisher is professor of psychology at the University of Saskatchewan. His writings include *Social Psychology: An Applied Approach* and *The Social Psychology of Intergroup and International Conflict Resolution*.

Allison Houston has recently published in the *International Journal of Conflict Management*, and is now studying toward a Ph.D. in the United States.

Loraleigh Keashly is assistant professor of psychology at the University of Guelph, Ontario, Canada. Her interests are in social conflict, informal third-party intervention, group identity in conflict development and resolution, and abusive behavior in the workplace.

Vassiliki Koutrakou is currently a research fellow in the Department of Politics and International Relations at the University of Kent, working on the UKC Mediation Monitoring Programme, and a part-time lecturer at Webster University, London.

Louis Kriesberg is professor of sociology at Syracuse University. His most recent book is *International Conflict Resolution: The U.S.-U.S.S.R. and Middle East Cases*.

John Paul Lederach is an associate professor at Eastern Mennonite College. He has wide experience as a mediator, mediation trainer, and consultant and is the author of a number of books and articles in English and Spanish.

Brian Mandell is a visiting associate professor at the John F. Kennedy School of Government at Harvard University. He is presently completing a book (with Jacob Bercovitch) on conflict management in the post–Cold War era.

Kumar Rupesinghe is now the secretary general of International Alert, an organization which promotes methods of peaceful conflict resolution. His most recent books include *International Conflict and Governance* and *Early Warning and Conflict Resolution.*

Deborah Shmueli is a lecturer in the Department of Geography at the University of Haifa, Israel. Her research interests are in environmental policy, planning and dispute resolution, and the development of quantitative methodological tools for use in public policy.

Kjell Skjelsbæk served in the Norwegian Institute of International affairs and in the United Nations Institute for Training and Research. His most recent publication was as co-editor of *The Multinational Force in Beirut 1982–1984.*

Ariella Vranesky is a research associate at the Center for Urban and Regional Studies at the Technion, Israeli Institue of Technology. Her research interests include alternative dispute resolution, citizen participation, and environmental planning.

Mike Walters spent thirteen years as a member of military intelligence. He is currently a research fellow at the University of Kent and is involved in the UKC Mediation Monitoring Project.

Keith Webb is a lecturer and director of studies of the International Conflict Analysis Programme at the University of Kent. His most recent publication is as joint editor and contributor to *Theory and Practice in Foreign Policy Making.*

Paul Wehr is a member of the sociology faculty at the University of Colorado at Boulder, where he has developed the Social Conflict curriculum and the Conflict Resolution Consortium. His books include *Conflict Regulation, Justice Without Violence,* and *The Persistent Activist.*

Index

About the Book

Mediation is rapidly becoming one of the most important methods of settling conflicts in the post–Cold War world, practiced by virtually every actor and dealing with every conceivable issue in the relations between states. This book represents the most recent trends in and thinking about the process and practice of international mediation.

A coherent, analytical, well-integrated text, complete with real-world examples, the book examines the mediation efforts of various actors, as well as various methods of mediation. Each chapter combines theoretical with practical concerns, making this collection ideal for classroom assignment.

Jacob Bercovitch is senior lecturer in international relations at the University of Canterbury (New Zealand). His many publications in the field of conflict management and mediation include *Social Conflict and Third Parties: Strategies of Conflict Management, ANZUS in Crisis: Alliance Mismanagement in International Relations,* and *Mediation in International Relations*. In 1993, he was the Lady Davis Professor in International Relations at the Hebrew University of Jerusalem.